SOCIAL POLICY OF THE AMERICAN WELFARE STATE

Harper Series in Social Work
WERNER W. BOEHM, *Series Editor*

SOCIAL POLICY OF THE AMERICAN WELFARE STATE

An Introduction to Policy Analysis

Robert Morris
BRANDEIS UNIVERSITY

HARPER & ROW, PUBLISHERS
New York   Hagerstown   San Francisco   London

Sponsoring Editor: Dale Tharp
Project Editor: Robert Ginsberg
Production Supervisor: Stefania J. Taflinska
Compositor: Port City Press, Inc.
Printer and Binder: The Maple Press Company

SOCIAL POLICY OF THE AMERICAN WELFARE STATE:
An Introduction to Policy Analysis

Library of Congress Cataloging in Publication Data
Morris, Robert, Date-
    Social policy of the American welfare state.
    1. Social policy—United States. 2. Housing policy
—United States. 3. Public welfare—United States.
I. Title.
HN65.M614   361'.973   78-15898
ISBN 0-06-044618-8

To Sara

CONTENTS

EDITOR'S FOREWORD

When Harper & Row established a textbook series on social welfare, we hoped to stimulate the writing of books that would serve the burgeoning undergraduate population as well as the graduate group of social work students. We have been guided by the best judgments we could muster about the path to follow in creating textbooks that reflect both the present needs and future requirements of the profession. Obviously, as we go on, we shall find that some books hew closely to tradition and others venture far into new territory. In welcoming Professor Morris to the Harper family, we believe that we are simultaneously filling a gap and opening up a frontier.

Despite the fact that the number of books in social policy, especially those that focus on social welfare, is gradually increasing, there are few, if any, which, like *Social Policy of the American Welfare State*, succeed in treating the several domains of social policy both comprehensively and analytically. Professor Morris has developed a paradigm which permits him to examine the several dimensions and attributes of social policy and their relationship to each other. While thus filling a gap, Professor Morris also breaks new ground in tackling the implications of his own analysis for practice. He asks how we can begin to create professionals competent in dealing with social policy, what backgrounds and identifications they might have, what is or ought to be the scope of their activities, and what tools they need. Here I believe Professor Morris breaks new ground and opens up a debate of interest not only to social workers but also to practitioners of other social policy professions. Whether or not one agrees with him is less important than the fact that he blazes a new trail which cannot fail to clarify the field, its core, and the areas contiguous with other fields.

Given the increasing concern with and interest in policy not only in social work but also by educators, lawyers, and political scientists, and especially in view of developments in health and education, Professor Morris' book contributes to the enlightenment of members of these several professions. Conceptual clarity coupled with precise delineation of programs and issues will make this book a useful tool not only for undergraduate and graduate students but also for the scholar in the field.

WERNER W. BOEHM

PREFACE

This volume was begun as an introduction to the general subject of social policy as it is developing on the American scene, an introduction for students and citizens puzzled by the proliferation of welfare programs.

The rapid growth of United States governmental welfare programs is now a commonplace aspect of American life. In terms of simple dollar expenditure in relation to national income, American welfare has nearly reached the level achieved by those European states which were once considered pioneers in decent dealing with human needs in an industrial age. Instead of viewing this growth as a great achievement, many have strongly criticized it as a jerry-built hodgepodge of unconnected bits and pieces of social legislation which have not satisfactorily dealt with persistent human needs. This dissatisfaction is summed up in the complaint that the United States has no social policies or, if it has some, that they are regressive and punitive. While many needs are now met by government programs which were ignored 40 years ago, the criticisms stress the omissions, the gaps, the contradictions. To many it would appear that this growth has had a mindless quality about it, a blind and erratic and undirected groping out of a wilderness of human and national difficulties.

The intended introduction was soon enlarged to test whether the welfare evolution has in fact been as chaotic and thoughtless as it appears on the surface to be. I was early forced to ask whether it is possible that some pattern lay beneath the seeming confusion, a pattern which was not readily seen in either the rhetoric of political campaigning or in minutiae of programmatic detail. It soon became evident that any such search would have to consider a persisting reality in American life: that there are very few concrete or programmatic issues about which ordinary citizens have a widespread consensus. Rather, there are numerous and conflicting views about which issues are more rather than less urgently in need of attention, and there are as many differences about exactly how to handle those which are accepted as urgent. These differences of opinion are found among ordinary citizens, among experts, and among political leaders. There is also a conscious ambiguity about our national view as to the respective roles for the expert, the elected official, and the lay citizen in arriving at policy decisions. Often public views lag behind the understanding of leaders in any field, but we are reluctant to let such leadership act decisively in making decisions until widespread support in the general public can be generated. This wide consensus often emerges as slowly as public values shift. The margin between official leadership in guiding public thought and the tyranny of state manipulation of a passive electorate is very thin.

In much writing about social policy, two strands have evolved without effective synthesis. One has been concerned with the political dimension, analyzing the exchange between political forces and special interest groups in maneuvering a decision through the processes of government and executive branch administration. The other has concentrated on the technical side of designing programs or policies in which the engineering or drawing-board aspect of planning is stressed. The relationship between the two can be described retrospectively, but a theoretical synthesis has not moved much beyond those which helped shape the American Revolution and the Constitution.

In trying to understand whether or not the evolution of welfare programs has proceeded by calculation or design, I have chosen to review the 40-year growth of federal programs in a few fields in order to seek out any patterns which may hold together the seemingly erratic bits and pieces of legislation and action. The approach is admittedly subjective. It is possible that a long involvement in social planning has produced a belief that a pattern *should* exist for planning purposes, and I may therefore be finding what I have wanted to find. In defense of the approach, I would offer the view that not all patterning in human affairs proceeds from a universal, comprehensive, and logical or engineering design which is introduced through conscious acts for which all consequences are calculated in advance. The social as well as the physical sciences have uncovered many examples of underlying coherence and continuity which frame seemingly isolated or random behaviors of human beings, of social organizations, and of atoms. Of course, this coherence is not complete and much remains which is as yet unexplained, certainly in the behavior of individuals and of social organizations, due to emotional and other forces whose dynamics are only partly understood.

The empirical look, no matter how incomplete, can improve our understanding of how American society copes with its social problems, given the size and heterogeneity of both the people and the land. If an underlying pattern is discerned, this may help us cope with the admitted deficiencies of present arrangements to deal with poverty, mental and physical illness, deviance and delinquency, or criminal behavior. If no pattern is discerned at all, the argument for an increase in the mechanisms to introduce some more rational planning may be strengthened.

Some readers may see the conclusions of this exploration to constitute a defense of the status quo. This has certainly not been the intent. There are serious deficiencies in the ways we have chosen to handle grave personal difficulties. Certainly our mechanisms for conscious planning in the interest both of effectiveness and efficiency are primitive and incomplete. As a nation, we are still trying to improve the articulation of a few basic principles which both electorate and public officials can accept and count on over time. The more clear these principles become, the more they can serve as a guide for the development of or improvement in social programs.

The arbitrary construct of underlying social values which both sustain and constrain governments' actions may seem like another case of blaming the victim (in this case the electorate) for the difficulties they experience. I believe the evidence is quite clear that our national experience is not one of denying the plight of the victim. Rather, it is one of steadily enlarging the range of plights to be attended to by government and, at the same time, shaping the *way* we allow our governments to help. It seem inescapable that we must either live with an ambiguity inherent in the symbiotic relationship between citizen and official, or we must embrace some form of dictation. We can live with the fact that average citizens hold values shaped by their past, the kinds of information and stimuli to which they are exposed, and the knowledge which the past confers upon them. These views are changed, usually slowly, by the influence of leaders in thought and action. But elected officials are not free agents when it comes to changing public values; they are elected because they fit the electors' views about who represents their views and who will express their values in action. Only a few values are so widely held that most citizens share them. Public officials can move beyond these few views only at their peril, unless they are so convinced of the rightness of their differing values that they are prepared to press their views and resist efforts to remove them from office. The rub, of course, comes in first identifying just what those key basic values are, and then in selecting acts which do not do too much violence to them.

This set of dilemmas explains, at least in part, the surface untidiness which characterizes our welfare apparatus. I hope that our efforts to better serve humanity will be well served by an examination of underlying citizen attitudes which act as stabilizers and constrainers as much as they are stimulators of change. As a nation, we have changed much by creating a welfare state; we have changed less rapidly in the values which underly how we organize and express that state.

In this process, civil servants and elected officials come off not as badly as their sharpest critics believe. While there is no shortage of knaves and opportunists in public life, there are also many who are committed to civilized and humane efforts to improve the condition of the helpless. While political movements, pressure groups, and special interests have all played active roles in the past 40 years' evolution, civil servants and elected officials have also been just as active promoters of change and growth, albeit less recognized and much maligned. I suspect that many anonymous public servants have played important roles in advancing the responsibility of government for alleviating human distress. Whether this is good or bad is a matter of political philosophy about which people still differ.

There are certainly other ways of perceiving the underlying forces and processes of recent decades. Marxist and neo-Marxist analyses represent one of several alternative interpretations. In time, our study of the facts, as we can tease them out of organizational and personal behavior and out of history, will sharpen and improve our analysis. This will change the ways in which professions, technicians, political figures, and concerned citizens go about the business of civilizing the world in which we live. One thing seems inescapable. It is not possible to peaceably reverse the tendency for government to play a greater and greater role in the lives of individuals. As this power increases, so may the power of the state apparatus increase to override or to ignore the underlying values of the governed. In this event, powerful interests will contend to guide government or to capture it. The power may then be used in the interest of the many or of the few. It is not at all clear that the power will inevitably be used to help the few who are likely to be helpless, which is, after all, the function of a welfare state.

I am indebted to many who have contributed to this effort: colleagues and pioneers in the search for systematic ways to approach policy questions, their writing and their conversations; the several editors at Harper & Row who helped so much to introduce more clarity and simplicity into the presentation; Sylvia Pendleton for research assistance; and Barbara Isaacson for careful preparation of an often messy manuscript.

ROBERT MORRIS

Lexington, Mass.

THE SCOPE OF PUBLIC AND OF SOCIAL POLICY: A CONFUSION OF MEANINGS

The term *social policy* is popularly used with varied and ambiguous meanings. *Policy* is generally interpreted as meaning an organizing principle to guide action. It has long been used in reference to the positions taken by sovereign governments on matters of state. With the growth of corporations, whether profit making or not, the term came to be applied as well to the principles determining daily management procedures and eventually to the primary or basic aims of corporate entities.

However, the growth of governmental and corporate structures during the past 50 years has made this limited definition of policy obsolete, for many of their actions now affect almost all aspects of the lives of most citizens. Those principles of action which affect most directly citizens as individuals or group interrelationships have come to be called *social* policies, to distinguish them from policies more directly related to the more traditional areas of power, political control, or economic production. The borderline between acts which might be defined as social, political, or economic is necessarily unclear, but in general social policies are identified as those through which government seeks to correct inequities, to improve the condition of the disadvantaged, and to provide assistance to the less powerful. They include actions directed toward equalization of the well-being of all citizens, adjustment of social relationships, and regulation of aspects of living not dealing with physical safety, economic and commer-

1

cial activity, or foreign relations. T. H. Marshall, a founder of social policy theory, has defined this difficult new arena as "the policy of governments with regard to action having a direct impact on the welfare of the citizens by providing them with services and income." [1] The need for a better understanding of the concept of social policies—how they evolve and to what extent their development is influenced by professional or technical competence—has been forced upon citizen and public official alike, for public action now affects the lives of all, indirectly if not directly.

Ernest Becker, a distinguished social scientist and philosopher, has tried to understand how it can be that intelligent, reasoning human beings continue to create and to recreate worlds with so much violence, inequality, and suffering. He states that governments are one, if only one, device for giving meaning to group survival.[2] In recent decades we have turned to government to make wise choices on our behalf, yet at the same time we are often repelled by what governments do. Becker concludes that reasoning has failed thus far to influence man's fate, but that we now seem to realize we must choose between inaction or using reason to keep the world from destruction. In electoral campaigns we seek a compromise between our deepest emotional wishes for peace and plenty and equity and our reluctance to trust too much to the reasonableness and thoughtfulness of others, that is, to judgments expressed through government.

At one level William D. Carey notes that the election of 1976 seemed to be mainly a struggle over the transfer of influence and power, and not at all over the substance of the choices which political leaders must make once power is achieved. He notes poignantly:

> It is the substance that defines the quality of choice. What are the terms on which an affluent and technologically powerful nation proposes to conduct its affairs in a troubled world? For that matter, are affluence and power . . . to be continued goals of our public policies and the measures of effective leadership? If *not* affluence and power, then what? Candidates speak for or against the power of a national government or say "trust me"; but few discuss issues concretely.[3]

In many ways the election of 1976 tested certain broad premises underlying governmental policy. For example, one premise is the desirability of unrestrained growth—growth in the economy, in consumer goods and consumerism, in freedom, in size, in power, and, finally, in government. Against this view lies a deep, uneasy sense that unqualified and unlimited growth will not only exhaust physical resources, but will lead to

---

[1] T. H. Marshall, *Social Policy* (London: Hutchinson, 1965), p. 1.

[2] From his two significant books, *The Denial of Death* and *Escape from Evil* (New York: Free Press, 1973 and 1975).

[3] William D. Carey, editorial in *Science* 193 (August 13, 1976): 535. Copyright 1976 by the American Association for the Advancement of Science.

new confusion and disorder and even to limitations in human tolerance. Such concerns are not expressed in the course of an electoral campaign in which the acquisition of power seems to be the major aim, but they lie uneasily beneath the surface, appearing as distrust of governmental growth and activity, coupled with a yearning for ever increased economic and physical well-being. What emerges is a fear not only that we are reaching the limits of growth, but also that we are nearing the limits of confidence in political solutions to our continuing problems.[4]

DIMINISHING CONFIDENCE IN GOVERNMENT POLICY

For much of human history, individuals, organizations, and governments were preoccupied with physical survival—prevention of starvation and protection against enemies. The Industrial Revolution and its accompanying promise of relief from some of the pressures of physical survival allowed for an increase in individual aspirations and in governmental capacity to satisfy them. Nineteenth-century optimism about science and technology expanded to include new, hopeful beliefs for society. It was no longer sufficient merely to avoid starvation. Centuries-old hazards of the human condition suddenly became proper objects of public attention. Disease could be controlled, the pain of death and dying postponed, the frustration of drudgery and labor diminished. The material comforts an industrial economy could provide came to be seen as the right of all citizens, not merely a favored few. Where these conditions did not result naturally, people began to look more to the government to accelerate the progress toward a better world.

The fully developed expectation on the part of the people that government should assume this responsibility and governmental acceptance of its new role reached a peak of expression in American politics of the 1930s with the promise of a New Deal. Succeeding generations and governments adopted variants on the theme: Square Deal, Fair Deal, and finally the Great Society of the 1960s.

Governments at all levels became engaged in modifying the distribution of resources, in allocating jobs, in controlling working conditions, in providing health and social services, and in developing housing. In effect, all aspects of human and social existence became the proper concern of government. In communist societies these functions were totally preempted by the state, and planning for the delivery and distribution of all goods was closely controlled. In noncommunist societies the borderline between private activity and governmental intervention was subject to constant modification, experimentation, and change.

---

[4]See, for example, R. E. Miles, Jr., *Awakening from the American Dream* (New York: Universe Books, 1976).

By the 1970s the number of federal governmental aid programs of all kinds totaled about 1,000 (this figure includes only programs listed in the Federal Catalogue of Domestic Assistance Programs, so the number can be arbitrarily revised upward or downward). In 1975 half of the federal budget, half of local government budgets, and a fifth of the gross national product (GNP) were devoted to social programs intended to realize the expectations for the well-being of citizens.[5] But the results of this flood of programs became the focus of dissatisfaction. Consumers, professional experts, policy makers, and taxpayers all expressed their special complaints. Some argued that government was permanently incompetent; others, that policies were unwise or benefited the wrong persons.

This frustration over federal social problems was compounded by further disillusionment with governmental wisdom resulting from the expeditions in Vietnam and Southeast Asia which were maintained through both Republican and Democratic administrations, and from the distortions, manipulations, and dishonesty of the early 1970s and of the Nixon administration.

The swing of the pendulum from high hope to great disillusionment produced in 1976 a period of pause and hope. Could a new national administration regain some sense of the confidence which the past represented? Or would dismay and apathy deepen? There were polarized views as to the proper approach to action. A conservative, widely held view was expressed by Robert A. Nisbet, who concluded that the national government has so deeply penetrated the most minute aspect of the daily life of all citizens that a real tyranny has entered into our society, a tyranny more insidious and dangerous than the political tyrannies of fascism or of communism.

> "The most absolute authority," wrote Rousseau, "is that which penetrates into a man's inmost being and concerns itself no less with his will than with his actions." The truth of that observation is in no way lessened by the fact that, for Rousseau, genuinely legitimate government, government based upon the general will, *should* so penetrate. In the name of education, welfare, taxation, safety, health, and environment, to mention but a few of the laudable ends involved, the new despotism confronts us at every turn. Its effectiveness lies, as I say, in part through liaison with humanitarian rather than nakedly exploitative objectives but also, and perhaps most significantly, in its capacity to deal wth the human will rather than with mere human actions. By the very existence of one or another of the regulatory offices of the invisible government that now occupies foremost place, the wills of educators, researchers, artists, philanthropists, and enter-

---

[5]Advisory Commission on Intergovernmental Relations, *Fiscal Federalism*, 1. *Trends*, 1976 Edition (Washington, D.C.: 1976), pp. 7, 11, 17.

prisers in all areas, as well as in business, are bound to be affected: to be shaped, bent, driven, even extinguished.[6]

Nisbet argues that present practices are pragmatic, beginning with the best intentions, but ending by placing government at the center of all activity. The accumulation of petty rules and regulations conceals the real predicaments of human existence that trouble many citizens, making it impossible for the so-called practical programs to do much good in ameliorating the very difficulties with which they are intended to deal; they may, indeed, do great damage.

At the other extreme, others argue that our national commitment to deal with serious human dilemmas has not been strong or firm enough, so that we end up with half measures neither adequately funded nor administered.[7]

Most of the people probably fall between the extremes, wanting the government to attend to certain kinds of difficulties, provided governmental action appears to be well-focused, efficient, and not too preemptive of private life. This vague aspiration of the center probably explains why the national investment in human services—through a growing body of social programs—continues to expand. The most vigorous debates over alternative policies under quite different national administrations—Republican (Eisenhower, Nixon, Ford) and Democratic (Roosevelt, Truman, Kennedy, Johnson)—have produced a steady rise in federal budget expenditures, in the proportion of federal taxes going for social purposes, and in the variety and range of programs introduced. What has varied is the *rate* of increase. For this middle range of public opinion, the concern seems to be that the "system" is out of control and subject to no reasonable direction or management, not that it is too big or too small.

Federal action in the social area since the 1930s has generally taken the form of problem-specific legislation resulting in an ever-increasing number of new programs. But starting in 1968, both Republicans and Democrats began to question the effectiveness of this approach, and both parties proposed new policy guidelines. One proposed policy was to improve government operations while imposing a moratorium on new programs. Another was to create more programs and to increase funding for existing ones in order to secure a more sizable mass of intervention. A third and very beguiling policy would seek to cut back sharply the role of government. An extreme and idealized version claims that:

a shift of the center of government to the citizen, the person, [makes] a new paradigm possible for social policy. The government defines

---

[6] Robert A. Nisbet, "The New Despotism," *Commentary* 59, no. 6 (June 1975): 31–43.

[7] See, for example, James L. Sundquist et al. *Centrally Planned Change: A Re-examination of Theories and Concepts* (Urbana: University of Illinois Press, 1974), chap. 8.

problems; people experience predicaments. . . . The government
acts through implementation; people seek to understand their predicaments through theories about their predicaments. . . . a true
social policy will come into being (according to the popular paradigm), a governing principle will come into being, as people perceive
their social predicaments, form theories about these, and on the basis
of such theories make commitments which, if the theory is at least
practically sound, will start a development through constructive conflict and cooperation by which people will lead themselves out of their
predicament.[8]

The first two policy lines shift the attention of technical inquiry to the
means by which service programs can be made more effective or a bureau-
cracy can be better trained and better controlled to assure responsiveness
to human needs. The third approach advocates the complete abandonment
of existing approaches in order to start over again. It would build up new
social mechanisms through the widest participation of citizens, relying on
citizen self-help rather than on government.

Unfortunately, the last proposal leaves unanswered the question of
how the popular paradigm will come into being. What is the mechanism
through which 250 million citizens will begin to express constructive conflict and cooperation? Who will be involved in the confrontation—government agencies, or the policy-making units of the legislature, or citizens outside the government? The first two approaches also leave questions
unanswered. How can the existing procedures and programs be reformed
without destroying them?

Whatever the identifiable flaws in such shifts in policy, each could
constitute a long-range general goal. However, in order to serve as an
effective guide for action more middle-range social policy guidelines
would also have to be adopted. Examples of these are dealt with in succeeding chapters, but a brief reference to them can be made here.

THE MIDDLE RANGE: SOCIAL AND SECTORAL POLICIES

Middle-range policies are best understood in terms of tangible human
dilemmas, not in terms of social abstractions alone. The following illustrate
some persisting human dilemmas for which some governmental action at
a middle range of policy is still sought, despite dissatisfaction with past
efforts. These middle-range policies may be better identified as sectoral
policies; they affect the entire society indirectly, but they focus on specific
sectors of human affairs.

---

[8]Quoted from an unpublished paper by Robert McClintock, Resident Scholar
in the U.S. Department of Health, Education, and Welfare, Office of the
Secretary, 1976.

Income Security The private economy has not been able to provide work and income for all persons at a level which meets their economic expectations. Public action is accepted for the retired, the physically disabled, the very young, and—reluctantly—for those unemployed through no fault of their own and for single-parent, female-headed families with small children. But the programs in effect keep some out of work whom the rest think ought to be working, even if at substandard wages. Other programs are at cross purposes—retirement programs are designed to get people out of the labor force, while work-incentive programs are designed to get others into the work force, neither working very neatly in relation to the other. The cost of such programs rises, regardless of boom or depression cycles. Meanwhile, hope persists that more jobs can be generated, but only as a result of "proper" governmental action, following which government should resume its narrower role of helping a few unfortunates who cannot work at all.

Health Guaranteed access to health services by government was first supported as a way to keep people off relief by keeping them healthy, but it became in time a right of citizenship in a humane society. Some improvement of access for the aged and poor minorities has occurred, but at the cost of depersonalizing health care and increasing expenditures. The inflated costs of medical care consumed 9 percent of the 1976 Gross National Product. Growing investment in high-technology curative programs produces a growing, not diminishing number of disabled persons.

Housing and the Urban Environment Decent housing at a reasonable price for all has been a vaguely articulated goal for decades. But a succession of governmental programs, designed to improve the physical quality of housing and to bring it within the reach of the poorest, seems to have coincided with a steady decline in the quality of the urban environment, ending in an ugly urban sprawl, wasting energy, and eroding the amenities of normal living. All this has incurred a further inflation, so that low-cost housing for families with modest incomes demands a rising percent of disposable income and becomes less and less attainable.

The Aged The elderly have been the object of major public programs to assure economic and health security. But the costs have proven unexpectedly high so that more and more of each generation's earnings has been siphoned off in rising taxes to assure this security for a growing percentage of the population retiring from productive work. At the same time, the idea of forced retirement to draw benefits has been increasingly challenged by the aged themselves, and their new social, not economic, circumstances have attracted federal action—loneliness, isolation, deficient nutrition, housing, transportation. The boundaries of federal protection of the elderly have greatly widened.

Other Problems   A variety of other human difficulties continue to distress public and private citizens: mental illness, mental retardation, delinquent behavior (especially among youth), drug and alcohol abuse or addiction, and overinstitutionalization of the disabled. A group of programs which may, for lack of a better phrase, be called the personal social services are now underwritten by the federal government and these involve federal control on a wholly new frontier. They raise the question of how far the federal government's obligations extend into the individual's daily life and into the family domain. At the same time, the reasons for this development are compelling human concerns about real problems, and a faith—perhaps vestigial—that government can make a difference in reducing these hazards.

In the 1976 presidential election campaign one candidate announced a major task force on governmental actions as they affect the family. The statement was so loosely phrased that it could mean either a wide-ranging assessment of many government programs or a narrow study of the Aid to Families and Dependent Children (AFDC) relief program as it operates to break up natural family ties, but whatever its meaning the fact that the statement was made at all confirms the movement of government into the family domain. The basic decision must be made as to whether to withdraw a little or to improve the programs' impact on family life. But in either case further decisions must be made—in what areas to withdraw, how can the programs be made more effective, and so forth.

Older views held that giving financial relief to poor widows or deserted mothers or giving health examinations to poor mothers was a sufficient expression of our national desire to help those in trouble. But we have discovered that if we give relief under strict controls, we encourage troubled fathers on the edge of survival to desert, so that their children can be fed. And if we remove controls, we risk encouraging whole family units to withdraw from the labor force altogether. If they do, can we conclude that family life is strengthened or weakened?

A desirable policy would be one which gives all individuals maximum choices about how they shall live, but such a policy becomes one of public financial support for private choice making. The cost of such a policy may prove higher than most citizens want to pay, and the results may increase inequity rather than reducing it (is it equitable to guarantee the same income to one family that works 40 hours a week and to another family that does no work?). But if we feel that this type of policy loses sight of social or collective needs, what course should we follow?

These are, of course, oversimplified formulations, but they still reflect emotional responses which are widely expressed. Single-action remedies are thus found wanting and social policies become more complex as we move from the generalized aim of helping those in trouble to guiding principles to direct actions to realize that aim.

The sectors we have listed are representative areas for social policy action. They suggest that social policy seeks to realize the largest of man's aims, to shape a more perfect world, but that it does not specify just how that perfection will be achieved or how it will alter our social and political forms. Policy seems to reflect man's effort to improve life's conditions with the imperfect techniques now at hand and in the face of many contradictory wants and beliefs. But saying this much tells us little about what social policy is. Does an accumulation of programs or any one program of services constitute a policy? And whose policy do we mean—that of the Congress, the president, 'the government,' or 'the people'?

CONFLICTING DEFINITIONS OF SOCIAL POLICY

Social policy slowly came to mean that area of organized human activity which somehow sought to impose reason and order on a mass of rapid and often untidy change. But the concept of social policy in the public mind developed as haphazardly as the social changes which led to its rise. Considering the explosion of diverse wants and aspirations, it is not surprising that the term has acquired many different meanings and has been used as a label to cover many different approaches. At least four common usages can be distinguished. Each has some validity and some defects.

Social Policy as the Sum of Society's Actions: Societal Policy

Social policy is sometimes considered to be the sum of all choices made in society governing the nature of relationships among individuals and social units. One especially ambitious effort to encompass all of man's knowledge into one science is that of David G. Gil, who argues that

> social policies constitute a society system of interrelated . . . relationships among individual units and society as a whole. Social policies . . . regulate the development, allocation and distribution of statuses, roles and their accompanying constraints, rewards and entitlements among individuals and social units within a society.[9]

It is clear that in the aggregate a set of behaviors and decisions reflects the current balance in any society's views about a social problem. This is perhaps self-evident, since this broad use of the term means that the social policies of society follow from the behavior of individuals, laws, acts of groups, etc. Such usage might be better termed *societal policy,* or *social norms.* For example, until 1860 American societal policy permitted the coexistence of slavery in the South and absence of slavery in the North. After the abolition of slavery in 1865 society still permitted racial discrimination. Since 1950, however, the nation's sum of actions has shifted

---

[9]David G. Gil, "A Systematic Approach to Social Policy Analysis," *Social Service Review* 44, no. 4 (December 1970) : 411–426.

in the direction of abolishing, or at least reducing, racial discrimination. If one adds together the combination of legislatve enactments, court decisions, and attitudinal changes, it would appear that, while discriminatory attitudes and behavior still exist, the national society overall has embarked on an antiracist policy. Such societal policy may be too slow moving, but it does represent some measurable line of norm development.

Such a broad concept of social policy thus becomes more a matter of historical reconstruction, that is, the recognition, after the fact, of changes which have taken place. It is doubtful whether it lends itself to the development of a discipline in social policy development since, at least in the United States, we do not have a monolithic society in which all aspects of social relationships are controlled and planned from any center. At best, such a usage of the term helps those engaged primarily in political activism, a career for which formal study has been unnecessary.

Social Policy as an Appeal to Do Something Comprehensive

In another usage, social policy is defined as the aim of a group of citizens for action on a particular problem. Thus, it is frequently argued that the nation requires a family policy, a national health policy, an income policy. In its more elementary sense, this usage simply identifies an area of human relationships in which advocates of action want society, through its mechanisms of government, to respond to a need, although the direction and details of action are not specified. In this usage, a comprehensive approach is usually preferred to a piecemeal one. A comprehensive approach is one in which all aspects are logically connected and neatly packaged, at least on paper, with no loose ends.

There is a tendency for advocates to conclude that if programs of action or behavior do not conform to what they desire or believe to be "right," then a policy on the subject is lacking. For example, in the human resource or social welfare area, it is commonly argued that there is no policy about the family or about health or about children, but such a conclusion ignores certain underlying realities. While there is certainly not "a health policy," adopted as such by the Congress and implemented by the federal government, certain sets of decisions and acts can be said to define American society's attitude to the health of its people. The present cumulative actions—viewed in their broadest context—can be said to contain the following elements: a belief in the ability of science and technology to effect cures and the consequent emphasis on cures as opposed to prevention of disease; a belief in the usefulness of distributing and sharing the cost of such curative services through insurance, so that individuals are not personally confronted with the costs of the services they receive; a strong preference for supporting individual access to private physicians rather than to collective health services such as polyclinics; the appropriation of tax funds and governmental services, added perhaps reluctantly, to the health system to fill in gaps which the private system refuses to fill; and, finally, the appropriation of public funds to assure widespread access by all, regardless of income, to the kind of system which the foregoing components produce. Such a set of acts is a far cry from a comprehensive scheme, but it can be said to represent a national policy, being the best compromise which conflicting and contradictory forces can achieve.

Social Policy as Acts of Government

In a third sense, social policy seems to refer to a set or group of programs, developed either by government or by private organizations, to deliver particular health or welfare services or a combination of health and welfare services to achieve some loosely defined general aim. Thus, it can be said that there is a policy concerning child health when programs have been enacted for well-baby clinics, for maternal and child health services, for immunization, and for nutrition. In this usage, it is not clear where the term *policy* differs from the details of program organization; it is sufficient to believe that the fact of "doing something," that is, the existence of a set of programs, is an expression of society's having some policy about a particular problem.

If we consider a narrower usage, for example, social policies as representing the specific enactments of government, we immediately encounter two levels of complexity. If "enactments of government" is interpreted as meaning legislation passed by Congress, how do we deal with the often contradictory intentions of many acts. If "enactments of government" is interpreted as meaning the sum of actions taken by the three branches of government, how do we reconcile the often contradictory effects of such actions.

We must recognize that we can refer to an act of Congress only at a particular point in time. Legislative history is replete with instances in which the Congress enacts legislation in one session and enacts quite contradictory legislation on the same subject in a following session, without troubling to repeal the former. Federal income maintenance policies originally were designed to provide emergency cash or in-kind income to people who had no work and who would, lacking such income, starve to death. But succeeding income programs, attempting to deal with the complexities of income distribution in America, produced an elaborate superstructure. There are income programs to fend off starvation, but there are also income programs to discourage people from working (social security retirement) and, simultaneously, income programs designed to force people to work (the work incentive program of public assistance). To make the situation even more complicated, the income programs originally designed for emergency relief were based on the assumption that only the unemployed would lack the minimum means of subsistence. But if means of subsistence was taken as the standard for need for relief, then the borderline between the unemployed and those who had low-paying jobs became more difficult to maintain, and programs such as the food stamps program were developed to give additional income to people who, although working full time, were considered poor. The boundaries between relief and income redistribution became progressively blurred.

Rather than concluding from such an accumulation of contradictions that our nation lacks a policy, it can equally well be argued that our policy as regards income maintenance is one of rectifying the major distortions in income security without at the same time completely destroying our basic economic system. One may argue that our basic economic system should be replaced by a system in which all the means of production are managed by the national government and all citizens in effect are employees of one vast corporation: the state (as in the Soviet Union or China). Equally, one can believe that human needs are best met by an infinitely complex economic system with many relatively independent producers offering employment opportunities, with the state moving progressively and pragmatically to correct inequities and to bring about continuous equalization of opportunity and condition.

There are social policies embedded in both the above approaches, and in either it can be said that there is a clear guide to action by the national government. Unfortunately, at least in the United States, the national government is not simply the legislature. The executive branch has as much influence over the nature of policy as does Congress, exercised in the executive's capacity to formulate operating regulations which govern the development of any program enacted by Congress. This power of the executive is further enlarged by a tendency of Congress to enact programs with general purposes and with guidelines, but to leaving the organization of administrative details to the executive branch. For example, Congress may enact a mental health program to return care for the mentally ill from hospitals to a community basis, but executive regulations can, and have, assured that mental health services are primarily controlled by a medical profession oriented to hospital care as the treatment of choice.

The situation in the United States is further complicated by the existence of a third, coequal branch of the national government, the courts, which in recent decades have become a major force in shaping social policies. When a court decides that a patient in a mental hospital must either be given active treatment or be discharged and that a patient cannot be constrained against his will, it can no longer be argued that the formulation of policy about the mentally ill is solely within the hands of either Congress or the executive branch. When the courts order busing of school children to reduce school segregation, educational policy is no longer solely a legislative or executive matter.

This three-tiered government forces one to consider the distinction between policies advanced for consideration and the ones actually adopted by all three elements through the checks-and-balances of constitutional government.

Policy as Daily Administrative Guidance

The term *policy* may also be used to refer to the rules and regulations which govern the day-by-day delivery of specific services, in other words, policy is defined as the operating guidelines for formal organizations which deliver human services. Thus, an income maintenance program can be governed by a policy which requires that able-bodied recipients register for work or take any work which is offered. Mental health services may have a policy of not accepting chronic alcoholics and drug addicts or, on the contrary, of especially trying to reach alcoholics and drug addicts.

Like the other common usages, this narrowest concept of policy also presents difficulties. In terms of the delivery of services it may be said that an agency has a policy to close at 5:00 P.M. or to offer emergency services at night and on weekends or to require a client's consent form to secure information from other agencies. Such minor administrative policies may also reflect wider social norms, as when an agency in the 1940s could require segregated entrances for minorities or could refuse applications from black applicants. An agency may or may not apply a rigid work test before giving relief or a psychiatric service may or may not admit alcoholics. But such policies are of a wholly different order from the societal norms or the national directions we have just discussed. They certainly do not address directly the larger questions of income distribution and mental illness which originally gave rise to the demand that organized society deal with these problems.

It may be evident from this brief listing that some groups use the term *policy* to identify specific achievements they want to aim for, whereas others use it to identify a general desire to deal with some loosely defined social difficulty without distinguishing among the diverse and often irreconcilable wants of constituencies, which may impede any course of action.

In effect, the broadest definitions of social policy are so general that they defy any attempt to construct a professional discipline or a governmental structure which can simultaneously handle all of the dimensions of life. The broader use is, therefore, most valuable in trying to identify a state of affairs in society at a given time without doing more than suggesting tension points requiring action. Similarly, the narrowest definition does no more than deal with minor organizational symptoms of the basic social problems with which we are concerned. What remains is a substantial middle range of subject matter touching on reasonably identifiable social difficulties which are sufficiently troublesome as to warrant organized intervention by some social entity. These troublesome issues are likely to be ones which provoke substantial controversy, at least as to means, if not ends. Opponents can agree that there should be equity and stability in income for the entire population, but disagree vigorously on what constitutes equity and how any agreed-upon definition might be achieved. The matter next to be considered is whether a more utilitarian concept of social policy can be formulated.

ADDITIONAL READINGS

Anderson, Wayne, Bernard Frieden, Michael Murphy, eds. *Managing Human Services*. Washington, D.C.: International City Management Association, 1977.

Gilbert, Neil, and Harry Specht. *Dimensions of Social Welfare Policy*. Englewood Cliffs, N.J.: Prentice-Hall, 1974.

Marshall, T. H. *Social Policy*. London: Hutchman, 1965.

Rein, Martin. *Social Policy*. New York: Random House, 1970.

Schorr, Alvin. *Explorations in Social Policy*. New York: Basic Books, 1968.

Titmuss, Richard M. *Essays on the Welfare State*. New Haven: Yale University Press, 1959.

A FRAMEWORK FOR UNDERSTANDING SOCIAL POLICY: SOCIETAL NORMS, PUBLIC POLICY, AND SOCIAL POLICIES

The term social policy may be more usefully developed from the sense in which it is defined in the Oxford English Dictionary, "a course of action adopted and pursued by a government, party, ruler, statesman, etc.; any course of action adopted as advantageous or expedient." [1] Schorr and Baumheier expand this definition by identifying social policy as

> the principles and procedures guiding any measure or course of action dealing with individual and aggregate relationships in society. It is conceived as intervention in and regulation of an otherwise random social system. Established social policy represents a subtle course of action with respect to selected social phenomenon, governing social relationships in the distribution of resources within a society. [2]

Elaborating on these definitions, social policy can be seen as a guide to action in future unanticipated situations. Policy identifies the general principles which an individual party or a government uses to make choices and decisions in unfamiliar circumstances which may arise in the future.

---

[1] *Oxford English Dictionary*, compact edition (New York: Oxford University Press, 1971), p. 171.
[2] *Encyclopedia of Social Work*, 16th ed. (New York: National Association of Social Workers, 1971), p. 1362.

15

Policy is, therefore, a guiding principle. It is a guide to action to be taken by individuals or groups capable of influencing the course of events.

For purposes of this volume, this usage of the term is to be distinguished from an ethical concept or a set of values; value may be fervently held and yet not lead to action. Policy is to be distinguished by the fact that it involves a choice to be made by an individual or a group, resulting in actions by which the lives of others are to be affected.

This usage also needs to be distinguished, from ideology, primarily by the flexibility inherent in a view which is treated as a guide rather than an immutable law. Ideologies are significant in shaping the course of human events, but they are frequently rigid in operation and deviation from the ideology is considered to be treasonable. Rigid adherence to ideological purity may result in a form of self-destruction or failure in action.

Thus, we will here interpret policy as a guiding set of principles employed with flexibility by public officials able to make choices affecting large numbers of other persons to assure decisive action when unanticipated conditions are met.

A Typology for Social Policy Analysis

The foregoing definition, to be useful, needs to be considered against a framework of those other dimensions which affect both the evolution and implementation of guiding principles. If one examines the various uses of the term policy more closely, a new pattern begins to emerge. The idea of social policy can be seen to consist of several elements, each of which needs separate attention and each of which has an effect on the rest.

Society's aspirations   The aspirations of a society are in the nature of *preamble goals* for a society, much like the statement in the American Declaration of Independence that "all men are entitled to life, liberty, and the pursuit of happiness."

Social norms or societal policy   Societal policy represents the accumulation of values and normative standards which a society builds up over time. These norms determine what a society will allow its organized structure of governance to do on behalf of its members. They are an unwritten blend of what a people think their society ought to be, what they wish to do collectively for the good of all, and how they prefer to act to achieve such ends.

Collective acts take place at two levels, that of government and that of nongovernmental informal or primary associations. Social norms control activities at both levels, but government is likely to be more rigidly limited because its acts can affect everyone. Informal associations are less rigidly constrained because their acts may affect only those who are members of the associations. Informal associations can test out variations in normative behavior and can, over time, alter the norms of the whole society, sometimes by trying out ideas which everyone is later willing to adopt and sometimes by forceful imposition as in the case of dictatorial societies.

Thus policy as social norms means the premises, values, and general mind-set of the country. Such values shape our political choices, and our scientific and technological pathways for exploration.

Public policy   Public policy provides a guide as to the aims of governing to which priority is assigned and as to the means which are acceptable to or preferred by a particular government. These guides are general in that they indicate which problems a government will choose to deal with and which way a government will choose to move when it is confronted with the necessity to take action. They are useful over time to assure some continuity in governmental behavior; they assure a sense of direction and provide a base from which to confront new or unexpected situations. In this sense policies are guiding principles for a government.

A government may choose a general policy of stressing its citizens' domestic well-being over acquisition of power in foreign affairs. When the well-being depends upon control over external resources, the policy choice is whether to concentrate on domestic resources alone or not. Within such a general policy, a government must also decide to what extent it will regulate the acts of its citizens in order to pursue the goal of general well-being, to what extent it will direct its citizens to act in their private capacities to satisfy their own needs; or to what extent it will provide for its citizens needs directly through government agencies.

Sectoral public policy   In the guidance sense, policy is not only general, applying to all of government. It can be *sectoral,* in that policy affects only a segment of a society, as in the case of health or child welfare policy.

Administrative policy   Policy also includes the rules and regulations which are adopted by private or by governmental agencies or units to govern their day-to-day activities.

We will concentrate in this book on the third and fourth elements, but will consider also how the first and second impinge upon the third, for the interaction of these four determines, over time, how social policies evolve.

Much of the recent discussion of social policy has assumed that development takes place as a result of political controversy, and this is essentially correct if, by politics, one means the maneuver for position and influence among political groups which have different objectives. Unfortunately, the ambiguity in language which we outlined in Chapter 1 introduces a rather sterile element into the political process. Political antagonists may argue that the "other" party is opposed to a preamble goal when, in fact, the argument is over the means to be used. Equally, the arguments may overlook the fact that general social norms can obstruct the adoption of particular public policies just as much as the views of extremist groups. These forms of political controversy lead to two indictments of American social policies: either that we lack a social policy altogether (e.g., we have no health policy) or that our social policies are destructive. This latter view is held by critics of the existing situation who are identified by their political opponents as conservative (or reactionary) or as progressive (or radical).

The later chapters will seek to establish that neither of these indictments is quite accurate. At the level of national government, consistent policies (in the sense of general guiding principles) can be identified for income maintenance, health, housing, personal social services, and children and the aged.

It will further be argued that the policies we have, however well or ill conceived and administered, have been constricted by societal policy, which represents the limits within which the general body of the electorate will allow its agents to function. This is not to deny that the norms of the citizenry are influenced by their political leaders. It is only to say that these social norms, however they have been shaped, do limit what governments are allowed to do.

This will lead us to a further consideration of the leadership role of government. Is government wholly passive or can it alter the constraints imposed by social norms without being disowned by its people? An examination of several social policy areas will produce some evidence that national government has sought to widen the boundaries of governmental action on social policy matters, often trying to go beyond the limits of approved norms.

Finally, our exploration into the development of social policy will lead us to distinguish between social policies which are advocated and those which are adopted. Usually this is discussed as advocacy by political parties and groups of citizens acting in unofficial capacities. For our purposes, we will look at the advocacy roles played by the executive and legislative branches of national government.[3] We will indicate how in several social policy areas either the executive or the legislative branch has taken initiative to advocate policies which went beyond the societal norms of a given period in history. While these efforts may have reflected pressures from constituency groups, we will focus primarily on the official acts of governmental units to translate advocated into adopted policies, regardless of the origins of the advocacy.

---

[3]In recent decades the courts have also played an active role in advocating the adoption of social policies, but these judicial efforts lie outside the boundaries of this volume.

Our analysis of American social policies will thus use these elements for a paradigm:

1. Underlying social norms which shape and constrict as much as they direct governmental action

2. Public policies reflecting the guiding principles with which governments meet new situations

3. Sectoral public social policies

4. The leadership role of governmental units in moving beyond or in modifying social norms

5. The distinction between advocated and adopted policies

The interplay among these elements produces one dynamic in the evolution of the American society and in the role of its government vis-à-vis the wants of its citizens.

THE CREATIVE TENSION: SOCIAL NORMS VERSUS PUBLIC POLICY

The succeeding chapters trace a few index social-policy areas in American life. But before examining them in detail, it will be useful to assess what has been happening in the United States regarding social policies over the past 50 years. The basis for assessment is derived from evaluation of the exemplars of national policy discussed in succeeding chapters.

The central character of American social policies has a direction and a continuity. It is shaped by a few basic attitudes or social norms shared by most citizens as well as by their public officials. This societal policy— the sum total of laws, habits, mores, and practices—appears to consist of the following.

Preference for private or marketplace decision making There is a preference for allowing marketplace forces the widest and fullest expression, that is, to find the solution to problems through the interaction of many decisions made privately, if at all possible. The term *marketplace* as used here refers to private party decision making, sometimes mediated through some economic exchange between parties. Such marketplace exchanges exist among nonprofit and governmental units, but the conventional usage does not extend to those exchanges, since government has a power to enforce decisions commonly considered to be absent in private activities. As used here, the term reflects a vague confidence that individual decision making is preferred above all other forms of action.

As social and economic structures have become more elaborate, especially since the Industrial Revolution, more and more decisions which govern the distribution and access to goods and services have been made by corporate entities and collectivities. Simple, one-person choices have become virtually impossible since these entities decide on the basis of corporate interests what goods and services can be produced or provided. Of course such corporate-serving choices respond to a degree to the aggregated wants of many individuals, but the choice of action is determined primarily by corporate units' need to satisfy their members—to show profit. Thus the belief that the *market* will respond to individual wants or needs is diminished by the recognition that we as individuals get what others are willing to do or to produce for us.

This disjunction between individual and collective wants and responses leads to the discovery that the market does not keep up with expectations as fully or as rapidly as we would like, and, more serious for our purposes, it does not adequately meet all wants with equal efficiency. Thus some groups remain relatively neglected, giving rise to the second facet of our normative social framework.

Belief in government aid to the weak and helpless With the recognition that the market does not serve all individuals' needs equally comes the belief that government should act on behalf of vulnerable individuals and groups. The accepted definition of vulnerable individuals is limited mainly to certain groups who are perceived to be relatively weak and helpless— the aged, widows, orphans, the crippled, and, by recent extension, anyone in serious trouble not of his or her own making, as, for example, unemployment following an acceptable work history.

Continued belief in the saving virtues of work If we assume that hard work by the individual will bring about the satisfaction of each individual's needs, then private decision-making is to be preferred. The vulnerable are then defined as those who are deprived of work by forces beyond their control—the widowed, the aged, the ill, the uneducated, and so on. The poor are poor because they are lazy.

Continued optimistic view of progress through science The nineteenth century belief in progress toward a better world through science and technology leads to belief that actions can be seen as short term on the assumption that science will abolish current difficulties.

Preference for shared responsibility The sharing or division of responsibility among the several layers of government is basic to our system. As an extension of this, there has always been a preference for shifting or distributing costs of any government action as far away from the individual as possible. If possible, let small insurance premiums anticipate large costs. Or levy small taxes to protect a few against grave trouble, and levy those taxes through "painless" payroll deductions for the federal government rather than levy local taxes which are more visible and "painful." If responsibility for any problem is assigned to the farthest removed level of government, the happier everyone is, for a time. But if the 'pain' of costs builds up too heavily and quickly at any one level, a blocking reaction sets in.

These five preferences are the parameter of public policies. They establish the direction in which policies are, by and large, permitted and expected to develop. The public, national policies on issues such as income, health, old age, and housing, have grown in volume and specificity, but remain guided by the sense of direction and continuity of our basic norms. The fact that the norms are implicit, rather than stated explicitly as the basis of government policy does not make them in any sense less powerful in determining decision making in public policy.

Although public policy is thus always limited by the basic norms, it would be a mistake to assume that it is unchanging. The norms themselves undergo change and policy sometimes pushes beyond the implicit limits. The guiding norm of responsibility for vulnerable groups has led to the many social welfare programs that account for a large proportion of federal budget and governmental activity. These programs have by now become so extensive in relation to other actions in the social fields that they represent an unexpected change in policy direction which goes well beyond the intent of the original concept of responsibility. The scope and dynamism of public programs produced by these policies has given such programs a vigorous life of their own. Their existence has expanded the limits set by another social norm as the reliance upon private actions and decision making has in many areas been overshadowed by public decision making and the range of subjects considered suitable for public intervention into private lives has widened.

It may be concluded that a new stage in policy evolution has been reached. Governmental actions have now moved beyond these sanctioning preferences or societal policies. A tension or strain has been introduced: either the government programs will be pulled back within the old confines or the social norms will alter as a result of leadership changes introduced by governmental action. Present evidence suggests that it is the constrictions of social norms of the past which will give way and that the new, wider platform for public policies in social needs will be used for the next generation of governmental actions.

Gone is the need to defend governmental action and policy as a basic violation of old norms. Instead, controversy now rests on such questions as: How much further shall the national government go? What is it possible and desirable to expect out of government action? How will the boundaries between government and private actions be redrawn? How much private disposable income will citizens permit to be used for public provisions? How will private action be used?

If this analysis is correct, certain assumptions about the debate over specific public policies will have to be altered. It has long been assumed by liberal-minded activists who seek to enlarge government actions that obstacles inhere in the nature of the governmental system and in the blocking capacity of some powerful groups, but the very societal guides upon which these advocates rely and upon which they call for justification may prove to be the difficulty. All desire a better world, but the guiding principles by which this better world is to be approached are circumscribed. It is the cumulative effect of public policies and actions which constitute the vanguard pushing beyond the old guidelines and creating new ones, albeit slowly.

Others who argue for a cutback in governmental action, whether for conservative reasons or because of a radical mistrust in government, will find that some of the normative impulses serve to push toward more government rather than toward less.

The distinction between norms and policy can be drawn thus: guiding social norms are the result of an accumulation of preferences produced by a people as they shape their specific society. This accumulation represents the most widely held, deeply felt beliefs, although smaller groups with divergent views or preferences coexist within any society. The dominant beliefs and norms are embedded in innumerable laws and organizational modes of behavior, as well as in personal and informal group mores. These norms are not amenable to specific alteration by acts of government, although they do change slowly over time as social forces work their way through inherited belief systems and norms.

Public policies, meaning the explicit sectoral actions of government, are less grandiose, although they are also cumulative. They do not cover all of life. Such policies are discerned through the actions of public officials and the legislating elements of government and cover relatively specific aspects of a society's life. These policies can be expressed by individuals or by political parties. They can routinely conform to social norms, or they can express leadership action taken by public bodies to respond to new conditions which require new steps outside of or beyond the prevailing norms. Such leadership action makes public policy the cutting edge of social change and helps a people to exploit the opportunity for change which a new social situation demands. In some instances public officials may seek to introduce public policies for relatively specific aspects of social life quite at variance with the underlying social norms, with the result either that a variant approach must be imposed by some force upon a people not yet ready, or the proposed policy becomes a subject for perhaps decades of debate and discussion during which public acceptance emerges. As we will discuss later, the 50-year-old effort to secure some form of national health insurance may illustrate such a lengthy process. In this sense public policy contains another level of guiding principles which are introduced by individuals or by parties to guide public actions of public officials. Such policies may lead or follow social norms, but they do guide government actions over time.

Thus the evolution of social policy occurs through the tension between pressures exerted on governments to act beyond the confines of social norms and the restraining influence of the norms on too precipitate movement. Except in periods of great upheaval and catastrophe, the result is to ensure that new assumptions of authority by government over the lives of citizens are tested and that if too little action is taken or the testing is too prolonged, the pressure for movement builds up.

Evidence for this type of creative tension between norms and policy is first found in the following tables. Tables 1, 2, and 3 show how governmental allocations in social welfare, income maintenance, and health have grown since 1950, but especially since 1965, regardless of changes in political party control of government. Table 4 documents the incidence of costs on income classes. What *has* distinguished the policies of different parties is a difference in emphasis on what increasing government actions will concentrate on and on how government should use its growing influence. The continuities and the cutting edges of change will be explored in succeeding chapters.

THE SOCIAL COMPONENTS OF POLICY

In all these views of social policy there is further confusion resulting from ambiguity over the meaning of the term *social*. Is social policy distinct from public policy? If they were coequal, one could make an arbitrary choice as to which term to use, but it is reasonably clear that social policy means something different from public policy. There can be public policy, meaning the policy of the national government as reflected by Congress, the executive, the courts, or all three together regarding the economy. Economic policy can be mandated nationally by a control of money supply, by a decision to fund public service employment as the last resort, by encouraging inflation, or by accepting a high level of unemployment.

Economic policy is not quite the same as social policy. By and large, economic policy deals with macro levels of society—with aggregates of consumers and producers—and is based on economic concepts about the behavior of that artificial construct known as the economic man. But it is now widely recognized that economic policy is affected by a set of circumstances not contained in economic theory. The state of a culture, psychological motivation, the character of family ties all alter and affect the individual's actual behavior so that it is different from that predicted for the abstract economic model. Acceptance of the idea that women with small children ought to compete in the labor force changes the nature of that labor force. The belief that people should have a minimum income changes the functioning of economic rewards. What is not altogether clear, however, is the way in which these less firm social considerations are to be treated at the level of national policy. Are they to be incorporated as a part

TABLE 1

Public and Private Expenditures for Social Welfare Programs, Selected Years, 1950–1975 [a]

Fiscal Year	Total[b] (Public-Private)	Public			Private
		Total	*Federal*	*State-Local*	*Private*
		Amount (in Billions)			
1950	$35.7	$23.5	$10.5	$13.0	$12.2
1955	50.6	32.6	14.6	18.0	18.0
1960	80.1	52.3	25.0	27.3	27.8
1965	119.9	77.2	37.7	39.5	42.8
1970	213.8	145.8	77.3	68.4	68.0
1975[c]	394.3	286.5	165.9	120.6[d]	107.8
		As a Percent of GNP			
1950	13.5	8.9	4.0	4.9	4.6
1955	13.3	8.6	3.8	4.7	4.7
1960	16.1	10.5	5.0	5.5	5.6
1965	18.2	11.7	5.7	6.0	6.5
1970	22.3	15.2	8.1	7.1	7.1
1975[c]	27.4	19.9	11.5	8.4	7.5
		Percentage Distribution			
1950	100.0	65.8	29.4	36.4	34.2
1955	100.0	64.4	28.9	35.6	35.6
1960	100.0	65.3	31.2	34.1	34.7
1965	100.0	64.4	31.4	32.9	35.7
1970	100.0	68.2	36.2	32.0	31.8
1975[d]	100.0	72.7	42.1	30.6	27.3

SOURCE: *Advisory Commission on Intergovernmental Relations (ACIR) staff compilation based on U.S. Department of Health, Education, and Welfare, Social Security Bulletin, January 1976; Alfred M. Skolnick and Sophie R. Dales, Social Welfare Expenditures, 1950–75; and U.S. Department of Commerce, Bureau of Economic Analysis, Benchmark Revision of National Income and Product Accounts: Advance Tables, March 1976. From ACIR, Significant Features of Fiscal Federalism, 1976 (Washington, D.C.: U.S. Government Printing Office, 1976), pp. 19–41.*

[a]Includes: income maintenance, health, education, and welfare and other services.
[b]Includes the following amounts of duplication resulting from use of cash payments received under public and private social welfare programs to purchase medical care and educational services: 1950, $0.4 billion; 1955, $0.6 billion; 1960, $1.4 billion; 1965, $2.0 billion; 1970, $2.8 billion; 1975, $5.6 billion.
[c]Preliminary.
[d]Federal general revenue sharing is included as state-local expenditure. In fiscal year 1974 an estimated $3.1 billion in general revenue sharing receipts were spent for social welfare purposes. Estimates for 1975 are not available

of economic policy? Is there a distinct social component of economic policy or a completely separate policy which affects economic behavior?

One common treatment of this subject avoids any attempt to distinguish among policies—all are equally social, be they economic or not. Anything governmental or public is social. A situation can be labeled a social condition when that condition becomes a problem to or is important to a particular society. This requires that the condition be one which the existing institutions cannot handle to the satisfaction of enough members

TABLE 2

Public and Private Expenditures for Health and Medical Care, Selected Years, 1959–1975

| Fiscal Year | Total (Public-Private) | Public | | | Private |
		Total	Federal	State-Local	
		Amount (in Billions)			
1950	$12.0	$3.1	$1.4	$1.7	$8.9
1955	17.3	4.4	1.9	2.5	12.9
1960	25.9	6.4	2.9	3.5	19.5
1965	38.9	9.5	4.6	4.9	29.4
1970	69.2	25.2	16.6	8.6	44.0
1975[a]	118.5	49.9	33.8	16.1[b]	68.6
		As a Percent of GNP			
1950	4.5	1.2	0.5	0.6	3.4
1955	4.5	1.2	0.5	0.7	3.4
1960	5.2	1.3	0.6	0.7	3.9
1965	5.9	1.4	0.7	0.7	4.5
1970	7.2	2.6	1.7	0.9	4.6
1975[a]	8.2	3.5	2.3	1.1	4.8
		Percentage Distribution			
1950	100.0	25.8	11.7	14.2	74.2
1955	100.0	25.4	11.0	14.5	74.6
1960	100.0	24.7	11.2	13.5	75.3
1965	100.0	24.4	11.8	12.6	75.6
1970	100.0	36.4	24.0	12.4	63.6
1975[a]	100.0	42.1	28.5	13.6	57.9

SOURCE: *Advisory Commission on International Relations (ACIR) staff compilation based on U.S. Department of Health, Education and Welfare*, Social Security Bulletin, *January 1976; Alfred M. Skolnick and Sophie R. Dales,* Social Welfare Expenditures, 1950–75; *and U.S. Department of Commerce, Bureau of Economic Analysis,* Benchmark Revision of National Income and Product Accounts: Advance Tables, March 1976. *From ACIR,* Significant Features of Fiscal Federalism, 1976 *(Washington, D.C.: U.S. Government Printing Office, 1976), pp. 19–41.*

[a]Preliminary.
[b]Federal general revenue sharing is included as state-local expenditure. In fiscal year 1974 an estimated $0.6 billion in general revenue sharing receipts were spent for health and medical care. Estimates for 1975 are not available.

of that society. Thus, a condition or situation with which established institutions and agencies can cope to the satisfaction of most members is not yet a social problem, although it may be a problem to individuals or groups within the society. Only when a problem becomes sufficiently important to enough members of society, meaning that enough are dissatisfied with the ways their institutions are handling it, does it become social. Once defined as a social problem, it requires collective action. Thus limited, the only collective action which matches this concept of a social problem is one which involves the institutions of government, for they represent the desires of citizens and their means for acting collectively on those desires.

TABLE 3

Public and Private Expenditures for Welfare and Other Services, Selected Years, 1950–1975 [a]

Fiscal Year	Total (Public-Private)	Public			Private
		Total	Federal	State-Local	
		Amount (in Billions)			
1950	$2.0	$1.3	$0.6	$0.7	$0.7
1955	1.8	0.9	0.4	0.5	0.9
1960	2.7	1.6	0.7	0.9	1.1
1965	4.3	2.9	1.6	1.3	1.4
1970	10.0	8.0	5.7	2.3	2.0
1975[b]	24.6	21.6	16.6	5.0[c]	3.0
		As a Percent of GNP			
1950	0.8	0.5	0.2	0.3	0.3
1955	0.5	0.2	0.1	0.1	0.2
1960	0.5	0.3	0.1	0.2	0.2
1965	0.7	0.4	0.2	0.2	0.2
1970	1.0	0.8	0.6	0.2	0.2
1975[c]	1.7	1.5	1.2	0.3	0.2
		Percentage Distribution			
1950	100.0	65.0	30.0	35.0	35.0
1955	100.0	50.0	22.2	27.8	50.0
1960	100.0	59.3	25.9	33.3	40.7
1965	100.0	67.4	37.2	30.2	32.6
1970	100.0	80.0	57.0	23.0	20.0
1975[c]	100.0	87.8	67.5	20.3	12.2

SOURCE: *Advisory Commission on Intergovernmental Relations (ACIR) staff compilation based on U.S. Department of Health, Education and Welfare*, Social Security Bulletin, *January 1976; Alfred M. Skolnick and Sophie R. Dales*, Social Welfare Expenditures, 1950–75; *and U.S. Department of Commerce, Bureau of Economic Analysis*, Benchmark Revision of National Income and Product Accounts: Advance Tables, March 1976. *From ACIR*, Significant Features of Fiscal Federalism, 1976 *(Washington, D.C.: U.S. Government Printing Office, 1976), pp. 19–41.*

[a]Excludes public assistance, included in the income maintenance table. Includes food stamps, surplus food for the needy and for institutions, child nutrition, institutional care, child welfare, economic opportunity and manpower programs, veterans' welfare services, vocational rehabilitation, and housing.
[b]Preliminary.
[c]Federal general revenue sharing is included as state-local expenditure. In fiscal year 1974 an estimated $0.4 billion in general revenue sharing receipts were spent for welfare. Estimates for 1975 are not available.

Seen in this light, illness becomes a social problem only when the ways in which medical institutions cope with it are seen as inadequate by a large segment of the population. The same can be said about unemployment, crime, income, and so on. When this critical state is reached, any action taken through the formal mechanisms of society becomes social action, and its guiding principles become social policies. When medical or police or income institutions take care of illness or poverty in ways which satisfy enough citizens, then it is not a social problem. If institutional methods are altered to the satisfaction of most citizens, one can say that

TABLE 4
The Narrowing of the Gap in Direct Tax Burdens Borne by Average and Upper Income Families, 1953–1975

Type of Tax	Average Family[a]			Twice the Average Family[b]			Four Times the Average Family[c]		
	Tax as Percent of Family Income		Percent Increase	Tax as Percent of Family Income		Percent Increase	Tax as Percent of Family Income		Percent Increase
	1953	1975	1953–1975	1953	1975	1953–1975	1953	1975	1953–1975
Total	11.8	22.7	92.4	16.5	24.6	49.1	20.2	29.5	46.0
Federal personal income tax	7.6	9.6	26.3	12.8	14.7	14.8	16.6	21.1	27.1
Social security tax (OASDHI)	1.1	5.9	436.4	0.5	2.9	480.0	0.3	1.5	400.0
Local residential property	2.2	4.0	81.8	1.8	3.2	77.8	1.7	2.5	47.1
State-local personal income	0.3	1.9	533.3	0.9	2.9	222.2	1.2	3.7	208.3
State-local general sales	0.6	1.3	116.7	0.5	0.9	80.0	0.4	0.7	75.0

SOURCE: *Advisory Commission on Intergovernmental Relations (ACIR) staff computations*, Significant Features of Fiscal Federalism, 1976 *(Washington, D.C.: U.S. Government Printing Office, 1976), pp. 19–41.*

[a]Estimates for average family earning $5,000 in 1963 and $14,000 in 1975 assuming all income from wages and salaries, and earned by one spouse.
[b]Estimates for twice the average family. Family earning $10,000 in 1953 and $28,000 in 1975 and assumes that earnings include $105 (interest on state and local debt, and excludable dividends) in 1975 and $25 in 1953; also assumes the inclusion of net long-term capital gains of $1,040 in 1975 and $350 in 1953.
[c]Estimates for four times the average family. Family earning $20,000 in 1953 and $56,000 in 1975 and assumes that earnings include $965 (interest on state and local debt, and excludable dividends) in 1975 and $265 in 1953; also assumes the inclusion of net long-term capital gains of $6,400 in 1975 and $1,730 in 1953.

social problem has been taken care of. It is then possible to identify the guiding policies which govern the acceptable solution; or it is possible to discuss alternative policies if the solution is not acceptable.

However, a large variety of public, governmental institutions and programs have evolved in recent decades to deal with conditions which fall within the foregoing definition of social, but yet are viewed as different from economic, cultural, or foreign policy conditions. An attempt should be made to see if an additional meaning can be given the term social policy when it is applied to this new cluster of governmental actions.

For the purposes of this volume the word social is used to characterize those aspects of government policy which can be directly traced to individuals in society rather than to the society as an impersonal abstraction. For example, public policy about income can be called social policy if redistribution among broad classes is intended or if needs of specific subgroups of persons are targeted (the aged or the American Indian family). Increasing or decreasing the rate of economic growth or increasing or decreasing national economic self-sufficiency are less likely to be considered here as social policy matters. Employment, income, or health programs affect and reach minorities, women, and the aged differently and the attention to these differentiations is also part of the social meaning. We can speak also of the social component of otherwise general policies when we take into account how policies intended to achieve wider employment are affected by the ways in which individuals and groups are differentially motivated. There exists a social dimension when we find unintended personal consequences of general policies, as when a policy to get working mothers off relief produces a generation of disturbed children because mothering care has been diminished by forced work policies.

The term also covers that cluster of public programs which are intended to meet the needs of vulnerable subpopulations. These can be rather narrow, such as the protection of abused children or the feeding of infants in low-income families, or they can be very broad, such as consideration of whether day-care facilities should be provided for all families who wish it, to permit mothers to pursue careers, or simply to relieve women from household drudgery. In this area the term refers to subjects usually identified with social (i.e., collectively provided) services or to welfare, as in the concept of the welfare state.

The term social therefore refers to the human impact of government, to alternatives in patterns of relationship, and to arbitrarily selected types of action addressed to the needs of vulnerable groups. In both the broad and narrow uses, we will be speaking of relationships across categorical lines. General policies affecting the economy can no longer be wholly isolated from effects on individuals and from the effects which individual and psychological phenomena have on economic policy. Health policy cannot be isolated from the reactions and the behavior of consumers. But equally, the setting up of organizational mechanisms to carry out any policy, social or otherwise, must consider the interface between the bureaucratic structure, its behavior, the behavior of persons who staff those bureaucracies, and the behavior of the persons who use them. These interfaces are here considered social for they also affect the ways in which any policy of government reaches individual citizens, whether those citizens are many or few, privileged or vulnerable.

None of these uses of our term stops at the level of criticism. It is necessary but not sufficient to note that work policies discriminate against minorities or that urban policies produce alienation and depersonalized environments. Such critiques are not social policies. When these critiques are linked specifically to explicit acts of government or are linked to explicit lines of action proposed to produce a more desirable state of affairs for individuals, then it can be said that the social dimension has a policy utility, as these terms will be used.

To recapitulate, policy is used in this text to denote a continuing guide for action by individuals or groups in a position to make choices over time affecting the lives of others in a flexible fashion. It is a nonidealized guidance mechanism. By contrast, societal policy or social norms (a variant on the common usage of the term social policy) may be said to represent the sum of actions, attitudes, and choices made in a society, often with contradictions but with rough identity, but a sum of choices so broad as not to be amenable to decision making by responsible individuals or groups. Public policy may be seen as the sum of what governments use as guides for their actions. And social policies represent those aspects of policy which directly address individuals and groups in a society and social relationships as distinguished from technical or economic relationships.

CRITERION MEASURES FOR SOCIAL POLICY ANALYSES

Our discussion thus far lacks measures by which citizen or scientist or policy maker can assess the direction of the evolution of public policies. Much attention has been given to the political process: how various subgroups exert power or influence to effect or prevent change and how society's political structure facilitates or obstructs change.

Less attention has been given to a more technical side of the problem. The term *technipol* has been coined to identify the twin functions which must be performed by anyone in the policy arena. At the level of organizational detail many technical facets have, of course, been elaborated. We have a plethora of devices to measure different ways of providing medical care, to control budget expenditures, or to prevent fraud. We have been less inventive when it comes to broader issues of policy which touch on the basic attitudes and permitted behavior in a given society. A start has been made by Lowi and by others to translate the old questions about "who gets what from whom" into more technical categories.

Lowi has suggested that the age-old questions about who gets what from whom can be traced out through a study of major policy types, classified according to their content. Public policies can be classified as: (1) *distributive* (the parceling out of public benefits among parties to the division, as in the case of "pork barrel" actions by Congress), (2) *regulative* (the control of the relations among parties, thus altering the rules by which they secure shares of the public benefits), or (3) *redistributive* (the reallocation of benefits and burdens among broad social-economic sectors of the population, rather than among organized narrow-interest groups).[4] In this formulation, it appears that distributive and regulative policies lend themselves to the creation of coalitions among relatively well-organized political entities, in or outside of government. Redistributive policies strike more deeply at the roots of society's values and structure and are likely to produce polarization among basic political forces rather than coalitions.

The social policies we will be discussing began as distributive or regulative ones, but over time have taken on a redistributive character. Thus they challenge deep-seated historical patterns of group behavior, and involve both the legitimacy of new governmental functions and certain unexpected limitations to private initiative. Patterns of the scope of government and the role of private initiative have strong roots in the past, but such marked changes have taken place in the last 40 years that a new level of decision making has been reached. Old norms about the proper scope for government no longer match the realities of government actions which touch the lives of all citizens directly and pervasively. Shall we try to return to old standards or construct new guidelines appropriate to the present reality?

For our purposes, the new distributive-redistributive character of policy requires a choice between two possible paths of program development in the future. Both paths raise questions about the much-widened scope of government intrusion into what has until recently been considered a private domain. Marmor, citing Friedman, has classified social welfare policies by the path they follow, that is, whether they are based upon a charity- or a middle-class perspective.[5]

---

[4]Theodore Lowi, "American Business Public Policy and Political Theory," *World Politics* (1964): 16, p. 107ff. See also David Gil, *Unravelling Social Policies* (Cambridge, Mass.: Schenkman, 1973) and Theodore Marmor, *The Politics of Medicare* (Chicago: Aldine, 1973).

[5]Lawrence Friedman, "Social Welfare Legislation," *Stanford Law Review* 21 (January 1969): 247, cited in Marmor, *Politics of Medicare*, p. 120.

Criteria	Middle-Class Program	Charity Program
Benefits	Broad demographic unit, not selected by means test	Needy persons selected by means test
Benefits	Earned, noncomprehensive, for a given problem	Given, not earned, more comprehensive
Financing	Regressive as with social security taxes, earmarked	General revenues, more progressive
Administrative	Centralized, nondiscretionary, clerklike with developed rules of entitlement	Discretionary, decentralized

While this formulation may not fit all situations, it provides one useful means by which to trace social policy evolution in the United States. This will be used in succeeding chapters.

Thus, the final framework for analyzing the evolution of American social policies consists of examining:

1. Social norms
2. Public policies
3. Sectoral public social policy
4. Leadership role in government
5. Advocated versus adopted policy
6. Criteria for assessing policy guidelines

IDEOLOGY BEYOND A POLICY FRAMEWORK

These elementary efforts to introduce a technical aspect to policy analysis, as distinguished from administration detail, complement rather than replace certain value or ideological considerations which underlie all policy actions. In social work as in many professions, the term *values* is used instead of *ideology* to express a faith in certain enduring beliefs upon which all professional, political, and technical behavior *should* be based. Some of these values are general, such as respect for individuality. Others represent more specific ideas, such as basing choices on a capitalist, marketplace system of organization, on government ownership and management, or on small-scale neighborhood forms of group association.

Such basic ideological preferences can constitute the core of policy as guidance but they require some operational framework for translation into action. Political structure or form of organization satisfies part of this requirement. The political processes of policy formation have been discussed in numerous case examples and will not be repeated here since our concern is with other less-publicized aspects of policy evaluation.[6]

It is evident that some structure, organization, or mechanism must be in place, or must be created, through which policies are shaped and moved. These structures are the formal mechanisms of any society, even if policy is perceived to have its original dynamic in the actions of individuals or of unofficial informal organizations such as associations or parties. Abstract concepts about policy require complementary attention to these mechanisms and also to technical tools, which will be briefly considered in Chapter 9.

WHY SOCIAL POLICIES WARRANT EXPERT TECHNICAL ATTENTION NOW

In a period of great flux, we may ask why it is not sufficient to hold strong ideological positions as a framework for evolution or to ask whether revolution rather than evolution in human affairs may not be more consistent with satisfying human needs. There are numerous illustrations, at least in the United States, that indicate the urgency of evolving steady policies in a situation of uncertainty. Policies are desired that do not straightjacket action and that avoid randomness in response. At almost every level of society citizens seek a society in which there is an opportunity for constructive employment for all. In the United States most prefer some looseness in an economic system where varieties of positions and opportunities for mobility and advancement are offered by a variety of nominally competing economic enterprises. A substantial proportion of the citizenry recognizes that this marketplace system works imperfectly and are prepared to accept some level of governmental intervention. This intervention is sometimes viewed as residual, meaning that it is intended to take care of areas in which the marketplace system fails (as, for example, when public assistance or public service employment is offered as the last resort). Others believe that progressive governmental intervention may slowly lead to sufficient improvement in the functioning of the economic system so that the economic wants of individuals are more adequately met. As recently as 1930, the idea of the national government's intervention in the economic system in even residual activities was fought out bitterly, but it is now widely accepted. What is not yet accepted (except by a minority) is the new boundary between private enterprise and government. This constitutes a minefield through which responsible groups and officials need to maneuver if they seek to develop consistent policies which will satisfy such conflicting desires.

---

[6]Readings listed at the end of Chapters 3–6 include references which outline the ideological facets of debate in each sector.

If we turn to a less economic arena—that of medical care—it is by now reasonably clear that there is no overwhelming public demand for a national, exclusive, governmentally administered health service. While compulsory health insurance remains a live option, the readiness to shoulder its cost is less definite. What does exist, however, is the determination to guarantee access to medical care for all, to remove the pain of paying for medical care as far from the individual as possible, and to retain some aspect of choice through private physician and hospital delivery of medical care. The costs of such a system in economic and human terms are now seen as very great (as will be discussed in Chapter 4), so that a new crisis can be said to have arisen and some steady guiding policy is necessary to confront it.

In a less well-defined arena—family policy—similar crises, conflicting wants, and difficulties emerge. We do not have a national position which says families must take care of all their members or that families will be relieved of explicit responsibilities. There is no national policy which seeks to move all mothers into work or to keep them from work. On the other hand, it is clear that most individuals believe that the family does constitute a fundamental social institution which needs to be sustained and that it constitutes the most flexible "social service" of first resort. At the same time, there is widespread acceptance of the belief that the family is overburdened in specific areas and needs to be relieved, primarily by public intervention. The real difficulty lies in how far to go. We are not ready to force mothers with small children into employment, but neither are we prepared to make it too easy for them to avoid it altogether. We have fairly well settled that families with severely retarded children can be completely relieved of the burden of care, but we are less certain when it comes to other forms of disability. Families had been presumed to be the final arbiter in matters of education, but the crises of racial discrimination forced a major shift in emphasis so that now a large area of ambiguity exists. The state is now attempting to force changes in family control of educational systems in order to remove gradually the vestiges of discrimination. At the same time it is seeking to avoid a complete abdication of family responsibility.

It may be clear from such illustrations that the formulation of guiding principles becomes more and more desirable and even necessary. Confidence in scientific skill is also found in the social arena, and the belief persists that difficulties can be resolved without too much encroachment on the private sector. Our expectations have grown enormously, fueled by a succession of New Deal and Great Society programs and carried into 1976 by presidential candidates who argued that our society is a great one, that it "can be gotten moving again," and that we are capable of mastering our destiny.

Unfortunately, the stated desire to resolve difficulties is frequently obstructed by a search for privacy and freedom from constraint and a fear that equity may mean equalization (the have's will have less). There is still a suspicion of "too much government"; there is an idealization of individual decision making; the acquisition of material goods and the search for pleasure are the modern-day interpretations of the pursuit of happiness promised in the Constitution. The citizens who believe that there must and should be a solution to these problems, may feel that they should not have to pay high taxes or be limited in their choice to solve someone else's problem.

Such contradictory passions underlie the urgency for developing a more clear-cut understanding about policy as a guide for progress. Income maintenance is perhaps the most sensitive area; it is here that Americans may be most sharply tested in their capacity to be both fair and reasonable. Scapegoating and attacks upon the welfare system abound, but it is no longer possible to consider the problem of the poor and of income mainte-nance in light of nineteenth-century charity. Unfortunately, much policy debate has been framed both by public and private individuals as charity. The free mobility of Americans, the imperfections of its economic balance between technological requirements in the work force and rewards for labor are quite severe, and while insecurity mostly affects the poorest, no income classes are immune from economic uncertainty.

The belief in private choice for medical treatment runs very deep, and yet the enormous inflation in the costs of medical care and the enormous gaps of resources in urban ghettoes and rural areas begin to erode faith in our ability to deal with such difficulties. When we turn to the problem of aging, there is a deep-seated desire to assure the minimum security for the elderly who are retired from the work force, but long extension of life and freedom of family members to move about conflict with the realities of trying to support an increasing proportion of retired persons, while ignoring the realities of long-term disability.

If we are to make any headway in relieving such social distress, there are quite practical reasons for developing guidelines for action and for training people to facilitate such action. Deep-seated conflicts of interest mean that any action taken is likely to be a compromise, at least among the major conflicting forces. Compromises seldom produce perfect solutions for any troublesome social condition. Therefore, although a succession of less-than-perfect solutions may modify its nature, the condition persists in the face of efforts to deal with it.

It may be discouraging to realize that some troublesome social issues are likely to be with us for a long time and are not amenable to clean-cut solutions. Differences among persons and groups, changing levels of aspiration, biological and physiological weaknesses, imperfections of any known economic system—all suggest that trouble will continue. In light of such reality, groups and individuals who make decisions affecting the lives of others need some guidelines. Goals, such as the abolition of poverty or illness, are essential but are too broad to fit the realities of decision making.

Hopefully a path can be charted which moves steadily, though slowly, in the direction of such ideal goals; and it is policy which holds groups and individuals on course as they form a succession of less-than-perfect solutions.

A second, more realistic reason for a continuous guide to action lies in our imperfect social science and social technology. Many ideological views argue that the adoption of their proposed course of action is the only remedy for poverty, illness, or mental disease if adopted completely. No such remedies have been completely adopted by any society and, therefore, remain untested theories. Since our techniques for social intervention are imperfect, responsible individuals and parties require guiding principles with which to test imperfect intervention devices making continual adjustments and improvements over time. Without steady middle-range policies based on goals and past experience, interventions become erratic, discontinuous, and random rather than building toward definable goals. Policy, therefore, draws a basic premise from its parent discipline, politics: learn to distinguish the possible and the impossible and then do what is possible. In the United States as elsewhere, it is natural to aim for the impossible. Policy, therefore, rides that uneasy course of balancing striving for the probably unattainable ideal, doing the possible, and avoiding the pitfalls of expediency, randomness, and impulsive experimentation without cumulative knowledge. It is this uneasy no-man's-land between expediency and the ideal in which government must act and in which a new discipline must evolve to inform the processes by which policies are developed and acted upon.

We have touched on contradictions between aspirations and reality in American society which, if not resolved, may erode confidence in government altogether. One consequence, of course, could be the creation of a wholly new governmental structure, but one cannot ignore the possibility of another consequence, namely, the growth of anomie and the breakdown in organized capacity to deal with problems, resulting ultimately in decay and nihilism.

In this text we, of course, cannot supply a solution to these dilemmas, but we can explicate an approach to analyzing social policy which through improved understanding of and discipline in policy development can provide a guide through the difficulties ahead. Policy promising neither too much nor too little can have a stabilizing effect on collective efforts in American society. Such efforts seek to improve progressively the way in which persisting social difficulties are managed without, at the same time, tearing the American fabric apart by violent internal conflict. Whether such a middle path can succeed remains to be seen.

Without proposing global solutions or specific programs, this volume will seek to perform a few limited tasks. It will seek to sharpen what the term social policy means. It will try to discover whether implicit, as well as explicit, social policies can be identified in certain areas commonly considered more social than economic: income, medical care, housing, and personal social services, and care of the young and the aged. If such policies can be identified, an attempt will be made to review what disciplinary techniques and tools are currently available to improve the development of guiding principles for the future. Such tools may be used to alter the evolution of implicit policies or to improve those explicit policies which have established their utility. Such questions as these will be examined.

1. Can the concept of social policy be given meaning as a basis for equipping professionals and citizens to better deal with the subject matter or content of social policy?
2. Are there levels of policy which distinguish between the state of a society, the directions governments take, and the details of program administration?
3. Do we have anything which can be called national social policies or do we at random act as a nation?
4. If we do have national policies, do they have any continuity or are they an accumulation of contradictory ad hoc reactions by government to problems?
5. Do tools, techniques, and concepts exist for a separate field of inquiry which also provide the basis for a separate career in policy development? Or is action, if any takes place, the result solely of political exchange among competing special interests?

Certain conclusions, based on the analysis of examples in Chapters 3 to 7, guide the treatment of such questions. First, the national government has, through many changes in national administration, adhered to a few basic principles as it acts on the social needs of its citizens. These principles constitute public policies and provide continuity in guiding national acts, contrary to the widely held view that the nation lacks consistent social policies. They conform to the best definition of policy available—a set of guiding principles by which accountable persons or groups make public decisions in reasonably consistent directions as they meet new and unanticipated situations.

Second, social norms generally circumscribe or set the boundaries for public policy action. These wider societal policies change slowly, and public policy (i.e., governmental choice) sometimes goes beyond these normal constraints and eventually alters the basic content of societal policies.

Third, the American system is at a new plateau in this evolution of social norms. As an unanticipated consequence of the incremental build-up of governmental actions conforming to social norms, and guided by public policy, the weight and scope of national governmental actions is now so great and so widely accepted that the very norms which once circumscribed national policy have been altered. Government has become a leading force in modifying basic social norms, not only the follower of random political forces. We are ready to make new choices, unprecedented in the American system of government.

Fourth, we can now question commonly held assumptions about the sources of resistance to and pressure for change. These new insights of American policy processes provide a basis for elaborating the technical, analytic side of policy analysis just as we have already probed the political dimension of a technipolitical process.

ADDITIONAL READINGS

Cullingworth, J. B. *Problems of an Urban Society.* Vol. 2, The *Social Content of Planning.* London: Allen and Unwin, 1973. Chaps. 5–6.

Gil, David. *Unravelling Social Policy.* Cambridge, Mass.: Schenkman, 1973.

Glennerster, H. *Social Service Budgets and Social Policy.* London: Allen and Unwin, 1975. Chaps. 2–5.

Graham, Otis. *Toward a Planned Society.* New York: Oxford University Press, 1976.

Titmuss, Richard. *Committment to Welfare.* London: Allen and Unwin, 1968.

INCOME MAINTENANCE POLICIES: CONTINUITY AND CHANGE

Income, whatever its form, is the fundamental means by which citizens exchange or secure access to the goods produced by any society. It is not surprising, therefore, that the most important and sensitive area of social policy is that affecting income distribution. This holds true in economies organized on "free enterprise" capitalist lines or those organized on market-controlled socialist lines. Conditions of life are at stake. Too rapid change in the distribution pattern produces unsettling reactions ranging from passive resistance to strikes, riots, and revolts. These arise in all societies regardless of economic form. Some control of income by the state is omnipresent and sometimes omnipotent.

Social policy concerning income can be distinguished from economic policy in that social policy focuses primarily on: (1) assurance of minimum requirements for survival for all members of a society and (2) the distribution of income among various group and class strata (i.e., the proportion of the population with high, middle, and low income and the difference between the highest and lowest income). Economic policy may take these social dimensions into consideration, but they are not its primary concern.

Attention to these questions in the United States has been characterized by a continuing pressure for change following a consistent line of evolution from minimum assurance of survival to income redistribution. The evolution of American income policy resulting from the tension between pressure for and resistance to change can be divided into four major phases: the period before the 1930s with minimum or no federal obligation, the New Deal period of the 1930s with the emergence of federal responsibility, the Great Society period of the 1960s with an enlargement of the guiding principles, and the 1970s with an attempt to control government responsibility.

LIMITATIONS OF SOCIAL NORMS AND THEIR EXPANSION

Implicit social norms, as we have postulated, have both stimulated and limited American approaches to income policy. These underlying concepts have found differing expressions at different periods in history but have remained remarkably stable. In regard to income maintenance, they can be briefly summarized as follows:

1. Primary responsibility is expected to rest with the individual and the marketplace. Perhaps this is an inheritance from pioneer days when it was assumed that any willing individual could acquire his own share of an apparently unlimited supply of land and resources and provide for his own subsistance. The Protestant ethic, and its Puritan expression provided a powerful religious justification for such an approach, with its emphasis on individual paths to salvation. With the evolution of an industrial society, the uncertainties and inequities of corporate control of employment opportunities were gradually recognized and steps were taken, often after violent conflict, to correct the worst abuses. But until the 1930s, with a few exceptions national action in the more industrialized states, was primarily regulatory—control of working conditions, hours of work, and monetary policy. Income dilemmas were not considered a matter of governmental responsibility, and it was still expected that an able-bodied person could take care of his own needs if he would only work hard enough.

2. Government, whether local, state, or federal, has always played a role in income maintenance. However, even as that role gradually expanded beginning in the eighteenth century, it was considered to be less desirable than, and only supplementary or complementary to, the free operation of the market place. However, the gradually increasing total amount of government income maintenance activities has increased the government role so that federal expenditures now represent over 20 percent of the GNP or of all of the goods and services produced in the economy.[1] Much of this expenditure is for direct income support for individuals or classes.

3. Government's supplementary role has been justified primarily for segments of the population considered to be vulnerable and helpless and

---

[1]Charles Schultz et al., *Setting National Priorities: 1973 Budget* (Washington, D.C.: Brookings Institution, 1972) tables 1–3, p. 11.

therefore needing and deserving public attention—aged, sick, widows. In the eighteenth century this was a modest obligation, but in the twentieth century the governmental responsibility to satisfy this concept has to an obligation representing nearly half the national budget.

4. Eligibility for most governmental programs is conditioned by present or former work.

5. Most national income maintenance policy has been predicated on a joint federal and state partnership.

6. Faith in science or technology to abolish poverty has persisted so that most income programs are assumed to have a short life (retirement for the aged excepted).

The national policy is guided not only by this set of stable principles, but also by another set of principles which are less stabilized and have been constantly expanding. In the earliest period, government, first local and only later national, was considered to have some responsibility for the helpless members of a pioneer society, primarily orphans and widows. In time, with the evolution of an industrialized nation in the late nineteenth and early twentieth centuries, the concept of governmental responsibility was expanded to include assuring minimum survival to especially disadvantaged groups, first as a matter of charity and then by the 1930s as a matter of right. But the concept of an essential minimum was also steadily enlarged until it came to mean not prevention of starvation but a minimum of health and decency. The most recent stage of this development has been the use of income maintenance programs to achieve a higher degree of equity by a progressive raising of the income floor for all persons. This development is on the verge of reducing the spread between minimum and maximum income in the United States. The supplementary role of government may become more active and positive to reshape economic relationships.

Before the 1930s: Limited Federal Obligation

The current dominance of the national government in social policy matters obscures the fact that local and sometimes state governments were actively involved in elementary forms of income support from the beginning of the Republic. At that time policies were shaped primarily by charitable concepts: neighbors discharged a charitable obligation to look after the widows and orphans. They were often recompensed by tax appropriations for the most elementary forms of relief payments. Such tax payments to citizens to perform charitable acts could be justified when most citizens were poor. However, a small beachhead of national obligation emerged when the national government reluctantly accepted some responsibility for large numbers of veterans of the Continental armies, many of whom were destitute.

The role of the federal government remained minimal during the nineteenth and into the early twentieth century, except for its continuing obligation to military personnel, who were considered to have earned special claims on the national government. However, the land-grant and homestead legislation of the nineteenth century represents national policies conforming to the principles outlined above. In the early days of industrializing, the major tangible asset available to the national government was its authority over vast expanses of land acquired by purchase or expropriation. Through various mechanisms land was made available to citizens, sometimes with preference to veterans, sometimes in a kind of lottery open to all competitors. It is true that large tracts of land were turned over to the railroads as an incentive to "open up the country" and, indirectly, to provide jobs and economic development, but other large tracts of land were made available to individuals. In a sense land in the middle nineteenth century was the equivalent of contemporary dollar allocations from the treasury. The land distribution programs conformed to a basic policy of relying upon the individual and the marketplace, and yet also involved federal supplementation of the essentially private processes. They also involved a form of federal and state partnership since jurisdiction devolved to the states once land was acquired by individuals or by corporations.

By the early twentieth century the major industrialized states—New York, Massachusetts, New Jersey, Ohio, Illinois—had elaborated other state-level programs based upon older English poor laws of local residence and poor relief. A few states enacted statewide, modest pensions for widows with minor children and for the aged. By 1929 these expenditures were estimated to total some $500 million, almost entirely state or municipality administered.[2]

The 1930s and the New Deal: The Emergence of Federal Responsibility

The depression years and the enactment of the Social Security Act in 1935 are rightly considered watersheds in the evolution of American policy for welfare and especially for income maintenance. However, the significant breakthrough in this period was the assumption of an active role by the national government for income maintenance.

While this can be considered a major development in the history of the nation, it does not represent a new direction in policy if, by policy, we mean those guiding principles for action in unexpected and future circumstances. Social security legislation of the 1930s appears to conform in all major respects to the principles governing income maintenance outlined at the beginning of this chapter. Most programs were based upon past employment; income support was to be temporary (except for the aged), assuming that private work would be revived; continued income

---

[2]*Encyclopedia of Social Work*, 16th ed. (New York: National Association of Social Workers, 1971), vol. 2, Table 20, p. 1584.

support was assured only to the widowed, disabled, and aged; and programs required cooperation and cost sharing by three levels of government.

If not quite a revolution in policy or a major change in direction, at least two significant advances in the nature of these policies were made: (1) the belief was introduced that income provided should be closer to a level of minimum health and decency than to a bare subsistence; (2) a first step was taken to use federal policy to equalize income as well as to provide access to minimum income.

The Federal Emergency Relief Administration (FERA) represented the national government's use of its fiscal resources to provide cash assistance not only to the widowed and orphaned, but to able-bodied workers. This was clearly an emergency program based on the assumption that the economy would, in time, provide the major sources of income and that the marketplace would resume its normal function. However, through its use of cash payments, the FERA represented an assurance of access to minimum income, a responsibility previously assumed by state and local governments.

The Public Works Administration (PWA) and the Works Progress Administration (WPA) of the same period represented another facet of the same guiding principle, namely, that, at least for the able bodied, income and work went hand in hand. Over the life of the WPA nearly 8 million persons, formerly unemployed, were given jobs building highways, bridges, roads, public buildings, hospitals, and nursing stations, libraries, schools, and museums. Swampland was drained; water mains and sewer lines rebuilt; parks and playgrounds restored or constructed; the first National Guide Series to the United States were produced; and theater, music, and plastic arts were subsidized. In a peak year of 1938, 3,161,000 unemployed individuals were employed on such projects.[3]

By the time of America's entry into World War II both the FERA and the WPA were terminated, testifying to the emergency nature of these national administrations and to the continuity of basic policy which saw government as a complement or supplement to the marketplace economy.

The enactment of the Social Security Act in 1935 symbolized further the continuity of American social policy as now expressed in the public policy of the national government. First, the Social Security Act assured access of minimum income for certain vulnerable populations, namely, the elderly, widows, and orphans. This policy, however, was no longer left to impulses of local government or to the uncertainties of annual appropriations. Instead, a form of compulsory annuity was introduced, compulsory for almost all the working population (certain excluded groups such

---

[3]See Donald Howard, *W.P.A. and Federal Relief Policy* (New York: Russell Sage, 1943); A. E. Burns, *Federal Work, Security and Relief Programs*, Research Monograph No. 24 (Washington, D.C.: U.S. Government Printing Office, 1941), p. 54.

as farm laborers, domestics, and employees of religious organizations and physicians were later covered), and contributed to by the beneficiary as well as by the employers. The assurance of security, meaning income access and nothing more, was riveted into our society by these devices. In the future it would be very difficult indeed to remove this access, at least for the working population.

A crucial issue was the compulsory nature of the policy. There was strong conservative opposition to the idea of any compulsory program, and a competitive preference· was strongly argued for some voluntary arrangements by which individuals would themselves choose whether or not to be protected under the new program. In the legislative controversy preceding the passage of the act those who favored a completely voluntary system, which would have returned the entire security program for the elderly to the marketplace, were counterbalanced by advocates of the Townsend Movement, which called for a straight and simple pension of a fixed sum to be paid to all older persons regardless of their work status. The proponents of the Social Security Act compromised by inserting the requirement that the annuity would become available only on retirement. This issue was left in doubt until final determination was made in the Senate Finance Committee in 1935. In the debate the president and his appointed Committee on Economic Security strongly supported compulsory annuities. The Congress represented the older policy, while the presidency represented the cutting edge of the new. The policy and position of the executive branch was finally adopted by the Congress.[4]

Regardless of the economic aspects of this decision, it represented logical consistency in a social policy which assured minimum income access only for persons who were considered by the society at any given time to be outside of the effective labor force. In the eighteenth century, women frequently and orphans often were considered wholly outside of the labor force. In the 1930s, in the midst of a deep depression, the elderly—especially those over 65—were also considered (whether realistically or idealistically) as effectively out of the labor force and, therefore, qualified for minimum income assurance.

The firmness of federal policy was further tested by the debate over where to place the administration of the Social Security Act. There was strong support among presidential advisors to place all administration within the Department of Labor, the federal department most clearly identified with employment and especially employment developments in the private economy. A compromise was reached whereby unemployment compensation would be administered by the Department of Labor and an independent Social Security Board would be established to administer the old-age pension program. This independent, permanent, new agency fell

---

[4]For a discussion of this debate, see Edwin E. Witte, *The Development of the Social Security Program* (Madison: University of Wisconsin Press, 1963).

within the old norms for the federal government in that it attended to the
needs of a part of the population considered most likely to be kept out
of the work force and also considered vulnerable. At the same time the
fact that its creation substantially widened the scope of the federal government's supplementary role would have consequences for the future shaping
of public policies. The new programs were located in permanent instru-
mentalities of the national government and thus marked a turning point in
the range of the national government's supplementary responsibility. This
evolution modified the underlying policy boundaries of the past in one
final respect: the administration of the old-age retirement program was
vested entirely in the national government, without the state and local
government partnership existing in most other activities.

Income security for widows and orphans was translated by the Social
Security Act into a program for mothers and dependent children. The
legislation was not as generous with children as it was with the aged, at
least with respect to federal sharing in the costs of security. But a federal
program provided federal contributions to state programs for mothers with
dependent children who qualified by lack of other income sources. The
national government did not assume a commitment to provide assured
income to this specially vulnerable group of citizens, but acted within
conventional boundaries by sharing costs and administration with state
and local governments and by limiting its share to the poorest, most
helpless.

The federal role of complementing the marketplace was, in 1935,
further enlarged by the introduction of a national system of unemployment insurance. This was intended to assure steady access to some income
for persons in the labor force but temporarily unemployed. Issues as to
whether to limit or to widen federal policy were argued. To ensure enactment the proponents of the program finally adopted compromises to maintain a central policy position. The insurance was limited to workers forced
out of employment through no fault of their own and the income security
provided was kept to a minimum. Some proponents argued for a federally
administered system with standard, federally determined premiums to be
paid employers and with standard federally determined benefits. Others
argued for a single fund, but one to be administered by each state. Still
others argued for maximum openness, with states free to choose between
a single unemployment insurance fund or several insurance funds set up
for each major employer group. While the details of tax level and of
insurance fund form are complex and significant, what proved most
important in the enactment of this legislation was the enlargement of a
well-established principle of governmental responsibility for income assurance. Between 1941 and 1970 the annual number of workers applying for
payments due to unemployment rose from 3,439,000 to 6,402,000. Average
weekly benefits rose from $11.06 to $50.34, representing about 35 percent

of average weekly earnings throughout the three decades as benefits sought to keep up with inflation.

The steadfast work focus of federal policy was further demonstrated by the introduction of a program for vocational rehabilitation of the disabled. The Committee on Economic Security, which spearheaded the original executive branch planning for this legislation, considered invalidism or disability insurance and recognized it as an acceptable form of protection. However, the complexities of developing and administering an insurance program for invalids were considered to be so great that the committee felt it should be the last item introduced to round out a full program of security. Those who argued for a comprehensive program for the handicapped and those who were opposed to any further extension of protection were satisfied by a compromise which provided for the rehabilitation of the injured so that they could return to employment. Balancing the executive determination to enlarge and the congressional determination to contain, the compromise measure joined the concern of government for a vulnerable group unable to work with the commitment to the marketplace and self-employment by establishing a program for education and retraining supported by the federal government.

The principle of shared responsibility between the federal and the state governments and with private industry was also strengthened and extended in this period. Except for the annuity program for the retired elderly, all other programs of the Social Security Act involved some form of joint federal and state collaboration and sharing in both administration and costs. The nature of the collaboration varies by program. Old age assistance, as distinguished from the retirement program, was administered by state governments with the federal government matching approved expenditures by one-half. Programs for mothers and dependent children were also state administered, with the federal government sharing in approved expenditures by one-third. Vocational rehabilitation proved to be a combination of state-administered programs and federal regulation and funding. Workmen's compensation was entirely state administered, with the federal government collecting and remitting taxes. Whatever the details of the form, the principle of federal-state sharing of both responsibility and financing was reaffirmed.

In another significant move the 1935 legislation sought to move the floor for income support from a bare subsistence level to one of minimum decency. The original social security legislation provided that the states must furnish assistance sufficient to provide "when added to the income of the aged recipient, a *reasonable* subsistence compatible with decency and health." [5] This provision was derived from legislation in pioneer states such as New York and Massachusetts. However, representatives of southern state were vigorously opposed to this introduction of a federal

---

[5] Witte, *Development of the Social Security Program.*

standard into a state's freedom of choice, primarily because it was viewed as a threat to the states' freedom to treat their minorities differently from the way in which others were treated. To secure enactment, this provision was dropped, but its proposal is another example of how executive branch activities sought to enlarge public policy beyond existing norms. In this case the proposal went too far beyond what the American society was then prepared to accept. If the language proposed had been retained, the balance in partnership between federal and state government would have been altered: a tool to press for greater income equalization would have been placed in the hands of a federal agency; and federal intervention into the lives of its citizens would have deepened and widened. However, federal efforts persisted into later years. A proposed policy was delayed, but finally was adopted by 1965 when the Department of Health, Education, and Welfare began its systematic use of a formula to fix a "poverty line" for counting the poor. This became the target for most social programs.

The 1935 legislation also represents a major advance in redistributive policy, which uses income maintenance as a means not only to assure minimum income, but also to reduce the disparity between income classes. The retirement program introduced a principle new to the American society, it payed relatively larger benefits to workers receiving low wages throughout their working life and thus discriminated slightly in favor of low-income workers at the expense of higher-earning employees who contributed more substantially to the income fund. This did not mean that benefits were strictly graded according to past income, but rather that there was a slight increase in benefits to the lowest paid while the higher-paid workers received slightly less than if the program paid an annuity based upon private pension plans.

In periods of overwhelming national emergency, the norms we have identified as governing income programs in the United States have been abandoned. During the depths of the depression public assistance income was federally administered throughout most of the United States. The fact that this was considered an emergency measure comparable to the kind of national mobilization which takes place in wartime is revealed throughout all of the debate of this period, in the very name of the Federal Emergency Relief Administration, and in its dismantling as soon as war and improvement in employment altered the economic profile.

Wartime introduced one interesting experiment in federal control of income maintenance indirectly through the health field. A large part of the work force was in the army; their wives were at the prime child-bearing age. The low army pay left them unable to meet the costs of child rearing and bearing. A wartime emergency program, the Emergency Maternal and Infant Care Program, was introduced to assure that the medical costs of child bearing and rearing for military personnel would be properly covered. Although not vast by comparison with other income maintenance programs, this program was the first which, while nominally handled through the marketplace of private medicine, did so under strict regulations introduced by the United States Children's Bureau and administered as a national program.[6]

The Social Security Act succeeded in sustaining the implicit social policies of the past: reliance upon the marketplace, government supplementation, with acceptance of limited federal sharing with the states, and a commitment to help assure certain disadvantaged groups of access to steady income. The legislation's major contribution brought the national government for the first time fully into the income arena as a matter of social policy, but without introducing any radically new thrust in policy.

Certain new and even revolutionary changes in policy were tested and by and large failed. The attempt to assure income, at least for the elderly, on a compulsory basis without requiring retirement from the work force was defeated as was the attempt to introduce a level of income for assuring health and decency rather than minimum subsistence. However, an approach to radical change was adopted. The retirement program was the first step in the long process of narrowing disparities in income in American society, and full federal administration and control was tested, even if on a depression or wartime emergency basis.

The 1960s—An Enlargement of the Guiding Principles

Between 1935 and 1960 most of the emergency relief proposals induced by the depression were dismantled, leaving only the basic income maintenance programs initiated in the 1930s. This period was characterized by inflation and economic boom with recession, but a combination of war and postwar economic expansion and growth in the national economic product produced a general belief that the basic economy was proceeding soundly and that substantial governmental interventions were no longer necessary. However, expenditures for income maintenance programs by federal and state governments did not decline; in fact they increased slightly. In 1935, at the depths of the depression, $22.4 billion were spent for these purposes; by 1960 the amount had increased to $24.4 billion.[7] Approximately half of these expenditures were in the form of federal payments to the states, representing continuity in the concept of federal-state partnership.

The persistence of government programs at these levels in a period of presumed economic health caused substantial anxiety, an anxiety increased by evidence that poverty continued at a high level even though the principle of access to minimum income still seemed to be at work. In 1959, for

---

[6]See Nathan Sinai and Odin W. Anderson, *EMIC: A Study of Administrative Experience.* Research Series No. 3 (Ann Arbor: Bureau of Health Economics, School of Public Health, University of Michigan, 1948).

[7]*Encyclopedia of Social Work,* 16th ed. (New York: National Association of Social Workers, 1971), Table 20, p. 1584.

example, it was estimated that about 22 percent of the American population lived below an arbitrarily defined level of poverty.[8]

The existence of such levels of poverty produced not only political
crises, but also a serious, if poorly articulated, doubt about the whole
economic system. Poverty was an issue in the political arena as the need
to increase expenditures to maintain income was argued. However, this
phenomenon also served to introduce a substantial challenge to another
guiding principle for government policy in the income field, namely, that
government existed primarily to supplement or complement the functioning
of the marketplace. The fact that nearly a quarter of the American population was not satisfactorily served in terms of income by the marketplace
raised grave doubts about the American economy itself.

These doubts led to a continuing search for better technical means
for identifying what is meant by the term poverty. In fact, the development of measures of poverty can be taken to represent one of the difficulties
in policy planning, namely, the absence of widely accepted technical tools
with which to carry planning forward. The instrument most widely used
to measure poverty was a measure of absolute poverty developed by the
Social Security Administration.[9] In its simplest form this measure is based
on the estimated cost of an economy food budget for families of various
sizes, representing the proportion of income expended by family types for
the purchase of food. Thus, if a family of given size and location spends
one-third of its income on food at an economy level, it is assumed that
income required to keep the family just at or above the poverty line
would be three times this figure; families with incomes below this fixed
figure are considered to be below the poverty threshold.

Although this measure is widely used and does represent a significant
advance over previous measures in the United States, it has nonetheless
been critized on several scores. It is considered to ignore accepted levels
of decency as distinguished from a stringent or even bare subsistence
budget. It also does not take into account price level variations in different
regions or climatic and other factors which affect the costs of budgetary
items such as food, shelter, transportation. With all its limitations, the
measure does, however, serve as a tool for national policy in that it does
establish a generally accepted fixed minimum below which families should
not fall.

Numerous proposals have been made to modify the social security
measure, but most of them have been concerned only with raising the
level of the poverty threshold. *Relative* measures of poverty are an important supplement to the social security index. The difference between
the income which most Americans consider to be "average" or real for

[8]President's Commission on Income Maintenance. *Poverty Amid Plenty—The
American Paradox* (Washington, D.C.: U.S. Government Printing Office, 1969).
[9]Molly Orshansky, "Counting the Poor—Another Look at the Poverty Profile,"
Social Security Bulletin 28 No. 1 (January 1965) : 3–29.

themselves and the income actually attained which falls below this real average is a useful measure of relative poverty in a dynamic society.

Plotnick and Skidmore have combined the official social security measure with a second relative measure of the poverty population.[10] Their modification divides a family's current cash income by the social security poverty line. This yields a welfare ratio which indicates the fraction by which the family's income exceeds or falls below the SSA level of minimum decency defined in absolute terms.

These measures do not adequately account for the effect of taxes or of in-kind transfers, such as food in-kind or subsidized housing or free medical care, although some attempts are being made by the Institute for Research on Poverty of the University of Wisconsin to introduce these variables.[11]

Bearing in mind these technical problems of measurement and the more general concerns about poverty and the economy, it is instructive to review the decade of the 1960s. The 1960s can be called the period of the Great Society. The boundaries of governmental supplementation of the marketplace were substantially widened, and the guiding principle once limited to assuring a subsistence minimum was broadened by the optimistically proclaimed "war on poverty." Underneath the rhetoric promising a campaign to abolish poverty lay an important shift in national policy, namely, the move from subsistence to prevention. The dimensions of this shift can be seen by a review of trends between 1965 and 1974 in social welfare expenditures considered to be related to income programs. Tables 5, 6, and 7 dramatically outline the increases in federal, state, local, and total expenditures on social programs addressed primarily to low-income populations. The relationship of such federal actions to the number of households considered below poverty during this period is clear, as is the effect of such actions on the poverty gap between the periods preceding and following the transfer of public funds.

The tables show clearly the great escalation of total amounts expended in the seven-year period. The programs all conform to the basic principles developed during the 1930s: they rest on the assumptions that a combination of job creation, education, and other incentives can reduce the number of families in poverty, that providing these incentives is a governmental responsibility, and that such governmental actions are essential to supplement the basic marketplace economy.

But job stimulation and cash relief were no longer seen as sufficient to reduce poverty and allow the market its old dominance. Deficits in education and in opportunity also had to be overcome by such short-term programs. Therefore, government financing was extended to include adult

---

[10]Robert Plotnick and Felicity Skidmore, *Progress Against Poverty*, Institute for Research on Poverty series, (New York: Academic Press, 1975), Chap. 2.
[11]Ibid., chap. 14.

TABLE 5
Social Welfare Expenditures, 1965, 1968, 1972

Year	Program	1965 Expenditure (in millions of dollars)	Percent	1968 Expenditure (in millions of dollars)	Percent	1972 Expenditure (in millions of dollars)	Percent
1965	OEO and related programs	359	(17)	0	(7)	359	(12)
	Other low-income programs	5,995		2,503		8,498	
	Other social welfare expenditures	31,420	(83)	34,205	(93)	65,625	(88)
	Total	37,774	(100)	36,708	(100)	74,482	(100)
1968	OEO and related programs	3,311	(21)	0	(9)	3,311	(15)
	Other low-income programs	8,698		4,379		13,077	
	Other social welfare expenditures	46,563	(79)	46,273	(91)	92,836	(85)
	Total	58,572	(100)	50,652	(100)	109,224	(100)
1972	OEO and related programs	4,695	(24)	0	(11)	4,695	(18)
	Other low-income programs	19,959		9,149		29,108	
	Other social welfare expenditures	80,362	(76)	70,707	(89)	151,069	(82)
	Total	104,016	(100)	79,856	(100)	184,872	(100)

SOURCE: *Robert Plotnick and Felicity Skidmore, Progress Against Poverty, Institute for Research on Poverty Series (New York: Academic Press, 1975), Table 1.3.*

TABLE 6
Basic Statistics of Pretransfer Poverty, 1965, 1968, 1972

	Pretransfer Poor Households		Total Pre-transfer Poverty Gap *(in billions of dollars)*	Average Per House-hold Poverty Gap *(in dollars)*	Total Pre-transfer Income of the Poor *(in billions of dollars)*	Average Pre-transfer Income *(in dollars)*
	Number *(in thousands)*	Incidence *(in per-centages)*				
1965	15,609	25.7	22.13	1,418	14.14	906
1968	14,933	23.2	23.79	1,593	12.95	867
1972	17,640	24.8	32.49	1,944	16.37	928

SOURCE: *Robert Plotnick and Felicity Skidmore,* Progress Against Poverty, *Institute for Research on Poverty Series (New York: Academic Press, 1975), Table 3.1.*

education, special employment programs, remedial medical and nutritional services, family planning, various child-care programs designed to relieve parents and to start children early on constructive careers, migrant services, youth corps for out-of-school youths to condition them to employment, counseling services, work-experience opportunities, and the like. To provide resources to the poor so that they could take an active part in remedying their situation special programs of the Office of Economic Opportunity (OEO) allocated large sums to local community action agencies which

TABLE 7
Composition of Total Social Welfare Expenditures to Pretransfer Poor, 1965, 1968, 1972, by Functional Categories

	Total Social Welfare Expenditures		
	1965	*1968*	*1972*
Total dollars (in billions)	74.5	109.2	184.9
Composition (in percentages)			
Cash transfers	48.5	41.7	43.3
Payments to farmers	3.0	2.8	1.7
Nutrition	1.2	0.9	2.0
Housing	0.4	0.4	1.0
Health	7.6	12.9	13.3
Welfare and OEO services	1.9	2.3	2.9
Employment-manpower	0.9	1.8	2.1
Education	36.4	37.1	33.7
Total	100.0	100.0	100.0

SOURCE: *Data from Robert Plotnick and Felicity Skidmore,* Progress Against Poverty, *Institute for Research on Poverty Series (New York: Academic Press, 1975), Tables 2–4.*

directed funds to local citizens' groups close to the thinking, culture, and needs of the poor.

Table 7 summarizes the nature of the expenditures in this massive program. Most of the funds were allocated to cash payments as a means of income support (43.3 percent) and to education (33.7 percent). Allocations to nutrition, OEO, and health services, less in volume but nonetheless significant, were primarily intended to overcome employment deficits, rather than representing a commitment to general public provision of health or welfare services.

A close analysis of this period indicates that, despite the surface confusion resulting from the introduction of many new federally funded services, most of them still conformed with remarkable fidelity to the basic principles which we have identified. This period still is characterized by a primary reliance upon the marketplace for employment, with governmental supplementation. It is based upon minimum income standards as an expression of decent treatment of citizens. There is little if any shift in the principle of federal and state sharing.[12] In 1965, for example, $37.8 billion were provided by federal funds and $36.7 billion by state and local funds. In 1972 the federal share had increased to $105 billion and the state and local share to $79.8 billion. While the federal share had steadily increased from 50 percent to 56 percent, the principle of sharing had not been abandoned.

One of the guiding principles has been especially powerful, namely, the federal readiness to assure more generous security for those clearly unable to take part in the work force—the aged and the disabled. Much of the social welfare expenditure to abolish poverty, 60 percent by one estimate, has concentrated on payments to the elderly and the disabled who, before transfer of public funds, were considered in poverty. Such groups in 1972 received a share of the total expenditures which some considered disproportionate, mainly through social security retirement benefits and Medicare. For example, programs which do not depend on poverty-line conditions of eligibility (Medicare and retirement) grew from $28 to $59 billion between 1965 and 1972; programs especially limited to those in the poorest economic circumstances (which do rely upon poverty-line determination of eligibility) increased from $19.6 to $41 billion. While the elderly and permanently disabled constitute the total beneficiary population of the first set of programs, they also constitute a large proportion of those in the second.

This principle may have been breached—or extended—by the fact that retirement benefits are paid regardless of income status of the recipients; only two conditions, old age and disability, are necessary to trigger federal action, not three as in the past, the third being low income.

A variety of economic analyses now permit some assessment of the

---

[12]Ibid.

results of this incremental shift in public policy regarding income. These econometric analyses are still in an elementary stage of development and, while limited by the nature of the data available, are still useful first-stage assessment tools. Between 1965 and 1972 the average real income of families, without public income-transfer programs, rose from $9,822 to $11,596.[13] The national unemployment rate fluctuated within a narrow range of 4.5 percent to 5.6 percent, and the rate of inflation increased perceptibly from 1.7 percent to 5.9 percent and then dropped to 3.3 percent.

Approximately one-third of all pretransfer poor households were lifted above the poverty line, as measured in absolute terms, by cash transfers (Table 8). In absolute and percentage terms households with aged heads benefited overwhelmingly in this removal from poverty, although a respectable one-fourth of households with nonaged male or female heads also were removed from poverty. Unfortunately, this movement has been quite unevenly distributed among population subgroups. For example, black households with female heads, a group which benefits less generously from these programs than do others, have grown proportionately, compared to other parts of the population. This unsatisfactory state is clearly connected with the prospects of various population subgroups entering the marketplace economy through regular employment. The aged and disabled are not expected, in the normative view, to be at work, but adult women are expected to work, even if opportunities are scarce. The latter are still afforded a lower level of economic security.

This picture of the effect of the programs of the 1960s should not be overstressed; it is suggestive only. This was a period in which by American standards unemployment remained relatively low and inflation reasonably controlled. Still, the number of persons requiring public income transfer programs remained high, and the movement out of poverty was mainly due not to a return to private employment, but to income maintenance programs. This finding has seriously disturbed those adhering to the basic principle that federal involvement in income maintenance can be transient and supplementary, decline over time, and be resumed only in episodic periods of depression. In fact, the number of persons dependent upon public funds and the sums of money involved both increased steadily during this period.

A number of explanations have been advanced to account for this rather disappointing result. The most pessimistic view is that the dynamics of a marketplace economy are such that relative poverty as distinguished from absolutely poverty can never be reduced. The economic system requires incentives to keep people in the work force, and these incentives must bring them income substantially above the income secured by those who are not employed. However, the wants and functioning of the bulk

---

[13]Ibid., p. 118, Table 5.4.

TABLE 8
Number and Percentage of Pretransfer Poor Households Taken Out of Absolute Poverty by Government Transfers, by Demographic Groups, 1965 and 1972

	Pretransfer Poor Households	Pretransfer Poor Households Made Nonpoor by Social Security		Additional Pretransfer Poor Made Nonpoor by Other Nonpublic Assistance Transfers[a]		Additional Pretransfer Poor Households Made Nonpoor by Public Assistance Transfers[b]		Total Pretransfer Poor Households Made Nonpoor by All Cash Transfers	
		Number (in thousands)	Per-cent	Number (in thousands)	Per-cent	Number (in thousands)	Per-cent	Number (in thousands)	Per-cent
1965									
All households	15,609	3,258	21	1,454	9	449	3	5,161	33
Households with aged heads[c]	7,512	2,699	36	880	12	222	3	3,801	51
Households with nonaged male heads, with children	2,761	75	3	182	7	45	2	302	11
Households with nonaged female heads with children	1,395	171	12	54	4	77	6	302	22
Households with nonaged heads, no children[d]	3,943	313	8	338	9	105	3	756	19

continued

	Pretransfer Poor Households	Pretransfer Poor Households Made Nonpoor by Social Security		Additional Pretransfer Poor Made Nonpoor by Other Nonpublic Assistance Transfers[a]		Additional Pretransfer Poor Households Made Nonpoor by Public Assistance Transfers[b]		Total Pretransfer Poor Households Made Nonpoor by All Cash Transfers	
		Number (in thousands)	Per-cent	Number (in thousands)	Per-cent	Number (in thousands)	Per-cent	Number (in thousands)	Per-cent
1972									
All households	19,557	4,685	24	1,370	7	603	3	6,659	34
Households with aged heads[c]	9,158	3,875	42	611	7	243	3	4,370	52
Households with nonaged males heads, with children	2,682	129	5	231	9	100	4	460	17
Households with nonaged female heads, with children	2,395	178	7	45	2	148	6	371	15
Households with nonaged heads, no children[d]	5,322	503	9	483	9	112	2	1,098	21

SOURCE: *Robert Plotnick and Felicity Skidmore, Progress Against Poverty, Institute for Research on Poverty Series (New York: Academic Press, 1975), Table 6.5.*
Note: Percentages do not always sum to total because of rounding.
[a] Unemployment insurance, workmen's compensation, veterans' benefits, and government employee pensions.
[b] Old Age Assistance, Aid to the Blind, Aid to the Permanently and Totally Disabled, and Aid to Families with Dependent Children.
[c] Includes unrelated individuals.
[d] Most are unrelated individuals, but childless couples are included.

of the population are such that employment cannot be offered to all persons, especially not to those with limited skills. Also, as people need more income to satisfy their expectations, the number of persons seeking work increases, because families with several wage earners have a greater total family disposable income. In a society where employment for mothers, wives, husbands, and teen-aged children is considered desirable, the volume of positions which can be produced is not sufficient to meet the demand.

It is also argued that the programs designed cumulatively during the 1960s did not concentrate on the poorest, but on a combination of the poor, the marginally poor, and those above the poverty line. The elderly who receive increases in social security benefits or Medicare payments are not necessarily below the poverty line, and while some elderly are through these increases removed from poverty, others below the age of 65 are not affected. In fact, one of the major incremental programs, food stamps, was designed to improve the position of the so-called working poor whose incomes hovered around the poverty line but might well be above it. The justification of this approach is not hard to see. It is argued that if the income of unemployed persons approximates the income of people who are fully employed at the lowest level of income but still above the poverty line, there is less incentive to remain in employment. Therefore, the condition of persons slightly above the poverty line needs to be improved relative to those below it. And for every improvement at the bottom of the income scale which results from a concentrated program focusing only on the poorest, there must be a consequent increase in income assured for those above the minimum. But since the functioning of the private marketplace economy does not smoothly assure these gradations, governmental intervention to provide supplements in the form of increasing income guarantees also increases government expenditures for a much wider segment of the population.

Finally, note must be taken of other unexpected consequences of a complex of income maintenance programs which have grown incrementally. First, there is the enormous variation in eligibility standards introduced in various categorical programs enacted by the Congress and in eligibility standards introduced by the states. Some people and families receive substantial cash transfers from these programs, and others in exactly the same objective condition receive no transfers at all. Some persons receive a combination of transfer benefits which raises them substantially above the average, whereas others fall far below it.

The chaos introduced by a series of incremental categorical programs all functioning within reasonable but broad national policies is well described by a series of reports by the Joint Economic Committee of the Congress of the United States.[14] It is possible for some households, depend-

---

[14]*Studies in Public Welfare* (Washington, D.C.: U.S. Government Printing Office, 1973), see especially Paper No. 6.

ing upon location, size, and age, to receive as many as 10 or 11 different kinds of benefits which together have a high cash value. By 1970 there were 100 separate public welfare programs. In the committee reports 1059 households in the sample studied (units which received benefits) received benefits in a minimum of 144 unique combinations. For example, in one community a female-headed family of four was found to have an average monthly combination of benefits totaling $714; in the same city a male-headed family of the same size received only $371. Some families receiving five or more benefits are likely to have total incomes above the federal poverty standard, but more families are entitled to fewer benefits and fall far below it.

The tangle of eligibility contradictions is also such that at least half of the persons who are likely to earn some income in private employment actually are worse off in employment than if they had not worked at all. Earning some income makes the families ineligible to receive certain welfare benefits such as payment of medical expenses, access to food stamps, housing supplements, and so on. This results in a "notch effect"; the keys to benefits are shaped by income earned. Categorical programs are intended to take care of segments of living: to assure access to health care, to improve housing, and so on. Each program is affected as much by the wants of the systems providing services as by the needs of poor people. There are many keys to eligibility but no master key has yet been devised to eliminate the notch effect so that each program change does not adversely affect some group.

Whatever the explanation for the relatively disappointing results from this venture into prevention, a reassessment of public income maintenance programs was demanded by 1970. The fact that a relatively good economic situation did not reduce the role of government in its "interference" with or supplementation of the private marketplace sharpened the debate. Some argued that the venture into prevention was ill advised and that a more cautious return to basic guiding norms was essential. Others argued that the complexities of the modern economy require a further expansion of the government role, but with more complex and comprehensive planning to ensure a better expenditure of funds, not a reduction. For both, however, the belief persisted that the guiding principles remained acceptable and need not be substantially modified. Probing experiments to go beyond these principles were not yet persuasive in their effects, but no one argued the abandonment of income maintenance.

The 1970s: Controlled Responsibility and Management Reform

The Nixon era represented an attempt to withdraw from the preventive policy and to return to the basic principles with a new focus, namely, the partial dismantling of the existing income maintenance programs and their reconstitution conforming to contemporary standards of business management. In this period it was assumed that a cap could be placed upon the total federal investment in order to stem the increase in the federal share. The principle of government responsibility was not denied, but it was to be controlled. At the same time the welfare system was to be simplified, its management rationalized. It is not altogether clear whether in this period the faltering first step taken in the Social Security Act to use income maintenance to equalize or reduce the disparity in income spread was to be continued or not. From some points of view, arguments for welfare reform, based on some variation of a negative income tax or family assistance plan, seemed to suggest the introduction of greater equalization of benefits paid but not necessarily of greater equity in the economic structure of society.

The search for a simplified and presumably equitable income maintenance program concentrated in this period almost entirely on public assistance and did not substantially alter the historic trend in workmen's compensation or retirement. For these programs, except for improvement in benefits, the basic principles as laid down in the 1930s were presumed to be sufficient. True, the demographic shift toward a larger proportion of older persons in the population, the tendency toward earlier retirement, and a significant increase in permanent and total disability among the adult population increased the cost of social security retirement programs beyond that originally anticipated. However, concern over the increased cost was expressed in debate over various financing forms rather than any major change in this basic component of the income system.

When one turns to public assistance, the situation is quite different. An attempt was made to rationalize more thoroughly the national responsibility. The Supplementary Security Income program was adopted in 1972, whereby the federal government finally assumed full responsibility for a minimum national standard of security for parts of the dependent population outside of the labor force; the elderly other than those on social security, the blind, and the permanently and totally disabled. This was clearly consistent with the ongoing social norm for government.

Although the full responsibility was assumed by the federal government, the principle of state and federal sharing was retained in that state governments were enabled to maintain higher than minimum benefit standards for this population by contributing the additional costs. The net effect of the program was to raise significantly the level of income for this population in southern, western, and poorer states without an increase in burden to those states, while the older industrial states of the northeast and far west were placed in the unenviable position of maintaining their higher-than-average standard only through their own taxation. Nonetheless, the principle of sharing the responsibility seems to have been significantly modified, with the federal government finally taking total responsibility for an average minimum to prevail throughout the country.

In 1972, 15 million individuals received some payments from federally assisted or state relief programs. By December 1975 about 4 million aged, blind, and disabled were transferred to the new SSI program with a national uniform floor of income, leaving some 11 million under the AFDC and general assistance programs which depend on state-determined standards.[15]

Those who transferred to SSI in southern and southwestern states benefited most directly. In six states (Georgia, Mississippi, South Carolina, Indiana, Tennessee, and Texas) average payments for the aged had been below $60 a month, whereas the new SSI minimum became $140 for individuals and $210 for married couples. In three states (Alaska, California, and New Hampshire) the average payments had been above $110 so that their elderly benefited, but not as significantly as in the southern states: Actual SSI payments averaged $102 for aged couples, $142 for blind couples, and $139 for disabled couples. The difference from the national minimum reflects income received from other sources and differences in living arrangements.

Fifty-five percent of the aged, 51 percent of the disabled, and 61 percent of the blind received increases in income under SSI. In seven states (New Mexico, South Carolina, Tennessee, Louisiana, Mississippi, Ohio, and North Carolina) 90 percent or more of aged or disabled individuals or couples received SSI payments above former state levels. On the other hand, in eight states (California, Delaware, Massachusetts, Minnesota, Maine, Iowa, Arkansas, and Alaska) less than 10 percent of the aged or disabled units received an increase.

By 1975 average payments, including state supplements of federal minimums, ranged from $82.23 a month in Indiana to a high of $145.93 in Massachusetts. By contrast, AFDC payments to mothers ranged from a low of $14.39 per recipient in Mississippi to a high of $111.77 in New York.

For the rest of the dependent population, primarily families with dependent children and unemployed fathers, the early 1970s was a period of experimentation without clear direction. The program of Aid to Families with Dependent Children for unemployed parents continued with full state and federal sharing of cost and administration. These families were generally not considered suitable for permanent government intervention; aid was presumed to be assurance of a minimum access to income until employment could be secured. Various devices were tested to encourage them to seek employment in the private sector: recipients had to register for job training and for work and deserting fathers were pursued by legal means. However, such special training programs and harsh incentives were soon cut back. At the same time, a search was introduced for a more standardized program for underpinning the income of marginal families.

---

[15]Lenora Kennedy, Dorothea Thomas, and Jack Schmulowitz, "Conversions to Supplementary Security Income from State Assistance," *Social Security Bulletin* 38, No. 6 (June 1975); and Annual Statistical Supplement 1975, Social Security Bulletin, Tables 157, 175.

The most widely debated of these standardizing measures was the variation of a family assistance plan or some form of the negative income tax introduced in the hope of devising some formula whereby standardized income levels related to family size could be adopted uniformly. Families would be entitled to income to bring them up to the standards. Assistance would be based on a sliding scale so that the combination of public payments and earned income could increase as an incentive to seek employment up to some maximum figure, at which point public payments would disappear. However, as earned income declined, public payments would automatically increase so that in no instance would the family fall below a minimum floor, usually set around $2400 or $3000 per year. Such a major reorganization has not been adopted; it remains a proposed rather than an adopted policy. But it has been proposed in some form by at least three national administrations.

Small-scale tests of a negative income tax system were experimentally undertaken between 1966 and 1969.[16] The tests were mainly intended to ascertain whether workers would withdraw from the labor force in any significant numbers if some minimum income were assured, combining benefits and earned income at levels higher than it was possible to achieve without the program. While the payments were not large, they did measurably improve the income of low-income workers with some employment. Over the three years of experimentation average payments made to continuous husband-wife families ranged from $91.03 per four-week period in the first year to $96.84 in the third year. Black families received somewhat higher-than-average payments, $97.65 rising to $102.83 per four-week period, and Spanish-speaking workers received $86.96 rising to $100.32.

The research was complex and the results not altogether clear. In general, it appeared that there was some slight negative effect on the labor supply, meaning that a measurable percentage of families with earned income subsidized reduced their total work hours over time, as compared with a control population which had no such income supplement. But this effect was small; the percentage of withdrawal from employment accounted for about 5 percent of the estimated economic cost of the program. Black workers did not show the negative effect. Labor withdrawal seems concentrated among workers with especially low earnings and high family expenses. The fact that black workers did not withdraw may be accounted for by the fact that unemployment among black workers in control families was especially high in this period.

When one looks at the response of all family workers, not just the husband, it appears that the effect of such an income program on work is even less; experimental and control families both reduced their work hours, although experimental families did so slightly more rapidly; and

---

[16]See *Journal of Human Resources* 9, No. 2 (Spring 1974), whole issue.

when work hours were increased, the experimental families increased their work total too, but less rapidly.

These studies also sought to ascertain whether there were any other social effects of such income guarantee. The findings suggest the following.

Experimental families (receiving the guarantee) are *more* likely to buy a house, but this effect was more pronounced in families with higher incomes. Rent payments also increased suggesting movement into better housing, or at least out of public housing.

Health and other aspects of life style were not significantly affected by a program of this brief duration. Attempts were made to test whether such programs would reduce family break-up and lead to more stable family life. The findings were inconclusive but suggest that when income assurances are more generous (i.e., a higher income achieved by a combination of earnings and guarantee) then such families do tend to stabilize.[17]

Other attempts to alter the income system concentrated on improvements in managerial efficiency. The federal government first encouraged states to reorganize state and local governments into larger units of administration with more comprehensive data systems to assure management control of expenditures. Under the guise of returning more responsibility to the states, federal administration of public assistance, in fact, increased the volume and detail of federal control. However, federal controls of a system based primarily on state determination of family incomes and eligibility for AFDC families, were founded on the use of statistical devices and management control procedures. Sampling methods were used to determine whether or not payments were made appropriately, and the federal share of payments to the states could be withheld on the basis of post hoc audits after the expenditures had in fact been made.

These efforts at management control occurred at a time when federal agencies for this purpose were demoralized by reductions and transfers, and state governments were increasingly harassed by large state budget deficits. The resulting confusion and dissatisfaction were increased by difficulties in launching the Supplementary Security Income program. It had been assumed that the program, using standardized payments once eligibility is determined, could be absorbed by the social security computer system and handled mechanically. However, the computer system, quite suitable for standard retirement programs, proved less than perfect when it came to handling a dependent population in fluctuating circumstances and with marginal total incomes. The system could not respond rapidly enough to changes in human needs and the built-in variations, which came from a combination of minimum federal standards with some above minimum payments in some states, led to confusion, delays, and a great deal of human suffering.

---

[17]Ibid., p. 253.

Thus, efforts to improve public assistance programs only increased the demand for reform of the welfare system, although the nature of that required reform is still not clear at this writing.

INCOME REDISTRIBUTION OR CONTROL OF THE POOR

While most activity in these decades focused on raising the minimum income for the poorest in the nation, the issue remains whether the relative shares of national wealth or income are more equitably distributed now than in the years before 1935.

A common measure of distribution is the proportionate share of personal money income received in the aggregate by the lowest, the highest, and the middle quintiles in the population. By such measures, it would appear that some redistribution did in fact take place as a result of government income actions during the depression of the 1930s and also government regulation of income during World War II. Between the middle 1940s and the 1960s, there was a slight reversal and since then, despite the Great Society programs of the 1960s, little change has occurred.[18] Income distribution among unrelated individuals did continue to rise, although slightly, in favor of those falling in the lowest quintile. Tables 9 and 10 trace this trend from 1929–1971.

But federal programs worked unevenly to carry out such redistributing tendencies, slight though they were. Blacks tended to do less well, although they were not wholly excluded. For example, old age, survivors disability and health insurance (OASDHI), while treating all beneficiaries alike, has not completely closed the income gap which separates black and white workers who retire or become disabled. OASDHI benefits are based on earned income, and in the private economy blacks, on the average, earn less than white workers. As a result, retired black workers receive an average of 80 percent of the benefits received by white workers because they earned less in their working years; disabled black workers receive an average of 85 percent of the benefits received by white disabled workers. (Between 1958 and 1973 black workers had mean taxable earnings of only 69–73 percent of the mean taxable earnings of white workers.)

A Note on the Social Component in Income Maintenance

The federal policy regarding income has usually been treated as an economic matter, although it may be clear from the foregoing discussion

---

[18]See Winifred Bell, Robert Lekachman, and Alvin Schorr. *Public Policy and Income Distribution* (New York: Center for Studies in Income Maintenance Policy, New York University School of Social Work, 1974); Michael Barth, George Carcagno, and John Palmer, *Toward an Effective Income Support System: Problems, Prospects, Choices* (Madison: Institute for Poverty Research, University of Wisconsin, 1974).

TABLE 9

Percentage of Personal Income Received by Each Fifth of Families and Individuals and by Top 5 Percent

Families and individuals ranked from lowest to highest	1929	1935	1944	1947	1957	1962
Total	100	100	100	100	100	100
Lowest fifth	12.5[a]	4.1	4.9	5.0	4.7	4.6
Second fifth		9.2	10.9	11.0	11.1	10.9
Middle fifth	13.8	14.1	16.2	16.0	16.3	16.3
Fourth fifth	19.3	20.9	22.2	22.0	22.4	22.7
Highest fifth	54.4	51.7	45.8	46.0	45.5	45.5
Top 5 percent	30.0	26.5	20.7	20.9	20.2	19.6

SOURCE: *Winifred Bell, Robert Lekachman, and Alvin Schorr*, Public Policy and Income Distribution *(New York: Center for Studies in Income Maintenance Policy, New York University School of Social Work, 1974), p. 6.*
[a]Lowest and second fifth combined.

TABLE 10

Percentage of Aggregate Money Income Received by Each Fifth of Families and Individuals, 1962–1971, Before Taxes

Families ranked from lowest to highest	1962	1964	1966	1968	1970	1971
Total	100	100	100	100	100	100
Lowest fifth	5.1	5.2	5.5	5.7	5.5	5.5
Second fifth	12.0	12.0	12.4	12.4	12.0	11.9
Third fifth	17.5	17.7	17.7	17.7	17.4	17.4
Fourth fifth	23.7	24.0	23.7	23.7	23.5	23.7
Highest fifth	41.7	41.1	40.7	40.6	41.6	41.6
Top 5 percent	16.3	15.7	14.8	14.0	14.4	NA
Unrelated individuals ranked from lowest to highest						
Total	100	100	100	100	100	100
Lowest fifth	3.0	2.4	2.8	3.2	3.3	3.4
Second fifth	7.4	7.1	7.5	7.8	7.9	8.1
Third fifth	12.7	12.8	13.2	13.8	13.8	13.9
Fourth fifth	24.1	24.5	23.8	24.4	24.5	24.2
Highest fifth	52.8	53.1	52.7	50.8	50.5	50.4
Top 5 percent	21.1	22.6	22.5	20.4	20.5	20.6

SOURCE: *Winifred Bell, Robert Lekachman, and Alvin Schorr*, Public Policy and Income Distribution *(New York: Center for Studies in Income Maintenance Policy, New York University School of Social Work, 1974), p. 7.*

that several other types of considerations have become important in the determination of income policies. These are the values which are implicit in the guiding principles. Human motivation as reflected in the willingness to remain in the labor force or to struggle to leave a state of economic dependency is primarily a social and psychological phenomenon and individuals do not always operate as the theoretical economic man is expected to function.

The development of modern, open economies, especially since the depression, indicates the extent to which social factors must be accounted for in income programs. The diversity of programs funded and modified as part of an attack on poverty illuminates the extent to which social programs are now a fixed part of any national approach to income maintenance: the provision of adequate education for the young to equip them for responsible lives in the working economy; the provision of day-care services in a society where women and mothers wish to work and often are expected to work; specialized training and retraining programs to reduce the segment of the population that lacks work skills suited to the modern economy; and supplementary employment opportunities to guarantee employment when it is not available in the private economy and to staff basic urban public services such as hospitals, sanitation, police, and fire departments.

Although it is easy to identify many social aspects in an area once considered primarily economic, it is less easy to identify the form which the social component finally assumes in income programs. The social component was long considered to consist primarily of individualized personal services provided by income programs, services in the form of counseling, encouragement, guidance, and the like. While personalization of income services is still valuable in order to assure a minimally decent administration of income programs, it has now been established that counseling and psychological services are not significant variables in removing people from economic dependency.

The social component has taken on a nonclinical meaning. It involves the nonwork, noneconomic aspect of income procurement and management in modern society as reflected by the variety of programs noted above.

POLICY ISSUES IN THE MID-1970s

Certain conclusions can be drawn from this recital of events. First, it is clear that the basic principles which have guided the development of federal income policies have been marginally, but not substantially altered.

Second, it is clear that efforts to expand or to add to these principles have been accepted reluctantly and have not been dramatically successful. There have been persistent episodic efforts by the executive branch to extend the scope of federal responsibility and to secure the adoption of public policies beyond old norms. These efforts have not received wide support, but some progress beyond the constricting norms of the past can be seen. Modest income redistribution has been effected and minimum federal standards have finally been secured at least for the elderly and disabled. The federal government has also become involved in managing a variety of social programs (such as training) which alter basic marketplace functioning, even though this intrusion is considered temporary.

Finally, the experience of recent decades casts a doubt upon the viability of these guiding principles in their present form in the period ahead. The belief that primary reliance can be placed upon the marketplace for that part of the population not clearly considered inappropriate for work—mothers, young adults, male heads of households—is no longer justified. Despite fluctuations in the economy, there appears to be a straightline growth in public expenditures for dependent populations of working age.

Abuses of the Income Provision System

Dominant in the public view is the concern over so called abuses of the system of income provision. From the inception of federal responsibility the charge has been leveled that some proportion of persons benefitting from income programs are "undeserving," that is, that they have concealed other sources of income or that they could secure income through work but avoid the search for work. The feeling has persisted that some persons benefit unfairly by contrast with others who either scrimp along on submarginal incomes or who work at any job no matter how difficult in preference to applying for some governmental benefit. When individual cases are cited, most citizens seem to agree that help should be given to the clearly "deserving" poor, such as the sick and the widowed. However, when programs are viewed as a whole and the tax cost identified, citizens are shocked and charge that there must be abuses, for it cannot be that so many need to be helped by others' contributions.

The facts are reasonably clear, but do not seem to clarify the issue in the public mind. The confusion exists between fraud and income redistribution. Certainly there have been cases of individuals who defraud income programs by concealing substantial earnings or assets. But agencies which have established strong antifraud departments have seldom found enough clear cases of abuse to cover the costs of looking for them. They have found that most charges of abuse can be accounted for by one of the following circumstances: (1) minor errors in which changes in income status are reported late, but only by a short time; (2) administrative errors of staff; (3) improvements in levels of income support so that a family of four may have an assured income of $5000 a year, a sum not overly generous at present price levels, but which is startling to taxpayers still accustomed to thinking that poverty can be relieved by an occasional basket of food; (4) claims made by persons not in dire distress, but claims which are entirely legal.[19]

It is the fourth of these explanations which may prove most troublesome in the future. For example, workers who are unemployed may claim unemployment compensation benefits even though other family members are working or hold assets in property or bank accounts. Unemployment benefits are in no sense attached to other income, but only to the fact of being unemployed. Some argue that such persons should exhaust other assets, thus converting unemployment insurance into a means-tested relief program. Others argue that workers should be forced to take any job and not be allowed to try to remain in their occupational field; an engineer should take a ditchdigging job rather than apply for unemployment benefits. The force of this argument would be strongest in a situation of a labor shortage. There are areas where fishermen or construction workers, for example, can work only half the year. If there is a real shortage of workers to fill other empty jobs, an inequity is perceived in that some workers can draw benefits and do no work—to fish or to repair their homes or go on vacation—while useful economic tasks are unperformed for lack of workers. The fact is that such situations are relatively rare; for the most part the empty jobs require high skills which unemployed workers lack or there is no significant number of empty jobs to start with. Where unskilled jobs are available they are likely to be in household service or stoop farm labor, and the effect of income programs has been to raise the level of wages which must be paid to attract workers to perform unpleasant jobs. Overall, of course, in the nation, there has been a persistent shortage of jobs, except possibly very menial ones.

Other examples of difficulty are encountered in other quite legal uses of income programs. Adult children who go to college or who wish to set up households apart from their parents may be legally entitled to income support if they cannot find work, although some would argue that parents should continue to supply their income, even if that forces them to delay establishing separate households.

These legal uses are further complicated when two families with similar incomes are not eligible for the same benefits. One family may be entitled to food stamps or to medical assistance and another may be

---

[19]Several studies suggest that most families with low income have modest standards by which to judge what income is right and necessary for them to live by. See Sidney Bernard, *Economic and Social Adjustment of Low Income Female-Headed Families* (Ann Arbor: University of Michigan Microfilms, 1965). He found that employed low-income families and families on public relief held about the same view as to income necessary to survival. Relief families saw public assistance as only one of several ways—part-time work, borrowing, selling numbers, etc.—by which the needed total could be secured. The total proved to be only slightly above the level of relief then being paid but sufficient to explain the minor cases of delayed income reporting, etc. Charges of great "rip-offs" and fraud were not uncovered.

ineligible, although their needs are similar, due to the vagaries of administrative regulations.

The significance of such arguments over who deserves what lies mainly in uncertainty over the future direction which income programs can take. The old debate continues over substandard relief given only to some persons on the basis of subjective judgments about "worthiness" versus income given as a matter of legal right because of an objective condition in which a person finds himself. The latter course has led to a slow but steady raising of the income and living-standard minimum for large numbers and has produced some modest redistribution of income. How much farther this process will go in the future may depend on our national ability to distinguish between identifiable fraud, which can be handled by improved administration, and the rising standards of living for all. The idea of income as a right requires acceptance of a redistributive income policy; increased benefits for all does not reduce relative poverty, while national resources limit the capacity to increase benefits without altering the shares of national income received by the more affluent.

Changes in Federal-State Shared Responsibility
The borderline between federal- and state-sharing responsibility is currently under major review. Because of the economic distress to which the states have been subjected, there is current pressure to transfer the total cost of financing all public assistance to the federal government, a tendency which has been resisted in the past and which, if accepted, would represent a major change in national policy. One obstacle is the absence of social techniques by which a national administration of programs can suitably adjust to the most varied of human needs which change from day to day among vulnerable groups.

National versus Regional Standards for Income
There seems to be growing a desire to reexamine the choice between national standards applicable to everyone in the country and regional and state variations in standards governing income. The Supplementary Security Income program represents a significant departure from the past reliance upon state-determined variations in income support. The continuing debate over welfare reform which could encompass some form of a negative income tax indicates another potential for modifying the historic tendency to allocate government support on an individualized basis. The trend toward reliance upon computerized management systems would seem to promote a further standardization of income procedures. If this direction is pursued, it is possible that a technical aspect of income maintenance would be significantly modified. Present income programs are in part determined by the processing of eligibility by personnel on an individualized basis. Entitlement by condition, such as that built into the social security system and workmen's compensation or unemployment in-

surance, might produce a more standardized entitlement for income maintenance programs.

Introduction of Children's Allowances and Disability Payments

Most income programs now in force apply to individuals in certain conditions of illness or unemployment or to families without income. Arguments are advanced in support of expanding the mechanisms for income support in two directions. One of these is based upon the special needs of children. Proponents urge that families be paid children's allowances, a sum for each child born and payments until the child reaches his or her majority. Such payments would be based on the fact of a child's birth, not on the economic status of the family. It has been argued that such an income program would benefit most persons with limited incomes, would avoid the stigma which comes from applying for "relief," and would bridge the gap which separates the poor from the working poor and the nonpoor families. Recently such programs have also been supported by those who believe that mothers and housewives should have available income paid directly to them rather than to the head of household, who may be a husband. Children's allowances are paid in Canada and in many European countries.[20]

Another extension would attach payments to the condition of disability. To a large extent this is now a reality as far as minimum income subsistence is concerned. However, the disabled have economic needs greater than those of the able-bodied. The disabled are often immobile or require at least some part-time care. It is argued that where there are no family members or where relatives are all employed, the disabled person should be entitled to a sum in addition to the minimum income relief payments now available to cover the costs of personal care. Such additional sums would be paid upon certification of the disabling condition and would not be dependent upon any means-test inquiry into other assets. Such payment programs are now provided to veterans with service-connected disabilities, and are found in several European countries.

Inequity versus Inequality

Finally, there remains the troublesome question of the relationship between persons entitled to income support, according to whatever basic principles are followed, and persons marginally above a level of entitlement to secure some relative improvement in their status compared to that of those being assisted. In other words, the debate over equity versus equality can be expected to continue without much resolution in the foreseeable future. There are no signs to date that the differential in income between those supported at the bottom of the income scale through public

---

[20]See, for example, Dorothy A. Projector, "Children's Allowances and Income Tested Supplements," *Social Security Bulletin* 33, No. 2 (February 1970): 3.

aid and those earning various levels of income by employment or investment is likely to be narrowed in the immediate future. What does seem to
lie ahead is a steady raising of the floor so that persons entitled to public
payments will have some absolute improvement in their situation, measured
by dollar income at least, while the condition of those above that minimum
can be expected to increase relative to the bottom as well.

Trends in Policy Development

Although prediction is risky, it certainly appears unlikely that the basic
principles which have governed income maintenance public policy to
date will be quickly altered, but slow changes can be expected. The
proportionate share of federal and state governments can be altered either
by some increase in the federal proportion or by a clear division of federal
responsibility for some categories and state responsibility for others.

Income programs will slowly move toward some redistribution of income by slowly extending the precedent established in the Social Security
Act of 1935 concerning retired persons. However, there is no sign that
national public policy will soon introduce any radical steps to eradicate
income disparities. Income inequities, however, can be expected to receive
continuing positive attention. Over time, the elderly, the disabled, and
more recently, minorities and women have been the beneficiaries of public-
policy programs or administrative arrangements which have slightly improved their status, and such incremental changes are likely to continue.

Despite the constrictions of general policy guides, it is also clear that
there has been an extension of the universality of some coverage, mainly
seen in the improved access to minimum decent income for minority
groups and the extension of some income supplement programs such as
food stamps to the so-called working poor. An increase in tax support,
but within the guidelines of the past, can be foreseen in the next decade.

Within such predictions administrative policy choices will affect the
ways in which certain more technical questions will be handled. (1) How
should the working poor, those with income at or just above the margin
of poverty, be assisted? Liberalizing public welfare payments and eligibility might be an answer, but there is a reluctance to mandate this in every
state for reasons already noted. Some form of an earning subsidy through
tax reduction might be one solution.[21] In this approach full-time workers
with low earnings would be entitled to preferential tax treatment when
filing income tax returns. The fact that over one-fourth of all poor families
have wage earners working at least 50 weeks in the year indicates the scale
of this measure. (2) Can the AFDC program be improved by mandating
other federal standards which would apply in all states? (3) How can the

---

[21]See Public Law 94–12, The Tax Reduction Act of 1975, *The C.Q. Almanac,
1975* (Washington, D.C.: Congressional Quarterly Publishing Office, 1976),
p. 95.

administration of assistance in the form of Medicaid and unemployment insurance be modified? These programs now represent a confusing and frequently unworkable melange of state variations with federal control exercised through postaudit devices.

ADDITIONAL READINGS

Barth, Michael, George J. Cavegno, John L. Palmer. *Toward an Effective Income Support System: Problems, Prospects and Choices.* Madison, Wis.: Institute for Research on Policy, 1974.

Burns, Eveline. *Social Security and Public Policy.* New York: McGraw-Hill, 1956.

Hochman, Harold, and George Peterson. *Redistribution Through Public Choice.* New York: Columbia University Press, 1974.

Joint Economic Committee of the Congress of the United States, Studies in Public Welfare. No. 5. *Intergovernmental Relations;* No. 6. *How Public Welfare Benefits Are Distributed;* No. 7. *Issues in Coordination of Public Welfare Programs;* No. 12. *Factors Influencing Family Instability;* No. 15. *Welfare in the '70's.* Washington, D.C.: U. S. Government Printing Office, 1973–74.

Lambert, Richard, and Sidney Weintraub, eds. "Income Inequality," *Annals of the American Academy of Political & Social Science,* 1973.

Levitan, Sar, and Robert Taggart. *The Promise of Greatness.* Cambridge, Mass.: Harvard University Press, 1976, Especially pt. 3 and chap. 3.

Marmor, Theodore, ed. *Poverty Policy: A Compendium of Cash Transfer Proposals.* Chicago: Aldine, 1971.

Morgan, James. *Income and Welfare in the United States.* New York: McGraw-Hill, 1962.

Moynihan, Daniel P. *The Politics of a Guaranteed Income.* New York: Random House (Vintage Books), 1973.

Piven, Frances, and Richard Cloward. *Regulating the Poor.* New York: Pantheon, 1971.

Steiner, Gilbert. *The State of Welfare.* Washington, D.C.: Brookings Institution, 1971.

Thurow, Lester. *Generating Inequality: Mechanisms of Distribution in the U.S. Economy.* New York: Basic Books, 1975.

HEALTH POLICIES: FIFTY CONTROVERSIAL YEARS

Next to jobs and the distribution of income, health policies have been the object of the most extended, continuous controversy in the history of American sectoral social policy. A continuous line of effort to shape public policy, first at the level of state government and then at the level of the nation, has been traced since at least 1900.[1] Societal policy has revealed remarkable strength and resistance to change. The guiding principles of the American society have been operative in the field of health as in the field of income distribution. In the twentieth century the field of health policy has been characterized by a persistent and continuous effort to move beyond the socially sanctioned policies of distribution and regulation (as those terms are used by Lowi) and to effect a significant redistribution. However, the results have been meager and unevenly distributed.

The effort to move in a direction apparently outside of the constraining limits of societal norms has been noteworthy in that it has been made

---

[1]See especially Peter A. Corning, *The Evolution of Medicare,* Social Security Administration, Research Report No. 29 (Washington, D.C.: U.S. Department of Health, Education, and Welfare, 1969). See also Roy Lubove, *The Struggle for Social Security, 1900–1935* (Cambridge, Mass.: Harvard University Press, 1968); Daniel Hirschfield, *The Lost Reform* (Cambridge, Mass.: Harvard University Press, 1970); and Theodore Marmor, *The Politics of Medicare* (Chicago: Aldine, 1970).

by both private groups and, at some intervals, the executive branch of the government. In this sense, health policy can be seen as an instructive example of the potential in and the limits to the executive when seeking by conscious means to introduce a change in direction at the level of government policy.

The fact that these efforts have not been notably successful has tended to concentrate historical attention upon the drama of the conflict between proponents and antagonists. It is the purpose of this chapter, instead, to identify where possible the nature of the proposed public policy and to separate such policy conception from the more global conventional ways of thinking and from the more limiting administrative uses.

Societal norms in health are in some ways similar to those prevailing in the income maintenance field. The belief in the operation of the private marketplace and the choices of individuals are principal guides to government action. Arrangements for the delivery of health services have consistently been left primarily in the hands of privately organized providers, and the tendency has been to enlarge this concept rather than to restrict it. As will be discussed shortly, for a brief period local and national governments did experiment with the direct governmental administration of health services for limited populations by means of city, Veterans Administration, and public health hospitals. However, in recent decades this activity has diminished; only the Veterans Administration remains as a strong force toward direct administration of services, and it, too, is under pressure to be absorbed within the private system through insurance.

The role of government is seen as complementary, regulatory, and limited, its primary function being to see that vulnerable groups are protected and that the burden of disadvantage does not become too heavy. Equality, while frequently a political slogan, has at no time been expressed as government action to assure it. Whenever government arrangements have been necessary, they have taken the form of a responsibility shared by the federal government with industry and private citizen, rather than with state governments.

Health policy at the level of government and at the level of the society, as in the economy, maintains a steadfast faith that science and technology will overcome all difficulties and that a greatly improved world for individuals and for the group will result primarily because of the inventive, imaginative genius of scientists and technologists.

The points at which health policy has sought to deviate from social norms help explain the bitter and continuous controversy associated with it. First, executive health policy has sought to redistribute health benefits among various sectors of the population rather than to act as a balance wheel in the normal marketplace distribution of those benefits. Second, government force has become an equal if not dominant partner with the private sector, mainly because of the weight of the public investment. Government's role, following societal norms, has produced the kind of increment in government obligation (to fill gaps and to satisfy societal expectations) which exerted a cumulative impact so that the simplified policy guides we have been discussing proved to be no longer sufficient.

As the succeeding review will indicate, the private sector has been unable to satisfy socially acceptable expectations about access to health services. The omission of some groups in the population from access to medical care at some point became so extensive and, therefore, so noticeable that it was no longer acceptable. For reasons not fully explained as yet, access for the poor, the aged, and minorities through large, impersonal, and distant public clinics became unacceptable; and this led to acceptance of government financing of private-system medical care for them. It is quite possible that the belief in the private sector as capable of dealing with this unacceptable limitation on access reinforced societal viewpoints on the use of insurance mechanisms as a primary means by which inequities could be rectified.

Insurance involves a systematic scheme by which funds become available to beneficiaries for the purchase of specified services. For a long time this was seen to be the simplest means by which Americans of all income classes could be assured access, namely, by assuring that the costs of medical care would be met without too much pain to the individual. This view has long been reinforced by all parties to the debate, including the medical professions, the insurance companies, and proponents of government action. What was unanticipated was that a dynamic would be set in motion by this continuous reliance upon insurance which would increase the share contributed by government until it became dominant in health financing.

A secondary, unexpected consequence was an introduction into the American belief system, of the idea that certain services, such as health, which are considered essential to all citizens and therefore become theirs as a matter of right, could be provided with minimal cost to the individual. If health bills could be met for many by insurance which cost no one too much, then there was no limit to the volume and type of services which could be paid for as a health charge; even those who could not pay the modest premium charges became entitled to the same coverage as all others, since health is so precious a commodity. Easy payment of medical bills seemed to be the route to fair access to health for all. As a result, the cost consequences of extending and enlarging access to the health system for more and more services produced more and more public allocations, until the public share reached a point where its distribution could no longer be considered as minor or supplementary.

Between 1929 and 1950 health services (public and private) rose as a proportion of the GNP from 3.6 to 4.6 percent, or by less than 27 percent over the 21-year span. But, between 1950 and 1970, the next 20 years, the proportion rose by 67 percent, or from 4.6 to 7.7 percent. In dollar terms total expenditures for health in 1929 were estimated to be about $3.5

billion. In 1974 this figure had grown to over $90 billion. Of this sum, public (primarily federal) expenditures rose from 13.6 percent of the total in 1929 to 37.6 percent in 1974.[2]

The scope of these public expenditures is the battleground of current debate over health policy. They are roughly distributed in the following categories: health insurance coverage for the elderly, health payments for persons of very low economic status, health benefits for injured workers, preventive health programs for mothers and children, rehabilitation of the injured and disabled, special primary medical services for the poor in ghetto areas, programs for veterans, and support of biomedical research. About 92 percent of all expenditures is in the form of cash payments to individuals to enable them to pay all or part of their hospital bills or in the form of assured payments to vendors as, for example, the purchase of medical care for the poor. Only 8 percent thus far involves direct provision of health services for some or all citizens, via the Veterans Administration, army, OEO, school health, maternal and child health, and public health programing.

The confidence in scientific solutions now offered by medicine is reflected in the purposes for which most of these sums are expended. About 91 percent of Medicare and 49 percent of Medicaid expenditures go for the payment of services in hospitals and by physicians for health. Medicare and Medicaid combined represent 60 percent of all public expenditures.[3] An additional $1.9 billion is allocated for the conduct of various forms of biomedical research, either by the National Institute of Health or by contract and research grants to private research institutions.

Unfortunately, the results of this trend in policy have been less than satisfying both to citizens and to political and scientific personnel. Some disadvantaged groups in the population, primarily minorities, inner city residents, and rural groups, are still relatively untouched. Redistribution has taken place, in favor of the elderly and to a lesser extent in favor of black minorities, but the scale of redistribution working through the private marketplace has been limited.

At the same time, as we have seen, the total cost has escalated, rising to 7.7 percent of the GNP. The cost of delivery of service to the individual has also risen dramatically; for example, care in a hospital for a single day, exclusive of surgical, medical, and diagnostic fees, runs in excess of $200. This escalation has suddenly confronted both policy makers and average citizens with the consequences of the policies they have thus far accepted.

[2]See *Encyclopedia of Social Work*, 16th ed. (New York: National Association of Social Workers, 1971), Table 39; and *Health U.S. 1975* (Washington, D.C.: Health Resources Administration, U.S. Department of Health, Education, and Welfare, 1975), Table A6.

[3]Derived from *Encyclopedia of Social Work*, table 39; *Social Security Bulletin*, Current operating statistics, April 1976, tables M18, M20, M35; and *Health, U.S. 1975*, p. 27.

The long-held belief that certain social benefits could become available by means which remove the individual from any confrontation of costs has been shaken.

As a result of these unanticipated consequences of the societal policies which have been expressed through public policies, a new set of issues have arisen. These policy issues are clearly social rather than scientific or technical in nature and have been brought about by a recognition of certain underlying social and economic trends. We should note some of these trends which are not subject to short-term change: the increase in population; the increase in the proportion of the population over 65 years of age from 4 percent in 1900 to 9.8 percent in 1970 and to an expected 10–15 percent by the year 2000; the resulting increase in the total demand for medical care which an aging population presents; the increase in the proportion of minorities in the total population, accompanied by the pressure to equalize their income status; the increase in the proportion of women in the total population from a ratio of 106 males per 100 females in 1910 to 94 per 100 in 1970; and the steady rise in educational level as open enrollment programs bring more than 50 percent of the American population to a level of at least one year of college education, as compared to the level of eighth grade which was the standard only 100 years ago.

Before considering the character of present policies, it may be instructive to review the evolution of American governmental policies. The following summary does not dwell on the political drama of public policy formation, but rather is an attempt to trace the evolution in public policy for health in order to better understand the current policy choices and to determine what guiding principles are still operative.

EMERGENCE AS A SUBJECT OF POLICY FOR THE FEDERAL GOVERNMENT: HEALTH INSURANCE, 1900–1950

The easiest starting point for understanding the evolution of public policy for health is the establishment in 1912 of the American Association for Labor Legislation's social insurance committee, an action which was to stimulate state governmental activity. But it would be misleading for our purposes not to take account of the character of health policy before this period.

Before 1910 the dominant position was that the federal government had no role concerning the health of its citizens other than the prevention of disease spread through broad-scale public health activities, mainly at ports of entry, and a responsibility for two special populations: veterans and seamen. State and local governments were considered to be responsible for any aspects of health care not left to individuals, which meant that they had basically the same practical role as the federal government, with one important exception: major cities took the responsibility for providing public hospital care for the poor and for those with infectious diseases. Although these hospitals were utilized primarily by poor families and especially by immigrants new to the culture, they were tax supported and therefore involved local governments in the direct administration and delivery of health care. In some eastern cities, such as New York, Philadelphia, and Boston, the city hospital networks were the pride and joy of local government; they were highly respected for the quality of care originally provided and they were much valued by medical schools as training grounds for physicians and by the medical professions as preparation for subsequent private practice. Some cities developed extensive locally administered ambulatory outpatient clinics.

The fact that these local programs involved direct governmental administration represented a deviation from an underlying societal approach in America to government. However, the deviation did not become fully developed. Between 1960 and 1974 the total number of state and local public hospital beds dropped from 953,000 to 664,000. Almost half of that figure represented special facilities for tuberculosis or for chronic or infectious diseases; large city general hospital beds represented the other half.[4] One can conclude that the underlying policy of relying upon the private marketplace showed its forcefulness and persistence as these ventures into governmental operation of some segment of the health system were attenuated and eroded.

At the federal level the same eroding tendency can be seen in the marine hospitals. While some do struggle to survive, most of them have been replaced by giving seamen access to the private sector through financial means, rendering the marine hospitals obsolete, underutilized, and by and large neglected. Only the Veterans Administration remains as a strong example of federally administered medical care, maintaining a nationally administered network of 125 hospitals, with 96,750 beds (33,472 for mental illness), a network of outpatient clinics, and various ancillary nursing-home and home-care services. This deviation from the more common pattern has been explained by the nation's sense of obligation to the veterans forced to devote some part of their lives to military service. But even the Veterans Administration serves predominantly a lower-income population, and over half of the acutely ill veterans with low incomes are believed to secure their medical care from normal private services rather than turning to available public programs.[5] Only services for chronic illness and mental illness are provided for and used by all income groups, perhaps because the crushing burden of paying for long-term care usually reduces previously affluent citizens to low-income status. But the Veterans Admin-

[4]*Statistical Abstract of the U.S., 1976*, Table 91, Bureau of the Census. (Washington, D.C.: U.S. Department of Commerce, 1976).

[5]A. Richardson, H. E. Freeman, J. Cummins, H. Schnaper, "Use of Medical Resources for Spancos," *Milbank Memorial Fund Quarterly* 45, No. 1, Pt. 1 (January 1967) : table 1.

istration is not immune to the cumulative effect of both public and societal policies. The debate over national health insurance has raised demands that veterans be covered by such insurance along with all other citizens, which would move the VA closer to providing fees for services rather than direct care. To date this view has not found widespread favor.

The first advance in government policy, aside from these special cases, was introduced by the social insurance committee of the American Association for Labor Legislation in the form of a standard health insurance bill. It reduced to legislative language a plan for protection in health, and it was pressed upon various state legislators in 1915, a period when state governments were considered the primary arena for public policy in the social welfare field. This bill can be taken as an early model of public policy, even though it was not widely adopted at the time. It called for the protection of all low-income workers, provided for cash compensation in the case of injury, and the payment of hospital and medical benefits to both workers and their dependents. This legislation conforms remarkably to the underlying societal policy imperatives which we have outlined. It provided for some protection of disadvantaged persons; it relied upon the marketplace for service delivery through the use of payments to individuals and providers as the element which would bring the private system and the individual into harmonious relationship.

By 1920 this effort acknowledged its failure and the bill was never adopted as public policy. What is significant, however, is the extent to which its defeat conformed to the underlying societal policy constraints we have been discussing. At the beginning of this initiative, major constituency groups in the United States proved to be polarized, but in unexpected form. The leaders of the American Medical Association suggested that it might eventually give official support to the movement, as did a committee of the National Association of Manufacturers. But the American Federation of Labor was vigorously opposed. For contradictory reasons over time, the members of the AMA and NAM turned against their leaders and became opposed even to this modest intervention of public policy in the private sector, whereas labor organizations slowly came around to supporting the movement.

In the 1920s, a period notable for its lack of governmental action in health, a new voluntary group, the Committee on the Cost of Medical Care, was constituted in 1927. The proposals by this citizen group once again conformed to basic constraints. It favored attempts to channel medical practice away from the solo practitioner, but still within the private sector, meaning, in this case, hospitals; group payment for medical care either through taxation or through private insurance or a combination of the two was proposed, but at no time did it recommend compulsory governmental health insurance. Other changes, such as extension of public health, the coordination of health services, and improvements in medical education, while ahead of their time, were not fundamentally controversial.

The Committee on the Cost of Medical Care can be said to have maintained some citizens' interest in health policy, but it was not until the crisis of the 1930s and the election of Franklin Delano Roosevelt with his New Deal programs that the subject of policy for health finally reached the federal government and an administration concerned with translating proposed policies into adopted ones.

For the first time, the executive branch clearly identified itself with a policy of federal intervention for the delivery of health services in some form. For the first time, a branch of government adopted a policy view about health which persisted for several decades, until the final adoption of Medicare in 1965.

The controversy over the incorporation of health insurance in the original social security legislation of 1935 has been obscured by the rhetoric of political debate. It would be mistaken to believe that a completely new public policy for the federal government was pressed upon the nation and defeated as a result of most reactionary forces. In fact, the executive branch, with the delicate support of the president, moved most circumspectly and its final proposals conformed remarkably well to the societal policies we have been discussing. Strong proponents such as Harry Hopkins, Eleanor Roosevelt, and others argued in favor of health insurance as the guideline for national policy. Other members of the executive branch, who spoke against the proposal, were not opposed in principle, but had a prior concern with the urgency in the depths of the depression of securing the enactment of unemployment insurance. Since the addition of health insurance to unemployment insurance would increase the number of powerfully organized opponents, they feared that unemployment insurance as well as health insurance would be defeated.[6]

For our purposes, however, it is significant that even the proponents considered radical at the time chose a public policy which proposed to deliver funds to individuals or to providers (vendors) bespeaking a reliance on the vigor of the private marketplace in health. Health insurance was seen as a way of assuring to all individuals minimum access to hospital and medical care by placing the financial means in their own hands. True, the policy had its radical aspects for the federal government in that it called for compulsory insurance, although on this issue, too, the proponents in the executive branch were divided and many would have accepted administration of the program through the private insurance industry as long as all persons were covered. Although the phrase "government health insurance" was commonly used in the debate, the administration remained uncommitted in the choice between a government-operated program of health insurance and a mandated compulsory system administered

---

[6]For a full discussion of this period, see Corning, *Evolution of Medicare;* Lubove, *Struggle for Social Security;* Marmor, *Politics of Medicare;* and Hirschfield, *Lost Reform.*

by the private insurance companies. However, even the most limited proposal of any form of a compulsory program appeared to open the door to
potential, if not real, governmental controls which were at the time considered unacceptable, especially in the midst of the administration fight
for major economic interests such as the Social Security Act and unemployment insurance. With the decision finally to withdraw health insurance
from the Social Security Act as introduced in 1935, the executive branch
temporarily suspended, but did not abandon its effort to secure the adoption of a different kind of federal policy in the field of health.

This initial battle at the federal level makes clear the balance of
interest which must be secured to adopt a public policy of any kind, let
alone one which deviates from societal policies. The American Medical
Association, the private insurance industry, and the private pharmaceutical
firms were organized to exercise most effective political leverage against
such policy, but it can hardly be said that they dominated the controversy.
Powerful congressional figures, powerful figures in the executive branch,
and some constituency groups were arrayed on behalf of this mild shift
in federal policy. However, what is noteworthy is that no massive support
was expressed by citizens in the United States. Instead, the primacy of
economic survival cast health policy in the shadow so that in the ensuing
balance of interests the proponents can hardly be said to have either been
powerfully organized or for that matter powerfully interested.

EFFECT OF EMERGENCY WARTIME ACTIONS ON POLICY PRINCIPLES: EMIC

By 1943 progress in World War II made it possible once again for
the executive branch to consider social policy for health. The publication
in the United Kingdom of an influential proposal for a national health
service, not national health insurance, provided the external stimulus to
the executive branch to resume its effort to secure the adoption of a new
national policy.[7] With encouragement, legislation was now introduced in
the Congress.

A temporary excursion into an adopted national health policy became
possible because of wartime pressures. With millions of young men in the
army, with low incomes, their wives were left to manage as best they
could. These wives were also young and at the prime of their child-bearing
years. The cost of medical care was onerous. The U.S. Children's Bureau,
which had pursued a mandate to monitor the needs of children since 1912,
undertook to propose a solution for the dilemma.

The issue first assumed prominence when the medical staff for hos-

[7]Sir William Beveridge, *Social Insurance and Allied Services* (New York:
Macmillan, 1942).

pitals attached to Ft. Lewis, Washington, was overwhelmed by demands to provide maternity services for wives of servicemen stationed at the camp. As early as March 1942, a committee of the Association of State and Territorial Health Officers recommended that

> the state health agencies develop plans to finance from Maternal and Child Health funds (administered by the Children's Bureau) the medical and hospital care needed by wives and children of men in military service . . . and to make more readily available medical and nursing services for mothers and children in critical areas.[8]

The American Red Cross reported a large need for such services at 240 army posts and inquiries by the Children's Bureau also identified widespread need for help. Funds already appropriated for maternal and child health services, which were administered by state health departments, were totally inadequate for the new demands, for the older MCH programs were limited to narrowly defined and especially vulnerable populations, whereas the wartime situation extended to large number of citizens never before considered to be in the orbit of the public program. As a result additional deficiency appropriations were sought by the Children's Bureau.

Although there was a readiness to finance emergency arrangements, numerous policy issues surfaced and had to be settled before even the emergency program could be enacted. Among them the following questions are significant for our purposes.

1. Was the Emergency Maternity and Infant Care (EMIC) program a step toward "socialized" medicine or to a national health program? Officials of the Children's Bureau argued that all the proposals were state programs; the federal government's only role was limited to setting minimum standards in the interest of national equity and sharing the costs. One congressman from Kansas said, "The only thing I can see about it is that it is drifting toward socialized medicine." When the chief of the Children's Bureau replied, "This is a war program and consideration of what happens next will have to be something else," the congressman responded, "It's just a leverage."

After the wartime emergency passed, the Children's Bureau argued for a continuation of federal responsibility although with changes based on wartime experience.

> The Children's Bureau has been on record since 1917 as being in favor of a public program for the protection of maternity and infancy. . . . those programs should be expanded as soon as possible so that there would be available everywhere in every State, a service

[8]Nathan Sinai and Olin W. Anderson, *EMIC: A Study of Administrative Experience*, Research Series No. 3 (Ann Arbor: Bureau of Public Health Economics, School of Public Health, University of Michigan, 1948), citing hearings before the Deficiency Appropriations Subcommittee of the House Committee on Appropriations, 78th Cong., 1st sess., February 11, 1943, p. 326.

for the protection of the health of mothers at the time of childbirth
and the health of children. . . ." [9]

It can be concluded that executive branch spokesmen, at least, supported
a federal program over many years and took advantage of an emergency
to try out ways for advancing proposed policies into adopted ones.

2. What should be the relationship between the federal and the state
administrations? The Children's Bureau could not assert that it was
"running" these programs nationally, but it could exercise significant influence through its obligation to supervise the expenditure of federal funds.
Some congressional spokesmen were concerned that some states might
deny help to some servicemen and give it to others, especially in the South,
while other spokesmen were concerned lest they be forced to give any
help at federal direction. The Children's Bureau policy was to set general
administrative guidelines, but to leave case decisions in state hands,
although it agreed that it would prefer to place more stringent requirements
on state administration.

3. Should cash payments be made to beneficiaries with all further
responsibility left to the mother? The Children's Bureau was firm in its
opposition to cash benefits arguing that

> under a plan based on cash allowances there would be no way to
> assure the enlisted man that care, and the amount and kind of care,
> will be available for either his wife or his infant. . . . The costs of
> care of individual sick infants would vary even more than the costs
> of maternity care and there would be no way to determine in advance
> the amount of a cash allotment necessary to meet these needs.[10]

Thus the argument defended a system of payment tied to case-determined
needs, which in the future could evolve into a system of benefits in the
form of vouchers for medical care or could even move in the direction of
publicly provided services.

The categorical approach was supported also on the grounds that it
was the only way to assure that physicians and hospitals would in all
cases receive payment, since the payments could not be diverted by the
mother for other purposes. And to clinch the argument, the Children's
Bureau argued that to go to a straight cash program would mean that
every wife would apply and the costs would rise by 90 percent or more.

4. Should payment cover hospital and treatment costs? Here the
Congress readily supported the Children's Bureau view that earlier programs, covering only prenatal and some postnatal costs, had to be aug-
mented by covering the hospital and emergency treatment associated with
birth itself.

5. Should the program be means-tested? The final decision was

---

[9]Cited in Sinai and Anderson, *EMIC*, p. 35.
[10]Cited in Sinai and Anderson, *EMIC*, p. 38.

clearly no, in favor of a broad entitlement based on army pay grades whereby most enlisted men (87 percent) but not officers became entitled to protection. Individual means-testing for eligibility was considered unsuitable for a program for servicemen.

6. Should the federal government set a fixed fee for payments? The Children's Bureau was empowered to establish fee scales to set limits to what could be charged and to discourage attempts by physicians to demand payments above the EMIC payment. Some flexibility was retained to permit states to adjust fee boundaries to local conditions as part of the state plan.

By 1946, 1,222,500 maternity cases and 230,000 infant cases had been approved for benefits.

EMIC pretested six policy steps which were later adopted as permanent characteristics for federal policy and also probed the potential for going beyond then acceptable boundaries.

1. The guiding and regulatory influence of a federal agency was much expanded in the health field by setting guidelines for eligibility and form and amounts of benefits under a state program. These guidelines were softened by providing for various advisory mechanisms to assure cooperation of health-care providers and of state agencies.

2. Beneficiaries of a federal-funded program were widened to a large segment of the population, no longer limited to the poorest and most helpless.

3. The means-test was almost abolished so that anyone falling into a clear population group was entitled to benefits without challenge. A residue of means-testing was retained by excluding from benefits all servicemen above a certain rank, but the exclusions were based on rank, not on total assets, and were limited to 13 percent of the total possible target population of all enlisted men.

4. Payments were no longer simple patient-physician matters. Boundaries were fixed limiting the scope of additional payments which could be demanded, and the route of payments went from government through a state agency to the provider.

5. Cost controls were introduced to private providers by the types of cost accounting procedures required by the EMIC program, if providers were to be reimbursed.

6. And, finally, modest experimental steps were taken to safeguard the quality of care provided. Standards of quality could now be overseen by a government agency and not left exclusively to the judgment of individual physicians or local medical societies.

The guiding policy of this administration was further described in the 1944 election campaign in which health policy was incorporated in an economic bill of rights. Here the administration's policy about health was defined to include "the right to adequate medical care and the opportunities to achieve and enjoy good health . . . and the right to adequate protection from the *economic fears* of old age, sickness, accident, and unemployment." The reference to achieving and enjoying good health can be considered one of those societal aims which have no specific policy tangibility but, when coupled with the other phrases in this campaign statement, it becomes clear that the public policy is seen as removing the economic inequities to access to medical care. This executive branch thrust was continued by President Truman. The Wagner-Murray-Dingle Bill, among other things, retained the insurance principle but continued to seek compulsory insurance coverage without means-testing. This proposed policy was once again defeated.

REDISTRIBUTIVE AND REGULATORY ROLES: POSTWAR ACTIONS

Medicaid and Medicare

The executive branch effort was continued without much vigor until 1950 when an alternative to comprehensive compulsory national health insurance was introduced. I. S. Falk, Director of the Bureau of Research and Statistics, Social Security Administration, suggested that a more modest next step might be taken by using the already enacted social security legislation to introduce some form of federal policy in the health field.

The Social Security Administration, rather than the Office of the President, noted that its protection for the elderly through retirement failed to protect against the single greatest cause of economic insecurity and dependency in old age; the high cost of medical care. By 1956 the executive branch introduced to the Congress proposals for health insurance only for those covered under social security, not for the entire population.

The nature of the policy debate did not differ materially from that of previous years. Any form of compulsory activity was opposed by some and supported by others. However, the underlying and continuing desire to do something for especially disadvantaged groups emerged when other legislation was introduced to provide some form of economic assistance for the medically indigent aged, if not for all social security beneficiaries. Initially, this was limited to the elderly who might be on the margin of economic dependency and therefore could not quite qualify for public relief, but still needed assistance with their medical bills. This narrowing of the Social Security Administration's aim to extend medical protection to all the covered elderly had significant consequences.

For several years debate continued between the executive and the legislature on two parallel lines: one pressing for medical-care protection for all beneficiaries of social security, the other asking for protection for only those who were on the verge of indigency. The first proposal became attached to what was finally adopted as Medicare legislation, and the second was incorporated in what finally became Medicaid. On the way to adopting Medicaid legislation, an interim enactment provided medical payments for persons of very low income regardless of age. It was not until 1965 that the Social Security Act was amended to provide medical protection for all retired older persons regardless of economic status.

Much of the policy debate in this period has been interpreted as the defeat of majority will by an obdurate minority. However, many observers have suggested that in the period of the Kennedy administration, during which Medicaid was enacted but not Medicare, there was no national pressure for the wider proposals which were then urged. We cannot determine exactly how the population was divided on the issue of reform and innovation versus reduced federal spending and activity, but we can estimate that the resistance probably included half the voters.

The final enactment of both Medicaid and Medicare in 1965 together represents a remarkable agreement between government policy and societal norms as we have understood them. And yet, these two pieces of legislation also represent a real and perhaps radical addition to public policy. While the marketplace of the private vendor remains primary as far as the delivery of health care goes, access using public funds was finally mandated for most citizens.

The definition of who is to be considered vulnerable and thereby entitled to governmental protection was broadened, although it still remained circumscribed; not all citizens were granted access to funds. Those on public assistance or near the level of indigency were seen as clearly unable to purchase the health care which was by now viewed as everyone's right and therefore were considered entitled to some means for procuring it. Social security beneficiaries may or may not need financial help for this purpose, but by and large they have limited incomes, sharply reduced from their working years, have increasing medical needs, and face escalating medical costs. This population came close to being identified in the public view as necessitous. Taken together, Medicare and Medicaid extended the authority of the federal government to about 16 percent of the population.[11]

We should note that these additions to public policy are concerned

---

[11]Based on estimated eligibility for medical care by social security retirees plus AFDC and SSI recipients. The *Annual Statistical Supplement, Social Security Bulletin*, published by the Social Security Administration, reports for 1976: Medicare enrollees, 20,361,000; SSI beneficiaries, 3,996,000; AFDC beneficiaries, 11,006,000; or a total of 35,363,000. The total may slightly overstate coverage, since not all AFDC or SSI beneficiaries may be able to effectively claim health benefits due to limitations in state regulations.

only with the right of the individual to purchase health care; they make no statement as to his right to health. They extended coverage for assistance, but did not consider the nature of the delivery of medical care. The extension relied on the scientific claims made by medicine—that seeing a doctor or entering a hospital would solve major health problems. It did not provide means for altering the health status or for evaluating the results as measured by the health of the population.

Medicaid, although limited to the indigent, was seen quietly by some of its proponents as providing a model for the future. To them, Medicaid was a step toward utilization of public funds for payment for a broad variety of both medical and health-related services, such as homemakers, chore workers for the disabled, and so on. Medicare was primarily limited to payment for hospital and doctor's services. Medicaid could be seen as potentially much more comprehensive. Although it was currently limited to the poor, and therefore means-tested, the legislation did open the door to extension to those not on public assistance, and therefore, might be considered a way of testing what would happen if a comprehensive program were extended to the entire population at some future time. Finally, Medicaid retained much more significant control than did Medicare over the objects, purposes, and directions of medical purchases. Medicare, although subject to complex billing procedures, leaves virtually all initiative to the individual consumer and his physician or hospital. Medicaid, by contrast, operates primarily through vendor payments which are administered by public agencies and their staffs on behalf of clients with the payments being made by public officials to private vendors. The system thus contains the potential to modify what kinds of health services are delivered, in what volume, and in what fashion.

The fact that Medicaid has not been extended beyond its original boundaries may suggest the dangers of this extension had been recognized and avoided through a continued restriction of the program to the indigent. Nonetheless, if one takes into account the 75 years it has taken to make this slight progress, it might be considered possible that a tiny foundation brick has been laid for the future evolution of public policy beyond its present limitations.

Facility Construction

Another example of federal actions along the redistributive axis of policy can be traced in the history of the Hospital Survey and Construction Act (popularly known as Hill-Burton after its sponsors). Construction of health facilities, except for the military, was virtually suspended during World War II. The pressure created by this backlog of construction was reinforced by the advances in medical technology stimulated by wartime discoveries. Public officials had been made aware of the startling findings of military and selective service physical examinations: a large percentage of American men fell below the minimum physical standards set by the army for its personnel. These factors combined to lead to a demand that each section of the nation be assured of a community hospital on the assumption that such facilities would attract physicians to those parts of the country which lacked adequate medical care, especially the rural areas. A common slogan of the time was "a hospital in every county."

The demand produced the Hospital Survey and Construction Act of 1947. Under its terms the federal government provided funds and other mortgage and construction assistance to sponsors of hospitals, to supplement funds raised locally by these sponsors. Certain standards were imposed by federal regulation as a condition for qualifying for federal aid. Among the most interesting was the requirement that the counterpart state agency for hospital construction ascertain where hospitals were needed and exercise control over the type and distribution of physical facilities. Statewide and regional councils were established through which these determinations were made. Proprietary and nonprofit groups could no longer raise their own funds and could not build where and when they wished. Governmental influence in the early years of the program was exercised to give preference to hospital construction in rural and suburban areas, while little incentive was given to build or renovate hospitals in the central core of major cities.

Over time this legislation was amended to extend to nursing homes, to chronic disease facilities, and finally to facilities in urban areas, permitting a major rebuilding and expansion of the decaying centers of larger cities. But at its inception the program was clearly intended to redistribute health facilities to underserved rural areas, and such a leveling of facilities did take place. Over a 30-year span some $12 billion were spent on hospital construction or modernization, 30 percent coming from the federal government. In 1948 some states had two hospital beds per 1,000 population and others had as many as 6; Alabama, Mississippi, Arkansas, Georgia, and Tennessee had the lowest ratio of beds. By 1973 these states were at or above the national average of 4.9 acute beds per 1,000, and some states previously having high bed ratios reduced their volume slightly. Poorer districts, including rural areas, have increased their beds and now closely resemble more affluent districts.

The movement of physicians to underserved areas did not follow as even a path since factors accounting for physician location proved more complicated than suspected. The construction of facilities did not operate as a sufficient attraction in the medical marketplace to redistribute physicians. In 1973 metropolitan areas had an average of 1 nonfederal physician for each 500 persons, while small nonmetropolitan counties had an average of 1 physician for each 2000 to 2500 persons. Southern states still have the fewest number of physicians relative to population, while the north central states still have the most.

Federal Regulation: Health Planning and Professional Services Review

We have thus far considered the growth of government's role in health financing and in facility construction. There have been equally significant increases in the federal government's regulatory power in the private health provider system. Several examples will be noted, if only to indicate that regulation as well as redistribution has become a way of life in federal policy.

In 1966 Congress enacted the Comprehensive Health Planning and Public Health Services Amendments, sometimes called the Partnership for Health Act. This measure advanced federal funds to stimulate the development of health-planning agencies throughout the nation. An incentive for what would otherwise remain a voluntary option was inserted by requiring, directly or indirectly, that hospitals receiving federal funds be party to some state and local planning agency of government. Such agencies, called comprehensive health-planning agencies, were established in 55 states or territories. They consisted of appointed spokesmen of state and local governments, hospital associations, professional health associations, and citizens. The escalation in medical costs forced many state authorities to use these units to attempt some control over costs. A first step was the state enactment of certificate-of-need legislation under which any new construction of hospital facilities required a certificate from an official agency certifying that the new construction was needed. Since total funds for construction were limited, this meant that the planning units would make priority choices among competing construction plans. Decisions were made through a mixture of evaluative assessment data and political influence, with planning agencies sitting nominally in judgment.

The National Health Planning and Resource Development Act of 1974 replaced the comprehensive agencies with a new form of planning—health systems agencies—which were given somewhat enlarged powers of enforcement. Their membership was enlarged to increase the role of consumers and to reduce the hitherto dominant role of provider agency members in decision making. At the same time decisions about large-scale program expansion or reduction (as well as capital expansion) and about manpower training plans became referrable to such planning units.

About the same time, federal legislation authorized a system for the regular monitoring and control of the utilization of health facilities in the hopes of preventing abuses in hospital, institutional, or physicians' services. Usually teams of physicians and other service providers establish, along with state rate-setting boards, the average lengths of hospital stay and the average modalities of treatment for major health conditions.[12] Then pro-

---

[12] In most states a public board is established which fixes rates by which hospitals and other providers are reimbursed by tax-supported programs. These rates apply mainly to Medicare or to Medicaid and to public welfare reimbursements.

fessional peer teams in hospitals review hospital stays and sometimes variations from average treatment modalities. Where there are charges outside
the average as determined by this process, physicians and other providers
are obligated to justify the variation to the satisfaction of the insurance
intermediary which makes actual payments. These intermediaries are
usually insurance companies operating under contract in each state. While
these reviews do not actually force providers into uniform practice, they
do force them to be especially conscientious about such average standards,
and there is a tendency for medical practice to revolve around this average.
Only in clearly exceptional cases or in the case of very strong-minded providers are deviations fought for.

This review mechanism is not yet in place throughout the nation since
it has had to be phased in by stages. It has had the effect of increasing the
power of insurance intermediaries, although the power is moderated by
judgments arrived at by the medical profession as to acceptable averages.
In effect, the system of payment for medical care becomes more mechanized, and clerical judgments, based on written reports, can more and more
influence the level of medical payments and the purposes for which they
are expended.

An Exception to the Rule

The long controversy over medical care cannot be left without noting
one little appreciated anomaly in American public policy—the Veterans
Administration. The VA is clearly a national health *service*, administered
by the federal government through full-time paid employees and linked
partially to the private medical care system through collaborative relationships with medical schools and other professional schools. True, this system
was established to provide for veterans who sustained injury as part of
their military service, so that the anomaly, if it is one, reflects a sense of
national obligation for its soldiers. But the system has been enlarged to
provide at least in-hospital care for all veterans whether or not their illnesses are due to military service. Ambulatory care was authorized for
non-service connected illness by the Veterans Health Expansion Act (Public
Law 93–82) to reduce the need for in hospital care. Nominally, this extension was intended for veterans who could not afford private medical
care; but in reality few, if any, questions are asked about ability to pay.
As an almost self-contained health system, the VA directly maintains and
administers over a hundred hospitals with some 100,000 beds, as well as a
network of outpatient medical clinics, nursing homes, and social services
for veterans under care but living outside of a hospital. Although designed
for a highly selective and limited population, in all respects it represents
a model for a national health service, not insurance. The acceptance of the
VA system may be the exception which proves the rule of societal constraints, but it may also be interpreted to mean that the boundaries of
normal value constraints are not as rigid as the fight for compulsory health
insurance has led many to believe.

THE SOCIAL EFFECTS OF POLICY EVOLUTION

While no direct cause-and-effect relationship can be claimed, it seems likely that the events of the past decades have played a part in materially altering the culture of health services. Certainly the burden of paying for medical care has been shifted. While national expenditures, both public and private, have increased more rapidly than most items in the Gross National Product, and while costs of medical care are now far above the common expectation of only a dozen years ago, the burden on the individual has been somewhat relieved by government assumption of financing responsibility. As has been noted, public funds grew from 13 to nearly 40 percent of all health expenditures, while private expenditures dropped from 86 to 60 percent. When private insurance, or private third-party payments are added in, the individual now pays less than a third of the total health bill out of his own pocket and less than 10 percent of all hospital payments. This has been true not only for the aged, although their benefits are more marked. Between 1966 and 1972 the proportion of personal health expenditures paid by the aged directly dropped from 53 to 28 percent, while government's share rose from 30 to 66 percent. For those under 65, government payments rose only from 20 to 26 percent and direct payments dropped from 51 to 38 percent, but private insurance (reflecting in part industrial labor health contracts) rose from 27 to 34 percent.[13]

There has been some redistribution of health resources. Facilities have been distributed throughout all parts of the country, poor and rich, rural and urban.

Very little can be said about the effects on the health of the population stemming from such a slow evolution of policy. But in one respect, at least, the long battle has had significant results both from the point of view of human beings and public policy. The federal policy of redistribution of access and monitoring distribution is now clearly established. Medicare and Medicaid are the source of a perceptable shift in the distribution of health services. The elderly and poor receive more medical care and pay less of the cost than was formerly the case. The elderly have benefited most dramatically, at least in terms of access to health services. While persons between the ages of 19 and 64 meet 71 percent of the cost of medical care from private sources, including private insurance, the elderly pay only 40 percent.

This shift in distribution has been subject to counterattack with the result that after 1970 the Medicare proportion of payments for the eldrely dropped overall from 44 to 38 percent and its share of physician costs dropped from 60 to 52 percent. The reversal was due in part to increases in the coinsurance or deductible amount for which the insured are held personally liable and even more to a sharp drop in the number of physicians willing to accept Medicare fees as their total charges. Between 1969 and

---

[13]Barbara Cooper and Nancy Worthington, "Age Differences in Medical Care Spending 1972," *Social Security Bulletin* 36, No. 5 (May 1973): 3.

1973 the proportion of physicians willing to accept full assignment of their fees to Medicare dropped from 61 to 52 percent.

However, it was clear in 1966, and it remains substantially true today,. that the elderly have been the beneficiary of a significant redistribution. In 1966 the hospital-days care for the aged rose by 25 percent and, even more vital, they were less dependent upon charity. Before Medicare 17 percent of hospital-days care for the aged were without charge, meaning they were treated as charity cases; after Medicare this figure fell to 3 percent.

The poor, among whom the aged constitute a large proportion, have also benefited, but not as dramatically. A full analysis would have to take into account regional variations, race, and urban location. However, we can draw a few conclusions suggesting how far these policies have directly benefited the poor in terms of access to medical care. Medicare and Medicaid meet 57 percent of all the expenses of personal health care for families with incomes under $2000, 84 percent for families with incomes under $5000. If a near-poverty level for a family of four is taken to be $5700, then government sources meet 46 percent of health costs for those below this level, but only 15 percent for those above it.[14]

If we turn to use of physician services we find that in 1964 nearly 28 percent of all poor families and 33 percent of nonwhite poor families had not seen a doctor for two years. In 1973 these percentages dropped to 17 percent of all poor and 18 percent of nonwhite poor, almost equalizing the relationship by color.[15] Interestingly, in the same period 17 percent of the nonpoor white population did not see a doctor for two years and this figure fell in 1973 to 13.4 percent. For nonwhite, nonpoor families, these proportions dropped from 24.7 percent to 15.3 percent. Thus the differential by physician access has been, in an aggregate sense, almost abolished.

By another measure, that of number of physician visits per year, the poor have fared a lot better. Between 1964 and 1973 the average number of visits per person per year for poor families rose from 4.3 to 5.6, while for the nonpoor the number rose from 4.6 to 4.9. The lower average number of visits by the nonpoor is probably related to their lower incidence of illness; this measure can tell us little about whether the amount of medical care received was appropriate for the amount required.

Although these data suggest that some leveling of access has occurred, others indicate the persistence of unequal access. Thus in 1973 only 5 percent of white medical visits were to a hospital outpatient clinic, while 16.4 percent of nonwhite visits were to clinics.

If slight, rather than dramatic changes have been produced for in-

---

[14]Data in this section from *Health U.S. 1975.*

[15]In 1964 nonpoor families were defined as those with incomes under $3000; in 1973 the figure used was $6000.

dividuals, the same can be said regarding the system of medical care itself. Except for hospital facility distribution and financing, the system has been remarkably unaltered. In the financing of hospital care significant changes have occurred, but still in the direction of shifting the cost burden rather than altering the practice of medical care delivery.

There has also been a redistribution in an unintended direction, for hospitals and physicians have benefited significantly through an increase in incomes. Hospitals are less likely to operate at a deficit, meaning that private philanthropic funds are less used to meet hospital deficits. In a sense, conventional wealthy contributors have benefited by being relieved of an obligation. The income of physicians has increased and in some categories has increased enormously, as in the substantial improvement in the relative position of radiologists, pathologists, and anesthetists as a direct consequence of reimbursement policies.

To illustrate the effect on the hospital system, between 1961 and 1965 (before Medicare) revenues increased annually by 10.4 percent, but between 1965 and 1976 revenues increased 16.4 percent. In the same periods semiprivate room charges increased by 5.6 percent and by 13 percent, respectively.[16] In this period all consumer prices rose, but not as rapidly. Part of the increase in hospital charges can be attributed to higher wages for nonprofessional workers, to a shorter work week, and to increases in the cost of equipment and drugs. The ratio of staff to patient census went up from 240 per 100 in 1961 to 301 in 1971, and average earnings rose from $3371 to $6028. However, private payments dropped from 27 to 11 percent of all income, and public payments rose from 8 to 39 percent, suggesting some correlation between funds pumped into medical care and rising costs. Between 1961 and 1971 private hospitals doubled the ratio of net income to plant assets from 1.4 to 3 percent.

There have been other social effects as well. Medical care has been more and more institutionalized and is now predominantly delivered in hospitals. Home visits and the delivery of medical care in any form to the patient's home has been significantly reduced. Hospitals have become larger and often less personal. Physicians' offices are often crowded and replace outpatient clinics of earlier times. The prescription of drugs and chemical therapies have increased enormously, with both great benefits and possible damage. With the rapid expansion in scientific means made possible in part by public support for the purchase of services or payment for research, the capacity to monitor and control the use of noxious or dangerous medicines has diminished. Attention to preventive health methods has declined as hospitals and physicians' offices have become the dominant focus of health services, while public health, sanitation, supervision of water supply have diminished in importance in health policy.

---

[16]Julian Pettergill, "The Financial Positions of Private Community Hospitals, 1961–71," *Social Security Bulletin* 36, No. 11 (November 1973): 3.

It appears that environmental protection efforts may some day assume the prominent position which public health once held in this field. Finally, medicine's concentration on scientific and technical cure has outgrown its attention to life styles and patterns of living as contributors to disease. At the present time arguments about the illness-producing effects of basic life styles are raised by private voices and have not yet become a part of national policy. Complaints that our illnesses are due to poor diet, speed, tension, and lack of exercise are not yet on a public policy agenda.

Thus, while the preamble of health legislation has argued that the purpose of the public policies adopted has been to improve and maintain the health of the people, the policies in effect have concentrated only on giving the population access to whatever services have been developed by the private providers—hospitals, physicians, the pharmaceutical companies, and so on.

A New Stage for Health Policy

What conclusions can be drawn from this long and painful struggle to achieve what may, in policy terms, seem to be rather minor advances? Whatever one may think of its merits, government officials have promoted one policy with persistence since 1935 and have produced perceptible changes in the way society assures the health of its citizens, doing so beyond the constraints which our society has imposed on public policy.

True, the fidelity with which public policy conforms to societal norms has been clearly demonstrated, but public policy can, albeit with enormous difficulty, lead the way to a change in societal policy through the slow, incremental enactment of specific pieces of public policy. In this example, the use of the federal government to influence the distributive effects in the health field has been enlarged. But the foundation has also been laid for future government action affecting the organization and structure of health care more radically than in the past. The unexpected consequences of actions made possible to date, that is, increasing government payment, may pull public policy further and further down the road of active intervention in the private sector. As interested groups and voters have come to expect more health assurance through their continued reliance upon science and more protection without direct personal cost, the more government expenditure for health services has increased. This in turn has produced anxiety about the scope of the cost and the possibility of containing it, which in its turn has forced some attention to ways to modify the delivery of services. A new plateau of public policy has thus been reached. It is no longer a question of whether government should act, but of how much and in what direction.

Direct intervention to modify the delivery system lies in the future, for any consideration of a national health service has not yet been introduced into the American debate. The minor experiments in governmental administration—city hospitals and clinics, EMIC and in the Veterans Administration—even appear to have lost ground in favor of a privately organized set of services.

But these dynamics have already produced a variety of governmental controls over the functioning of the health system which may some day justify reassessment from the point of view of their overall impact. Federal policy by and large determines what hospital and nursing home facilities will be built and where. This has been exercised cumulatively and incrementally, first, by the enactment of the Hill-Burton Law which provided for federal contributions to the support of hospitals, with priorities to assure that all geographic sectors of the country, even the most rural, have hospital facilities. More recently, this has been extended to the concept of certificate of need, whereby health systems agencies are entitled to question further expansion of hospital facilities and of their location. Many states have the capacity to deny a certificate of need, which effectively halts capital expansion although it does not yet positively direct construction in underserved areas.

The character of services provided is now mildly challenged by the requirement that all medical facilities subject the practices of their physicians to professional review bodies, in order to assure that there are no wide variations in the practices of physicians. True, this control is exercised on a peer basis, physician over physician, but it is mandated by national policy.

The Health Manpower Act of 1975 now largely determines the volume and type of medical education. While in the past this has been a reflexive policy, responding to the choices made by the medical professions and medical schools, recent enlargement of the policy provides for national priorities to be established by quasigovernmental bodies governing the types of health personnel required and their distribution. The priority guides will in the future govern the allocation of manpower training resources, which in their turn will govern the production of health personnel.

Finally, utilization review standards and control by fiscal intermediaries, such as Blue Cross associations, now determine what health services will in fact be paid for out of the more than 35 percent of the health bill met by public funds. Since hospitals and nursing homes and, to an increasing extent, physicians are dependent upon these funds for their incomes, this capacity in an administrative mechanism to determine what will be paid for in health care can become decisive. To date these choices have largely been left in the private sector, either in the hands of physicians to determine their average billings or in the hands of private insurance companies, but the principle at least has been established that the requirement can be federally mandated.

It thus appears that the operations of limited societal policies may produce an accumulation of small effects which can in time lead to a radical renovation of the health delivery system. But it is important to emphasize that radical change is not yet in sight.

THE CHARACTER OF CURRENT PUBLIC POLICY ISSUES

The current state of development of the national government's health policy leaves the following issues unsettled, and it is difficult to state with any certainty whether a national policy on these subjects does exist.

Should financing access to health services be extended from those special categories now covered to the entire population? This in effect would involve an attempt not as much to redistribute health services to benefit the entire population, as to remove from individuals the illusion that they do not have to bear some of the burden of medical costs and that these costs can be shifted to someone else. If all persons are covered and if demand continues to grow as it has, it seems inescapable that either the costs will increase or controls on utilization and the nature of provision will have to be introduced. Can such controls distribute a highly valued commodity—medical care—to persons equally, regardless of income?

With or without an extension of financial coverage, what, if any, shall be the federal policy to control the escalating costs of medical care, which have so exceeded increases in the GNP or cost of living? Specific pieces of legislation have been introduced, but there seems to be no indication that the national government has at any stage adopted a policy of systematically controlling the cost of medical care when, by this phrase, one means controlling the charges made by all medical providers. A method of some control exists in programs which set fee scales, but this is limited to use of the public dollar. Private payments are still the greater part (60 percent) of the total expenditure for medical care, and there is no indication that a national policy to control the imposition of charges to the private consumer is anywhere in sight. The only controls in the past have been negative in the sense that they are imposed only on aspects of medical care which are paid for by public funds. Can controls act in a positive sense to direct the delivery system to do more of some things (for example, ambulatory care in ghettoes) and less of others (says, cardiac bypass operations) ?

What are desired forms of organizing health services? If any answer is to be given to such a question as a matter of national policy, it is essential that a judgment must be made between the present private system and some alternative form. There have been modest experimental probes into alternatives. For example, encouragement of the creation of group practices was embodied in national legislation, and a few health maintenance organizations did result. However, the legislation did not require prepayment, and health maintenance organizations have been financially supported only on a small, experimental basis and without substantial continuity. Some alteration in the balance between hospital and primary care (the services of a doctor in an individual's community) has also been attempted, but without any clear national choice as to direction. The primary flow of support continues toward payment in the hospital. Modest sums have been expended to encourage the education of physicians prepared to practice family medicine, and some emergency funds have been used to underwrite the development of neighborhood health clinics in ghetto areas. But neither of these represents a permanent national commitment to assure the delivery of primary care services by family doctors or through neighborhood health centers.

At the extreme, we may some day have to decide whether to abandon our primary reliance upon a system of insurance and financing and substitute a program of health services. The model best known in the United States is the British National Health Service.[17] The British government acquired all the hospitals and placed their administration in the hands of regional hospital boards; the boards operate on behalf of the national government, but with a large measure of freedom, subject only to total funding provided by the national treasury. Physicians are paid by tax funds, either as specialists on hospital staffs or as general practitioners with their own lists of patients for each of whom the physician is paid an annual per capita sum. Physicians are free also to develop private fee-for-service practices within set limits. Physicians' levels of payment are negotiated with professional associations, all persons have a physician of their choice, virtually no charges are made for any medical attention or hospital care, and small sums are charged for common medicines. The system is complex, but its main features are the assurance of a minimum of physician attention to all, no cost barrier to medical care, and no fee for service complexities.

Many arguments have been raised for and against such a system. It exists in other countries in some form, but mainly in socialist or communist nations. The substitution of a health service for a health insurance has not yet been raised in general policy debate.

How will the purposes of the national health policy (other than the global purpose of assuring access) be defined? Small-scale programs are supported to provide presumably preventive health services for mothers of newborn infants, to provide special centers to concentrate on the needs of geriatric patients, or to pay for the care of industrially injured workers, such as miners. The occupational health legislation has provided modest sums in an effort to reduce health hazards in industry. And a program

---

[17]For a full discussion, see Gordon Forsyth, *Doctors and State Medicine: A Study of the British Health Service* (Old Woking, Surrey: Open University Set Book, Pitman Medical, 1966); and I. Douglas-Wilson and Gordon McLachlan, eds., *Health Service Prospects* (Boston: Little, Brown, 1973).

of environmental protection has been launched in an effort to clean up water supply and reduce industrial pollution.

In one sense, these national programs appear, when taken together, to amount to a federal policy to have both butter and guns. Primary reliance is still placed upon private providers and the curative miracles of modern science, which claim the bulk of public expenditure and of public manpower. On the other hand, parallel activities are also initiated with much less money and personnel to tackle great environmental health hazards. And even smaller sums are made available to private groups to experiment with alternative forms of delivery organization, such as group practices. But none of these can be considered more than small-scale testing experiments by contrast to the major policy of trusting the private system to function reasonably well for itself and government to step in to correct the most glaring inequities. However, as has been stated before, the volume and scope of the public investment on this policy are now sufficiently great and the contradictions and tensions which have ensued from it are sufficiently disturbing to open up the possibility that the field of health policy will continue to grow and to be controversial. There may be a stage when the nature of health services themselves will be altered or planned by government action, but such a shift in public policy to alter societal policies remains in the future. For the time being, the legislation most likely to be enacted remains rooted in the past—insurance to cover costs, with an increase in government regulation.

The subject of serious disability may prove to be as powerful a force to move government into new roles as is the anxiety over the cost of our present medical and health system. Federal policies of relying upon payment mechanisms alone have created within thirty years a vast addition to the health system, that of proprietary nursing homes which manage more beds than do all our hospitals. At the same time the prevalance of severe disability has increased. Between 1960 and 1970 the proportion of adults covered by social security who qualified for permanent disability benefits increased by 225 percent.[18] The elderly over 75 years of age are especially prone to severe disability which makes living at home difficult without some supportive personal services. And the proportion of older people is the fastest growing in the population. Serious auto and sport injuries are increasing in prevalence and possibly in incidence so that there is an increasing proportion of young adults with lifetime disability. Medical science now keeps alive large numbers of children who once died in the early years of life because of congenital disease or injury, but who now survive for long lifetimes of severe incapacity. To these must be added the apparent increase in cases of alcoholism, drug abuse, and

---

[18]P.R. Lerner, *Social Security Disability Applicant Study, 1970* (Washington, D.C.: Social Security Administration, U.S. Department of Health, Education, and Welfare, 1974).

mental illness, all of which are long-term conditions which impair functioning.

Our health system is focused on curing those conditions which it knows how to cure; it has little competence yet and even less interest in taking care of a growing population of the disabled. But inattention to their needs does not spare the health system, because for lack of proper attention these patients return often to acute hospitals, which can do little for them, or they unnecessarily end up in nursing homes, for which the health system must pay.

It is possible that the strain which this phenomenon introduces may force an alteration of the system, although the type of change cannot be clearly outlined. It is likely that some shift may have to occur in the proportionate amount of attention given to the chronically ill, which would demand in turn major changes in the training and practices of physicians, nurses, and hospitals. Such a shift is not likely to be welcomed nor is it likely to be introduced by present providers acting on their own initiative. An alternative to this type of shift in emphasis might be a new system for caring for this population, combining nursing homes and various home-care and personal services. The financing of such a parallel system would necessarily become competitive with the health system and increase the total of the nation's income spent on health matters.

ADDITIONAL READINGS

Anderson, Odin. *Health Services in a Land of Plenty.* Chicago: University of Chicago Press, 1968.

Corning, Peter. *Evolution of Medicare.* Washington, D.C.: Office of Research and Statistics, Social Security Administration, U.S. Department of Health, Education, and Welfare, 1969.

Donabedian, Avedis. *Benefits in Medical Care Programs.* Cambridge, Mass.: Harvard University Press, 1976.

Health Policy Advisory Committee (PAC), ed. *America's Health Empire.* New York: Random House, 1971.

Marmor, Theodore. *The Politics of Medicare.* Chicago: Aldine, 1973.

Somers, Herman, and Anne Somers. *Doctors, Patients, and Health Insurance.* Washington, D.C.: Brookings Institution, 1961.

Stevens, Robert, and Rosemary Stevens. *Welfare Medicine in America.* New York: Free Press, 1974.

HOUSING: ENLARGED AIMS—MINIMUM RESULTS

Providing shelter is another dimension of existence in which federal governmental obligations have expanded significantly. The expansion has accelerated since 1960, and the breadth of social concerns has been remarkable. Governmental concern about shelter was originally local and limited to the income and economic provisions already discussed. But the growth of urban concentration focused attention on minimal regulation of land use and standards for construction through local zoning and building codes and to a lesser extent on the provision of housing for poor families. In an unusual manner, housing policy seems to have completed a full circle. In its origins, at the level of local government, public concerns were deeply infused with a social purpose—concern for a deprived population, concern about adequacy of space, reduction of overcrowding, relative value of high versus low densities, and provision of essential amenities, then defined as access to running water, indoor sanitation, and air. The relationship between housing arrangements and population dispersion was even considered in the early debates in New York State. This early breadth of approach was followed by a long period in which the concentration of policy was on physical construction, stimulation of the private housing market, modest public construction for low-income families, and regulation of the land use. By the 1960s however, concern for the entire range of social as well as physical environments reemerged.

Physical Housing as Policy Objective

Origins of Governmental Intervention

Much of the pioneer activity by local government took place in older eastern seaboard cities, such as New York. In the 1890s, the needs of new immigrants and the jerrybuilt private-market, profit-making construction of housing with a short-term outlook produced an intolerable market situation: high density of population, the spread of disease, and the complete absence of minimum amenities in what was then considered decent housing.[1] A New York survey exposing such conditions found nearly 3000 individuals in one block of 39 tenements, with only 264 water closets, with 40 units of hot running water, and a high incidence of tuberculosis.

Findings such as these gave rise to widespread civic action and conflict with local political and construction interests. The reform movement prevailed, however, and state legislation was enacted providing for the establishment of a tenement commission to tackle the host of interrelated problems which this information revealed. Implicit was a concern for physical and social relationships affecting large numbers of human beings, but the terms of reference and the premises of the commission and its leaders concentrated primarily on physical and regulatory solutions.

It was believed that regulation of private construction by government was much preferable to public construction or administration of housing, and there was little confidence that government could effectively administer housing programs. This skepticism prevailed in a period when the corruption of local government processes was widely publicized. It was believed that strong regulation by a tough-minded administration could produce better physical standards in new and old housing. Such improvements were expected in themselves to provide the kind of "decent environment" which would resolve all other difficulties: reduced density population, access to air, and sanitary facilities would be sufficient. It is even possible to perceive some early glimmerings of concern about concentrations of poor families in segregated sections of the cities, the slums. The distressing conditions in which poor families found themselves and the concentration of low-income families in congested segments of the city were all blamed upon the profit-making motive to secure the maximum return from the minimum investment and the maximum use of the least amount of space. Since these circumstances were controlled by builders, it was presumed that tight regulation of standards might lead to a elimination or reduction of slums.

---

[1] For a valuable summary of the origins of governmental intervention, see Roy Lubove, *The Progressives and the Slums* (Pittsburgh: University of Pittsburgh Press, 1962), especially Chap. 5 on Tenement House Commission of 1900.

Beginnings of Reform

A major step toward federal policy was taken when the Housing Act of 1937 was passed as part of the New Deal momentum of the depression years. The act provided the first federal subsidy for housing. Programs of the 1930s produced public construction and administration of low-income housing, with federal support of locally initiated plans. During this period New York City provided housing for upwards of 500,000 persons—an entire city, produced with federal help, but planned, built, and managed by the local housing authority. Public housing elsewhere was undertaken, but not on such a large scale, and much of the programming was concerned only with basic physical structure, that is, the construction of safe, solid, unimaginative housing capable of being rented at a very low figure.

Proliferation of Programs

The housing shortage created by the halt in construction during the war years and the rush of discharged veterans to establish independent households was an important area of concern in the late 1940s. In 1949 amendments to the Housing Act of 1937 authorized a program of public housing, publicly administered and constructed, creating 135,000 units annually for six years. In addition, separate categorical programs were directed at slum clearance and urban redevelopment. The Federal Housing Act of 1949 contained as one of its goals the provision of a decent home and a suitable living environment for every American family. This objective has been more or less maintained in all succeeding administrations. However, such an ambitious objective needs to be examined more closely in light of the specific policies adopted in federal programs. By and large, the practical policies as distinguished from the stated aspirations conformed to the basic societal guidelines which have affected other programs—a reliance upon the private market, with government in a subsidiary or supplementary role, and some preoccupation with especially disadvantaged groups.

Within this framework, by 1968 a federal executive agency proposed the construction of 26 million new homes over a 10-year span in order to provide adequate shelter, to improve substandard housing, to replace substandard units, and to accommodate newly established families in a period of rapid family formation. This goal was to be achieved primarily by stimulation and incentive for the private construction market, and in fact by the late 1960s that market was producing about 1.5 million units annually. However, these new constructions did not necessarily address themselves to removing substandard units or to meeting the needs of families with low income.

A significant array of administrative agencies was established, including the Housing and Home Finance Agency, the Federal Housing Administration, and the Urban Renewal Authority. The most influential of these, the Housing and Home Finance Agency, functioned primarily through mortgage and construction guarantees. The incentives for the private market were directed primarily toward housing for middle- and upper-income families, on the assumption families with lower incomes could occupy the housing left behind by the higher income families, and thus the interests of all groups would be served.

A succession of complaints and pressures led to the enactment of a variety of specialized programs without fundamentally altering this approach. Large concentrations of the poor in low-cost public housing produced concentrations of social difficulty and distress and established that the simple replacement of substandard housing by sterile, sanitary housing exacerbated rather than ameliorated social difficulties, especially when such construction did not take into account the whole range of problems of social and group relationships and the decayed environments outside of the apartments. Urban renewal, the attempt to get rid of slums by bulldozing them, led to the charge that many of these programs were attempting to revitalize the inner city by attracting middle- and upper-income families to better housing, but without taking care of the families thus displaced from slum areas. In the period between 1949 and 1963 it has been estimated that the urban renewal program alone removed about 177,000 family dwelling units and 66,000 individual family units from the market and replaced them with only 68,000 dwelling units, of which only 20,000 were for low-income families. This led to the accusation that urban renewal, with the expenditure of several billions of dollars, succeeded in reducing the supplying of housing for persons of low income rather than increasing it. It was not only that families displaced by these programs were not provided with replacement housing anywhere, but in the period of disruption which ensued families with limited means were forced to move into higher rental housing without any assistance for making the transition.[2] Old neighborhoods and whatever supportive network of social relationships they contained were destroyed with the dispersion of previously more or less class-homogeneous populations into new and strange areas.

By 1966, the year in which the Demonstration Cities and Metropolitan Development Act (Model Cities) was enacted, the growth of federal commitment measured in dollar terms became dramatic. In 1940 and in 1950 it was estimated that federal grants to state and local jurisdictions averaged about $2 billion per year. In 1960 this figure increased to $7 billion, and by 1966 it was estimated that approximately $16 billion was expended in federal grants, plus some $12 billion available for residential mortgage guarantees. At this time the Presidential Commission on Intergovern-

---

[2]Bernard Frieden, *The Future of Old Neighborhoods* (Cambridge, Mass.: MIT Press, 1964); Scott Greer, *Urban Renewal and American Cities.* (Indianapolis: Bobbs-Merrill, 1965).

mental Relationships (the Kastenbaum Commission), appointed by President Eisenhower, reported that "federal grants, represented in the variety
of categorical programs, did not constitute a system. The program has had
such varied characteristics, and diverse objectives, and piecemeal organization, that this could lead to not only confusion but cross-purpose program
development." [3]

By this time and continuing at an accelerated rate until the 1970s,
the congeries of federal programs had by now become so intertwined with
the private construction of housing for persons of all income classes that
the old boundaries which constrained federal responsibility were no longer
applicable. Policy was no longer concerned with the disadvantaged alone
or with one-time emergency measures as in the post-war period. Federal
policy continued to be an accumulation of independent programs out of
which it is difficult to extract a clear set of policy directions. In 1966 when
various programs were consolidated in one super federal agency, the
Department of Housing and Urban Development (HUD), the federal
programs were roughly clustered into four categories defined by objective:

1. Urban renewal programs intended to improve central city environments, a program used in most cities to construct middle-
   class housing, to tear down slums, to alter the mix of population
   in the inner city, and to improve the environment through such
   means as nonpolluting transportation

2. Mortgage guarantee programs for all income classes, which
   strongly stimulated the construction of housing in suburban
   areas and even the experimental construction of new cities, both
   stimulating the dispersion of populations from the inner city and
   without strong enough incentives to increase significantly the
   volume of housing, especially for the poor

3. Programs to provide dwelling units at low cost to a limited extent
   through publicly administered housing and increasingly through
   various subsidy devices for builders, such as low interest rates,
   tax write-downs, and incentives in the acquisition of land, in-
   tend to reduce ultimate rental or sale price for the consumer

4. Modest programs for special groups, especially the aged and the
   disabled

While these programs were in some respects addressed to certain
social problems of certain special groups (the poor and the elderly), the
definition of policy objectives remained general: to improve the physical
quarters of all persons living in substandard housing. The focus on the

[3]U.S. Commission on Intergovernmental Relations, *Message from The President
of the United States. Transmitting the Final Report to the 84th Congress,*
1st sess., House Document No. 198, 1955 pp. 118, 139.

objective of physical housing ignored the social consequences of the actual results of the programs: conflicting claims upon the distribution of income by different economic groups, the disruption of groups with more or less homogeneous economic-class conditions, the relocation of persons of different status to common neighborhoods in the inner city, and the segregation of populations by income class in suburban areas.

EMERGENCE OF CONCERN FOR THE SOCIAL ENVIRONMENT: THE MODEL CITIES EXPERIMENT

The clear worsening of the condition of low-income families was for a time obscured by the value definition of "substandard." Between 1950 and 1959, for example, the percentage of unsound housing occupied by whites dropped from 18 to 14 percent and by nonwhites from 60 to 46 percent; the percentage of overcrowded units declined for whites from 12 to 8 percent and for blacks from 30 to 25 percent. But the definitions of "unsound" were not very tough; the gross disparity between white and nonwhite conditions could not be concealed for long, and the pressures for attention to minorities and low-income families segregated or hemmed into large city centers became irresistible. Housing policy was no longer a matter of simply stimulating construction or of giving attention to physically unsound housing. It had also to give attention to most troublesome problems of class and social relationships and to the dilemmas of population concentration and dispersion.

The consequences of previous policies which led to the concentration of poor, usually public-assistance families, in densely concentrated high-rise units, forced attention to the host of social problems with which low-income families are plagued. Federal programs by and large made no provision for tenant services which this population urgently required, and the running sore of low-income housing was difficult to ignore. The New York City Housing Authority was forced to establish a division of community services to consolidate its own activities and those of a variety of private agencies with a services budget of some $20 million per year, in order to attend to the most minimal social needs of the 500,000 people living in Housing Authority units. Recreational activities, vocational preparation, legal aide, homemaking services, literacy training centers, study centers, and the like, had to be provided as a palliative if not as a serious solution to the problems of living faced by low-income families in the city.

Pressures such as these found expression in the expansion of social programs of the middle 1960s. One of the interesting forward steps in federal social policy was embodied in the Model Cities legislation of 1965. A presidentially appointed task force reviewed the explosive situation in low-income and urban areas and proposed the testing of a new national approach to cope with these difficulties. The policy of the new program was to include: concentration of federal resources in order to assure a critical mass of effort directed at clear-cut objectives; coordination of the disparate and often contradictory federal program activities in the direc-. tion of this objective; mobilization of local leadership, especially from low-income populations, in the direction of joint action on the problems of urban housing and environment. The legislation as drafted by the President's office proposed that the new approach would be tested in 50 cities, would be financed entirely by federal appropriations, and would introduce into each demonstration city a federal administrator to provide an active influence rather than a simple monitor of the ways in which these federal funds were used to further the objectives of the program. The legislation was clearly redistributive in its intent and clear about its constituency. Its preamble states:

> The Congress hereby finds and declares that improving the quality of urban life is the most critical domestic problem facing the United States. The persistence of widespread urban slums and blight, the concentration of persons of low income in older urban areas, and the unmet needs for additional housing and community facilities and services arising from rapid expansion of our urban population have resulted in the marked deterioration in the environment of large numbers of our people while the nation as a whole prospers.[4]

The legislation was intended not only to provide direct assistance, but also to help the cities coordinate their other welfare activities aided by other federal social programs to encourage an economical use of all federal, state, and local efforts to improve the quality of urban life. The bill was intended to provide a demonstration of the effectiveness of a massive, comprehensive effort to rebuild or restore entire sections and neighborhoods of slum and blighted areas.

The Congress was unenthusiastic about many aspects of this proposal, and finally adopted a much more vague statement of purpose: "maximum opportunities in the choice of housing accommodations for all citizens and of all income levels." This phrasing replaced administration proposals which included such language as "counteract the segregation of housing by race or income." The Congress also weakened the draft legislation in a number of ways. It removed the proposal for a federal coordinator to be located in each demonstration and substituted funding for technical assistance from the various federal agencies whose programs affected urban housing. It also doubled the number of cities to be included in the Model Cities experiment and thus reduced the total sum of money available to any one. Finally, it removed the provision that all other federal programs

---

[4]U.S. Congress, House Subcommittee on Housing, *Hearings on Demonstration Cities, Housing, and Urban Development*, 89th Cong., 2d sess., 1966, p. 1.

relevant to urban housing give priority to the Model Cities areas and called instead for simple coordination of activities through HUD. The administration sought to increase slightly the margin of federal authority, and the Congress cut it back to ensure the more conventional understanding of partnership between federal, state, and local governments and private industry. At the time that Model Cities legislation authorized appropriations of approximately $2.3 billion plus $412 million of earmarked urban renewal funds, the Congress retained the antecedent categorical programs and funded them at the level of some $12 billion without any provision that these programs give priority attention to the purposes of Model Cities. These differences in concepts held by the executive and the Congress persisted throughout the 1960s.

The total effect of the administration's attempt to focus federal policy was thus reduced to only an addition to the accumulation of diverse, limited, and ineffective programs. The adopted national policy of the federal government (meaning both the executive and the legislative branches in agreement) succeeded in giving supplementary attention to especially difficult areas without significantly altering the traditional reliance upon the private marketplace to deal with the social dilemmas of housing. It has been estimated that by 1971 federal spending in urban areas ranged as high as $44 billion, including loan insurance and guarantees.[5] A more realistic figure which excludes loan insurance and guarantees would still approximate $10 billion, spent specifically for these focused urban needs. Out of this total, the Model Cities program secured annual appropriations of approximately $390 million per year, or about 15 percent of the total of HUD's urban programs, about $2.6 billion.

With the coming of a Republican administration in 1968, the Model Cities program was not immediately dismantled, but the whole thrust of federal policy began to shift in the direction of the "new federalism" and the experimentation with general revenue sharing. General revenue sharing not only provided for a more generous distribution of funds, some $5.3 billion in the first year, but shifted major responsibility for choice making from the hands of the federal government back to the local government and the local interplay of political forces. On the average, revenue-sharing allocations were double that of Model Cities funding and local pressures significantly reduced the saliency and priority position of low-income areas which, on the average, represented less than 10 percent of urban populations. By 1972 adopted federal policy continued to represent a limited attention to poverty areas or to their complex network of social as well as housing problems. But although the effort remained modest by

---

[5]See U.S. Congress, Senate Subcommittee on Executive Reorganization, *Hearings on the Federal Role in Urban Affairs*, 89th Cong., 2d sess., August 15–16, 1966, pt. 1, pp. 178–181; Staff Paper, Office of the Assistant Secretary for Model Cities, *The Basis for Analysis of Federal Aid Programs for Urban Impact*, 1971.

comparison with the thrust of other federal programs, it did persist as a beachhead of federal policy far beyond that of previous years.

The impact of the national policy in this decade of strong effort and altered priority-making has been summarized by Frieden and Kaplan.[6] These analysts conclude that dramatic improvements in living conditions did not take place through Model Cities largely because only a small share of all urban aid was devoted to Model Cities and there was a low level of overall national commitment to the cities over the decade. The 6 million residents in the final round of Model Cities programs receiving grants received proportionately less than other populations in urban areas benefiting from other federal housing programs.

One other conclusion can be drawn from the Model Cities experiment which has importance if one wishes to consider the public policy role of the federal government. Local governments, even where they vigorously supported Model-Cities planning, had great difficulty in actually securing and spending much increased sums on improving the conditions in their Model Cities areas in the time available. This raises a question whether cities can spend federal funds effectively on the problems of poverty areas, given the modest scale of this experimental approach. Roland Warren found that

> The agencies concerned themselves with Model Cities principally for two related purposes: to prevent any threat to their own domains and their own viability and, where possible, to benefit from the program by increasing their budgets or enlarging their domains . . . . if we had been serious about it, we would have needed a budget at least four times as large.[7]

Frieden and Kaplan state that

> no simple conclusion can be reached about the ability of cities to spend federal funds effectively. Large numbers of them applied to participate in the Model Cities program; both their plans and their planning arrangements were consistent with the purposes of the program. Along the way, the mayors endured many local controversies with citizen groups and undoubtedly paid a political price for their support of the program . . . but their commitment was slow to produce tangible results. The cities, like the federal government, and partly because of the federal government could not reorient their own agencies quickly enough.[8]

---

[6]Bernard Frieden and Marshall Kaplan, *The Politics of Neglect: Urban Aid from Model Cities to Revenue Sharing* (Cambridge, Mass.: MIT Press, 1975).
[7]Roland Warren, "The Model Cities Program, An Assessment," in *The Social Welfare Forum, 1971* (New York: Columbia University Press, 1971), pp. 153–154.
[8]Frieden and Kaplan, *Politics of Neglect*, p. 230.

Assessment of Federal Policy

The lesson is a sobering one. Once housing programs are institutionalized in any agency structure, be it governmental or voluntary, the process of change to alter the direction and thrust of those programs and agencies is slow and difficult to bring about. It apparently requires a significant, directed effort conducted over several years and with more substantial resources than are usually committed to assure that policy aims move programs and governments in new directions.

It is difficult to make a final assessment about the effects of federal policy, given the characteristics thus described. If one takes as a measure the removal of substandard housing, meaning housing with measurable overcrowding, without running water, and with measurable fire hazard, it can be said that federal policy has reduced, but not eliminated, the volume of substandard housing for both white and minority populations.

A somewhat more rigorous and socially oriented measure would include not only housing condition and overcrowding, but the ability of the occupants to afford adequate units. Such a measure is one of the interesting and significant examples of a social measurement which results from examining the cross-over relationship between several human activities—in this case, physical housing, family income, and the economy. By this measure, in 1970 there were at least 13 million housing-poor households in the United States. Of this total 6.9 million households lived in physically inadequate units, and an additional 6.2 million were living either in housing of excessive cost in relation to income or of inadequate size.[9]

Have conditions changed against such an enlarged framework? A clear answer is not possible. According to the 1960 census 8.5 million families were living in substandard (meaning dilapidated) housing and an additional 6.1 million were living in overcrowded conditions, but it is not known how much overlap there was, meaning families living in both overcrowded and substandard housing. If we were to limit ourselves to dilapidated housing conditions alone, it would appear that there has been some reduction as a result of all the programs now at work, from 8.5 million in 1960 to 6.9 million in 1970 as estimated by the Joint Center report. Whatever the details of the long-time trend, it is at least clear that the reduction in substandard housing has proceeded very slowly indeed.

Of greater interest for our purposes is the way in which a sufficient understanding of the nature of social problems begins to influence the direction of social policy. The introduction of the concept that excessive rental charges or home purchase charges constitute a factor in defining substandard housing shifts the possible direction of public policy in a completely new direction. It is doubtful whether regulation and incentive

---

[9]David Birch et al., *America's Housing Needs 1970–1980*. Cambridge, Mass.: Joint Center for Urban Studies, MIT-Harvard University, 1973).

to private suppliers of public housing will alone be sufficient to overcome this aspect of deprivation. But will our underlying societal policy norms permit an extension of federal responsibility to this extent? There has been reasonable support for the idea that the federal government should in some way participate in reducing the volume of substandard housing measured in physical terms. The chosen instrument has been the private marketplace which has functioned slowly to accomplish the end desired. Regulation seems to be moderately useful. But if the effect of regulation is to increase the cost of housing, when added to other inflationary tendencies, then the broader definition of deprivation leads to an increase in problems requiring public attention. But such attention to public policy can no longer be limited to regulation, for the federal government then becomes involved in the matter of income distribution. Traditionally, if a population is considered at a serious disadvantage, there is support for federal intervention. But has the point yet been reached where a strong federal attack on substandard housing as more broadly defined would be supported? The enlargement of mortgage support with the concomitant legislative difficulty in securing support for other public programs which can attack the other dimensions of deprivation and housing, would suggest that the time is not yet ripe.

The outlook, though, is not all bad. Some smaller-scale areas of social policy have begun to emerge so that the outlook may not be entirely bleak regarding federal responsibility for the social dimension of housing. What follows below may be said to represent the current inventory of federal aid. These programs continue to grow, not only in dollar value but in variety, so that the tools with which ultimately to shape federal social policy in housing are probably stronger and more generous than ever before. What is lacking is a sense of direction to be given this variety of programs from the standpoint of federal policy.

Provision of income to the poor   Public assistance may be said to be one of the largest underwriters of substandard housing in the country because the level of public-assistance is usually so low that families can afford only the lowest level of housing adequacy. Federal income policy as previously discussed has been made more uniform through Supplementary Security Income programs, at least for the elderly, the blind, and the disabled, and the executive branch continues to search for the means to reform income maintenance on behalf of other populations (families with dependent children and the unemployed).

The federal government has instituted some pilot programs to experiment in the use of direct cash subsidies for housing expenses. Such subsidy programs provide eligible families with supplementary payments usable only for housing to guarantee that their private payment for housing out of earned income does not exceed 25 percent of total income. Presumably this addition to the income of low-income families who are forced to compete in a high rental market will give them more access to better housing. In 1975 these housing allowances were extended experimentally to 24,000 families; $160 million has been authorized over several years' time.[10]

General revenue sharing This program could be used by local governments to supplement housing income for poor families, to mount other programs to reduce the cost of housing to the poor, to improve the conditions of housing stock through direct public programs or through the stimulation of local low-cost construction, or to reduce tax burdens. Such action would require pressure from local citizens to alter the priorities governing use of this federal income.

Proposals to enlarge special revenue sharing Special purpose revenue sharing limited to housing would lead to a community development program which would encompass Model Cities, urban renewal, grants for water and sewer projects, open space, beautification, neighborhood facilities, and housing rehabilitation. Whether or not a consolidated grant program to local governments, without the constraints of numerous federal categories, would be directed toward low-income populations or to especially troublesome social needs remains to be tested. Plans for such a program provide substantially new flexibility to local governments and reduce the requirement for local matching to secure funds. Presumably such a special revenue program would also introduce predictable future income so that long-term planning could be entered into. However, the level of funding contemplated is only the level of current expenditures, which means that available funds are eroded annually as inflation proceeds. Such specialized revenue sharing is intended to concentrate on metropolitan city areas (central cities and others with a population of 50,000 or more) and some urban counties, rather than being spread across all the 38,000 units of state and local governments. Since the formula proposed for distribution would take into account population, overcrowding, and poverty, the cities in greatest need might be expected to secure proportionately larger funds, whereas others ranking lower on these criteria might receive less.

The Housing and Community Development Act of 1974 makes a modest start along these lines.[11] But in 1977 the formula for allocating $2.5 billion in appropriated funds was already sharply challenged. Older cities with severe blight and unemployment were getting reduced allocations under a formula intended to help the economically depressed areas, while more affluent suburban and southwestern cities were getting in-

[10]*Experimental Housing Allowance Program: Initial Observations* (Washington, D.C.: U.S. Department of Housing and Urban Development, 1975).

[11]See William Frej and H. Specht, "Analysis of the Housing and Community Development Act of 1974," *Social Service Review* (June 1976) vol. 50, no. 2, pp. 275–292.

creased allocations. A mechanical economic formula has not yet been fine-tuned sufficiently to fit local problems.

Continuation of categorical programs If special revenue sharing for community development is not enlarged and extended, the preexisting categorical programs would undoubtedly continue: urban renewal, mortgage guarantee support, and the like. Among these are:

1. Mortgage construction support both for one- and two-family housing and for apartment housing

2. Subsidized mortgage arrangements so that interest paid on mortgages is reduced

3. Turnkey programs whereby contracts are entered into with private contractors to construct housing according to public specifications spelled out in contracts which, when completed, are purchased by local governments and rented to families eligible for public housing; these have led to the construction of somewhat smaller housing units

4. Sections 235 and 236 of the Housing and Urban Development Act, which reduce the interest families pay on FHA-insured mortgage loans or which provide subsidy to the mortgage holder who in turn will be enabled to charge lower rentals and still operate the property profitably; in 1969 a total of only 38,000 families received assistance through one of these means

5. The National Housing Act which provides very modest levels of financial assistance to nonprofit corporations such as labor unions, churches, and fraternal associations which seek to construct low-cost housing on a nonprofit basis; this operates through interest-free loans and technical assistance

6. The National Housing Corporation, a consortium of industrial and financial companies, which raises seed money through selling its stock to corporations

7. Continuation of Model Cities

8. New Towns development funding; this program has been erratic and insubstantial but a large number of new towns have been stimulated into development through private developers.

A few New Towns have actually been constructed in part and others are still struggling to find economic viability. One of the major aims of these New Town programs has been to test the kinds of living environments possible with the application of modern technology. Incidentally, they also test the feasibility of thinning out urban concentrations through the planned construction of new environments outside of large metropolitan areas or on their periphery. In a sense, the New Towns legislation provided minimal federal support to private developers' experimentation in creating better comprehensive environments for living which go beyond the simple construction of housing units. New cities presumably are planned to take into account the social, cultural, educational, and health requirements of the resident populations along with population and housing. Unfortunately, the discontinuity in support for this program makes it difficult to assert with confidence that it represents long-term federal support for comprehensive planning.

It would appear from the foregoing review that federal policy has remained within the constraints of social norms with one vital exception: the extension of government into actions which affect housing for all income classes, not only the poor. The extensiveness and breadth of federal involvement has now become sufficiently great for it to be difficult to visualize any retreat. The goal of social policy concerning the poor is still concentrated on improving the physical environmental conditions, but supplementary efforts to support beautification, to improve air and water standards, and to alter densities are all moves in the direction of wider social responsibility by federal action. The worst that can be said of the nominal steps taken thus far is that they are just that: they represent tentative probes and experiments with continuity, but limited financial support. Nonetheless, they represent steps in a clear direction.

In one respect, it can be said that the federal government has become significantly enmeshed in an almost completely social aspect—that of a housing mix. Federal intervention in housing has generally moved along the paths of market preference which appear to have followed the constant mobility of populations and this self-segregation by economic class and racial preferences. But marketplace preferences and national policy have encountered another national policy, one enforced by federal court decisions and congressional civil rights legislation. Together, these give to the federal government the instruments for modifying the natural distribution of populations in the market. Model Cities represents a small effort to redistribute the federal effort in favor of low-income groups in cities which are heavily dominated by the dilemmas of racial minorities. Civil rights legislation and court decisions impinge upon state and local tradition and law, undermining land-use policies which discriminate against racial minorities and discourage their moving into hitherto white communities.

Finally, a continuing demand for attention to the social needs attached to housing—recreational space, beautification, reduction of congestion, access to health, shopping, and social services—suggests that federal support is present to assure the presence of these amenities which were once considered privileges and are rapidly becoming matters of necessity.

Issues Concerning Age, Race, and Economic Class

If one moves beyond these components of social policy, other considerations emerge. An achievable aspect of federal social policy can be seen in the field of aging. A long accumulation of behavioral studies indicate that the elderly prefer to maintain their own housing, but in close proximity to families, that they seek relatively safe neighborhoods, that they require easy access to health, shopping, and social services, and that their morale is improved when there is some concentration of the elderly so that shared interests can be mutually reinforcing, but that they do not like age-segregated housing. Rosow and others have indicated the rich supply of mutual aid and support which the elderly give to each other when they live near their peers but also in a viable environment with other age groups as well.[12] Certain kinds of federally supported programs for housing provide that at least 5 percent of the constructed units be available and suitable for the elderly, but if these 5 percent of units are not subscribed to, other uses are usually sanctioned. There is nothing in present public policy which consistently uses such federal housing support to stimulate actively the construction of housing environments based upon this principle. Initiative is left to local sponsors. Federal support for the construction of special units for the aged has thus dealt with half of the policy potential—that of providing incentive for clusters of housing occupied solely by the elderly. Whether these units have appropriate access to other populations and to services has not been thoroughly investigated.

Modest federal support for the construction of service facilities, space for recreation, and the tentative explorations through new cities also represent a nascent federal concern with the wider environment which is being created. But these remain consistently at the level of experiments without strong federal support or direction. The shaping of environments remains, on the whole, in the hands of local and state governments through city planning and urban-use legislation or regulation. Federal policies on healthy environments—defined to mean air, water, and sewage predominantly—deal with growth but not the social aspects of the environment. Nonetheless, the activities resulting from these federal interests represent the development of tools which might be used systematically under the guidance of policies to influence the environments in which populations live.

Perhaps the most powerful issue which demands the attention of social policy now and in the near future is race relations. Many neighborhoods are relatively homogeneous in race or economic class as a result of tradition and history. Should these neighborhoods be systematically altered in order to bring about more heterogeneous neighborhoods and communities? Thus far, tools to alter the present balance or mix of populations have

---

[12]Irving Rosow, *Social Integration of the Aged* (New York: Free Press, 1967).

been made available to minority groups through civil rights legislation and occasional housing regulations. The most powerful of these may prove to be the school desegregation orders of the courts, with their consequent testing of forced busing as an instrument of change.

However, it cannot be said that a systematic national policy has yet emerged committing the national government to strong positive action for one or the other policy—homogeneous or heterogeneous neighborhoods and communities. Many federal programs are contradictory or act at cross purposes.

The adoption of a clear policy in this troublesome area is made especially difficult and unlikely because of the conflicting views held by segments of the American population. Various studies of populations' preferences indicate that few consistent agreements can be found among consumers of housing, although their behavior does fall into certain rough patterns.[13] Some minorities seek to remain in homogeneous communities, while others prefer to move outward into areas populated by different groups. Some persons prefer apartment living in high density areas of the cities, while others prefer open space. Upper-class, middle-class, and working-class families seek comfortable housing, but what each defines as comfortable varies not by race, but by culture and income. All income and racial groups have the same basic concept of what they want in housing— it should be decent and comfortable; but the definition of decent and comfortable varies in our large and diversified population.

The Future of Federal Involvement

Given this diversity, the most that can be expected of federal policy in housing is a proliferation of programs directed at specific and specialized problems—construction of neighborhood facilities, housing renovation, special subsidy for housing expenses for low-income families—and some policies designed to limit the most extreme arbitrary segregation in local actions. It can be expected that the development of new environments will proceed as a result of innumerable local decisions, rather than under the direction of national policy.

Confusion in the development of clear-cut federal policies, other than along the dimensions already outlined, can be explained in part by the displacement of earlier views about the power of desirable environments. At the turn of the century there was a widespread belief that changing the physical environment would improve people's lives. Subsequent experience showed that the intended effects were not secured. Concentration on

---

[13]Birch et al., *America's Housing Needs*; William Michaelson, "Social Adjustment to the Environment," in *Encyclopedia of Social Work*, 16th ed. (New York: National Association of Social Workers, 1971), pp. 291 ff.

physical housing did not necessarily improve either home or neighborhood environments, or at least not for very long. The replacement of dilapidated housing frequently resulted in less spacious units and an even greater population density. The historic accumulation of neighborhood informal reinforcing services were frequently destroyed and new forms of construction and building did not provide replacements except at a great cost and from a distance.

It has been established that changes in the physical environment produce improvement in the quality of the lives of the poor only when grossly substandard housing is replaced by constructions with reasonably good standards. As a result, the belief has emerged that social surroundings are more important than housing in what determines the lives of human beings. However, whatever conclusions are reached about the best, ultimate solution, the existence now of substandard housing and the concentration of racial minorities in that housing must be confronted, so the two views are still in conflict.

For a time, the Green Belt prospect and open housing (defined to mean small concentrations and small densities in suburbia) have also proven to be less than completely satisfactory. Suburban expansion has provided an opportunity for physical innovation and for population mobility, but families by and large have been found to bring with them their inherited cultural patterns, simply transplanting them to a new physical environment.

None of this is to argue that the physical environment is unimportant, but the nexus of socioeconomic relationships is now at the center of public concern. However, we must still deal with the physical fact of substandard housing, we must still confront the issue of concentration or segregation of racial and economic groups, and we must accept that we still know little about the intricate workings of social relationships. These factors make it extremely difficult to plan national policies in much detail except at the rather primitive levels we have discussed thus far.

The following issues can be identified as governing exploration and search for federal policies in the future.

High-density concentration   Given the historic development of population distribution and the urban base of our economic system, it seems unlikely that high-density concentration of residences will thin out.[14] Crowding in densities at some level does have undesirable consequences, but individuals and groups differ widely in how they balance the disadvantages against what they feel is desirable. The demands of available space and the economics of housing construction in urban areas have stimulated high-rise apartment living. The high costs of transportation, water, and

[14]Michelson, "Social Adjustment."

sewerage over a large area have encouraged the recent emergence of high-rise apartment house construction even in suburban areas once considered to be the primary domain of single residences. While many families have difficulties with high-rise living, many seem to prefer it because of the ease of access to urban resources, the security, or other social and practical amenities which are provided. It is possible that over time high-rise living may be found most acceptable for young families and those at the beginning of their careers, for single persons, and for the elderly, but this has not yet been established as a basis of policy.

Elimination of slums The issue of renovation of dilapidated housing and elimination of slums has not been resolved. There is accumulating evidence that some persons prefer to live in what was once considered a slum area, provided the quality of the housing there can be upgraded to meet some personal or cultural level of satisfaction which has not yet been standardized. Improving housing and amenities in such areas seems to be a major frontier for continuing public policy. The Model Cities experiment represents promising initiative at the level of federal government, but whether it will receive sufficient support to permit an enlargement of the federal effort remains to be seen.

Integration of social and ethnic classes Public actions to date have by and large served to break up ethnic segregation but without positive steps to control the reestablishment of homogeneous communities by suburban land use control and urban development procedures. Even less tested are actions to promote a mix of social and economic classes living in the same neighborhood.

Integration of age groups The progressive aging of the American population produces the need for some ultimate attention to the pattern of living to be provided for the elderly. For those who are physically vigorous, the varieties of cultural and economic choices already alluded to probably preclude a systematic national policy in favor of any particular pattern. However, when enfeeblement sets in, the social issues become dominant. Shall the public thrust be in the direction of institutionalization (as discussed in the chapter on health) or toward the production of supportive services to enable the elderly to remain in private residences? And what kind of private residences? As will be discussed in Chapter 6, it is likely that public policy will in time settle down to a clear-cut direction regarding this subgroup of the elderly population. But for all the others, it can be assumed that the federal government's action will be to permit the market of choices to determine the nature of relationships ultimately to be established.

Additional Readings

Aaron, Henry J. *Shelter Subsidies: Who Benefits from Federal Housing Policies*. Washington, D.C.: Brookings Institution, 1972.

Fisher, Robert. *Twenty Years of Public Housing*. New York: Harper & Row, 1959.

Frieden, Bernard. *Metropolitan America: Challenge to Federalism*. Washington, D.C.: Advisory Commission on Intergovernmental Relations, 1966.

Frieden, Bernard, and Marshall Kaplan. *The Politics of Neglect*. Cambridge, Mass.: MIT Press, 1975.

Gorham, William, and Nathan Glazer. *The Urban Predicament*. Washington, D.C.: Urban Institute, 1976.

Grigsby, William G., and Louis Rosenburg. *Urban Housing Policy*. New York: APS Publications, 1975.

Stegman, Michael. *Housing and Economics: The American Dilemma*. Cambridge, Mass.: MIT Press, 1971.

TOWARD A PERSONAL SOCIAL SERVICES SYSTEM: THE UNPLANNED EMERGENCE OF A FEDERAL POLICY

Thus far we have been considering examples of the developments in federal social policy which are within the commonly accepted view of what constitutes social welfare—income, housing, and health. But ever since the 1930s, a little publicized but persistent evolution has taken place to broaden the conception of what constitutes social welfare as an appropriate area of federal responsibility.

DIMENSIONS OF PERSONAL SOCIAL SERVICES

Public policy actions in social welfare were traditionally concerned with the provision of minimum income, the guaranteed access to health, housing, and educational services, and the management of a correctional system. This view of what is subsumed under the general heading of social welfare was enlarged in 1920 with the enactment of the first Vocational Rehabilitation Act. The act was initially seen as an adjunct to the existing educational and medical services in order to fill the recognized gap in social provision for military personnel. Vocational training programs to equip manpower for economic careers were seized upon as foundation for the development of special services for those disabled either in industry or in military service. In the succeeding 50 years, rehabilitation grew until it assumed a minor but established place in the spectrum of welfare services. A federal bureau was established, a network of relationships between federal, state, local, and private organizations was formed, a new profession of vocational counseling developed, and annual funding was assured year by year, rising in 1975 to over $750 million per year. Following World War II, the concept of rehabilitation was broadened significantly by an expansion of medical rehabilitation technology which added medical procedures for the physiological and psychological restoration of function to the established vocational procedures.

While this evolution was taking place, a more subtle evolution also occurred involving an area of welfare activity ambiguously identified as the social services or social work. In the following pages, the phrase *personal social service* will be used in place of the common but confusing terms *social work* (as a profession of counseling) and *social service* (as a basic and established set of programs).

This new profession gradually assumed a dual position. Social workers were employed in all of the other social programs. They performed a variety of counseling and guidance functions to help individuals deal with troublesome situations. This evolution can in part be traced back to the historical view that individuals who cannot manage their income, health, housing, and educational needs independently are somehow weaker than the average person and require specialists' assistance.

This concept of a social service adds a new area to the conventional welfare responsibilities we have discussed—income maintenance, the provision of health, housing, education, corrections, and (latterly) rehabilitation. These have been the publicly underwritten areas of modern life which require governmental sanction and support and which are addressed to the needs of individuals, especially of individuals who require some special attention in the interests of equity and public conscience.

In this chapter, two aspects will be explored: (1) the evolution of a policy about personal social services; and (2) evolution of an integrative policy about the "basic" services.

As a result of this evolution and elaboration in the use of a common term, these professional functions have come to be viewed as an independent new social service to be added to that of income, housing, education, and the like. It appeared that any society which provided adequate income, health, housing, and educational programs still did not have an adequate complement of social services suitable to modern, complex society.

In England, where income, health, housing, and education had long been taken to represent the social services, a fifth social service of equal stature was added, known as "personal social services." One function of the personal social services was to provide and to manage a residue of concrete services which special groups required, but were not conventionally provided by the older social programs. Examples are: (1) the provision of day care for children of working mothers or of single-parent families (where the head of the family must work while minor children are left at home); (2) the provision of homemaker services in cases of either long- or short-term illness or disability; (3) the management of day-care programs for isolated or disadvantaged persons; (4) the management of inter-system information and referral activities which would link together several programs for individuals with multiple requirements or which would reduce the overlap of functions among services.

A second function was to provide psychological counseling. The anxieties, ambiguities, and distresses of modern urban life were perceived as being great enough to require a publicly supported counseling service to help individuals cope more satisfactorily with them.

In addition, the rigidities of the other basic services such as income, housing, and health became severe as they involved larger and larger bureaucracies, so that an external and independent advocate on behalf of disadvantaged groups became increasingly necessary. The personal social services assumed this advocacy function to alter or moderate the rigidities of the basic systems so that they would be more responsive to individual needs.

As social workers pursued these functions, it began to be felt that not only the disadvantaged, but all citizens might need or benefit from the services. For examples, all families might benefit from access to day-care facilities and all children might benefit from the preschool experience. Thus the concept of special services for special groups has been broadened to the view that all families should have access to the personal social services, much as they do to education.

Despite these uncertainties as to what the personal social services really consist of, there has been a fairly consistent evolution in federal programs which take on the character of a federal policy. Defined one way, this evolving policy has been a federal determination to work continuously on the reorganization and rationalization of the complex of public activities loosely defined as the "basic social services." This policy of rationalizing established public functions has required either the creation of a personal social services system (as the fifth basic social service) or a more effective distribution through all of the basic systems of administrative and professional social workers. The evolution of this policy, if it is one, toward welfare rationalization illustrates the unwitting emergence of policy without a firm conceptual basis of the subject matter to be affected. Is the policy to be one of integrating well-established social systems? Is it to be the creation of a new personal social service system to join the others? Or is it to be the federal underwriting of an emerging profession, as in the case of vocational rehabilitation, to staff service systems?

The course of evolution has been one of constant change. The dimensions of the public action and its purposes both have been modified with amazing frequency. Sometimes it has appeared that the policy has been one of strengthening family life, and at other times, it has reflected a sole preoccupation with the reduction of relief dependency.

EVOLUTION OF A PERSONAL SOCIAL SERVICES POLICY

Expanded Concept of Social Welfare: 1935–1972
The roots of this development can be identified as early as the 1930s when the federal government first entered into the area of economic security of persons through emergency relief legislation. Several of the emergency relief programs, intended solely to give economic means of subsistence, also provided small units of specially trained social workers to deal with social problems on a case and clinical basis. Part of the motivation was to help especially troubled individuals to surmount economic dependence, but another part of the motivation was the pioneering development of a tax-supported, personal service counseling program to give help beyond economic support to individuals with a variety of personal difficulties.

In the years following the enactment of the Social Security Act, the Bureau of Public Assistance incorporated the antecedent private charitable beliefs that social workers were needed in the administration of public assistance programs to identify individual family variation in requirements, to formulate a plan of action, and to carry through that plan of action. These functions were for many years tied to the administration of relief payments.

In 1956, however, following long, persistent encouragement from the Social Security Administration, the Congress finally amended the Social Security Act to give statutory recognition to the provision of social services to families on relief. Social services were for the first time defined as something different from the administration of relief payments themselves, at least with respect to an adopted federal policy. In the initial years, the federal government undertook to match local funds for the payment for these social services. This represented the federal government's first statutory acceptance of the idea that a personal social service beyond income provision merited federal support.

In 1962 the federal share was increased from 50 to 75 percent in order to stimulate the states to develop such services more rapidly. The objective of these amendments was to reorient the cash transfer program to one which also stressed the rehabilitation of persons on relief. In a new departure, the staff was also to be used to prevent other vulnerable persons threatened with financial instability from becoming economically dependent. Unmarried parents, deserted families, families with adults potentially able to support themselves but currently not doing so, children with special problems, and the aged or disabled were cited as categories of persons justifying the attention of these newly sanctioned services. They were intended to help parents, improve home conditions, assume wider responsibility for the guidance of their children, and improve the management of their financial resources. As a token of this shift in emphasis, the Bureau of Public Assistance was renamed the Bureau of Family Services.

This broadly gauged program did not develop very rapidly. In 1967 the structure of the Department of Health, Education and Welfare was modified. Public assistance rolls and claimants were increasing rapidly despite the preventive promises of the 1962 amendments. The personal social services responsibilities already identified were separated from the administration of income maintenance programs. They were redistributed to a variety of other bureaus within the Department of Health, Education and Welfare, including Administration on Aging, Rehabilitation Services Administration, and the Children's Bureau. These three were bound together for coordination and management purposes in an overriding Social and Rehabilitation Service.

Meanwhile, the reorganization, in large part under pressure from the Congress, introduced a new work-incentive program which shifted the emphasis of the personal social services away from prevention and toward a concentrated effort to move dependent families off the relief rolls. A great deal of staff effort was redirected toward the procurement of job retraining services, and funds were mandated for the provision of day-care services for the children of working mothers in single-parent families. At this time, although the bulk of the personal social services was directed to persons on relief and could thus be considered simply as a part of the administration of an income maintenance program, the day-care services were legally extended to families in certain geographic areas which included families of low income in danger of becoming economically dependent, even though they were not yet on relief.

The separation of the personal social services from income maintenance signaled a major departure in public policy in the direction of a public service program unconnected with economic dependency. In the past economic dependency was assumed to have some association with personal deficiency or weakness on the part of recipients, but in the new conception income maintenance was assumed to be a consequence of defects in the economic order and entitlement a matter of right not requiring any specialized professional administration. Where relief recipients had personal problems requiring attention, these might be provided under public auspices since these families presumably could not purchase relevant counseling services from other sources.

This evolution, however, required some attention to the definition of boundaries for the new personal social services. One report of the secretary of HEW defined these services simply as "those human services rendered to individuals and families under societal auspices." [1] It was assumed that health, education, housing, and income maintenance served the general public as they sought their self-development, whereas the social services were identified as those needed by people with limitations and handicaps so severe that they could not maintain their independence without some supplemental assistance.

Unfortunately, the ambiguity about boundary and definition was not resolved and by 1968 the boundaries as defined made it difficult to separate the personal social services from the other agencies with the same generalized goals as those embodied in public assistance.[2] These goals are the three "P's": preparation (giving hard services to cope with obstacles such as day care and homemaking), participation (organizing consumers to express needs), and protection (the maintenance of equity).

This formulation still left the conception of the new approach mired in goals which were also adopted by other major or basic public programs. Administrative attempts to clear up ambiguities about the program continued until in 1971 the Community Services Administration of HEW produced the GOSS formula: goal-oriented social services. It proposed as the objective of the new services a decreased state of dependency for the individual on a scale which would (1) reduce the need for full institutional care; (2) provide community-based care as an alternative (halfway houses, etc.), (3) encourage the assumption of responsibility for care by the natural family, and (4) encourage maintenance of full independent status without public support. This emphasis is not only on a reduction in economic dependency, but on an enhancement of independent self-care on a progressive scale which is a major turning point in the evolution of federal policy.

The evolution of a program of personal social services can be traced in the volume of federal grants for such purposes. Following the 1962 Amendments to the Social Security Act, social service expenditures grew between 1963 and 1972 from $194 million to $1,600,000.[3]

These funds were distributed over a wide range of service activities. The most significant were: child foster care, 57 percent; child care, 16 percent; homemaker services, 6 percent; child protection, 5 percent; employment and training, 8 percent. Smaller amounts were assigned to support adoption services, information and referral services, strengthening family

---

[1]Jack Wedemeyer, *Policy Issues in Service Delivery* (Sacramento: Sacramento State College, 1969).

[2]See Martin Rein "Social Services and Economic Independence," in *The Planning and Delivery of Social Services* (Washington, D.C.: National League of Cities, 1969).

[3]See Social and Rehabilitation Service, Office of Financial Management Reports as cited in Paul Mott, *Meeting Human Needs: The Social and Political History of Title XX* (Columbus, Ohio: National Conference on Social Welfare, 1976). Much of the material for this chapter has been drawn from this text.

TABLE 11
Federal Grants for Social Services, 1963–1972

Year	Total Expenditures
1963	$ 194,000,000
1964	254,400,000
1965	295,140,000
1966	359,165,000
1967	281,589,000
1968	346,654,000
1969	354,491,000
1970	522,500,000
1971	692,433,000
1972	1,598,215,000

SOURCE: *Social and Rehabilitation Service, Office of Financial Management Reports.*

functioning, family planning, housing, health services, protection of adults, and so forth.

Setbacks and Consolidation: 1972–1975

In 1972 the HEW program was confronted with a new Republican Administration determined to slow the rate of increase in welfare programs. It had been expected that in 1972 the social services under the existing amendments would involve $4.7 billion of federal aid to the states in the form of matching grants on a 3 to 1 basis. The executive branch through the Office of Management and Budget (OMB) fixed a budgetary maximum of $2.5 billion for such funding. By administrative action the open-ended program was capped.[4] The federal government's promise to match personal social service state programs without limitation was rescinded.

At this time the national administration's effort to introduce a new approach to federal-state relationships led to a hope that the concepts of general revenue sharing could be extended and that the complex of federal categorical programs could be simplified by grouping several kinds of programs together in special revenue-sharing blocks. The hope was that this would not only give states and local governments more flexibility in how to utilize federal matching funds, but would also introduce savings in federal expenditures by reducing presumed overlapping and duplicatory expenditures presumed to exist among current categorical programs.

By this means the administration sought to retain a personal social services presence, while restricting the federal government's involvement.

[4]For a revealing analysis of the dynamics in federal-state relationships which finally led to this limitation, see Martha Derthick, *Uncontrollable Spending for the Social Services* (Washington, D.C.: Brookings Institution, 1975).

By a combination of administrative regulation and legislative amendment, a new title was finally added to the Social Security Act, Title XX, which provides the 1976 framework for federal support of personal social services. This statutory foundation was secured at the price of introducing an annual appropriation limitation on the amount of money available, but it gave a reasonably firm foundation for a continuing federal support to the evolution of a personal social services network.

An Independent or a Subsidiary Personal Social Service: Title XX

Title XX left unclear whether the personal social services commitment would be realized through the creation of an independent, publicly supported personal social services network or whether funds would simply be allocated to a variety of preexisting services (income maintenance, housing, mental health, etc.) each of which could acquire technical and professional personnel to perform functions within its own categorical boundaries.

In order to secure matching funds, states are required to develop plans for the social services, but are relatively free to choose what services they wish to offer, where they wish to offer them, and by what means. Certain federal guidelines are proposed and five acceptable goals are identified: (1) achieving economic self-support or reducing dependency; (2) achieving or maintaining self-sufficiency (as separate from or independent of economic self-support); (3) preventing or remedying neglect, abuse, or exploitation of children and adults unable to protect their own interests, or preserving, rehabilitating, and reuniting families; (4) preventing or reducing inappropriate institutional care by providing for community-based, home-based, or other forms of less intensive care; (5) securing referral or admission for institutional care when other forms are not appropriate and providing services to individuals in institutions.

Services considered appropriate for achieving these goals are not clearly defined, but choices are rooted in the antecedent federally supported programs for the elderly, the blind, the disabled, and children. At least one of the personal services must be provided for each of the goals, and at least three must be directed toward supplementary security income recipients.

At least half of the federal funds must be directed toward recipients of public assistance or SSI or Medicaid. Certain undertakings are not eligible for federal funding, including medical or remedial care, room and board for more than six consecutive months, child day care which does not meet federal standards, generally available educational services, capital expenditures, and cash payments.

The categories of eligibility reflect the persistence of federal policy in trying to reach beyond public-assistance recipients. All recipients of cash payments under AFDC or SSI are eligible. In addition, individuals and

TABLE 12
**Personal Social Services Activities in Federal Budget
for Fiscal Year 1977**

Service	Expenditure
Rehabilitation services	$776,000,000
Other services for children and youth	470,000,000 (of which 440,000,000 is for Head Start Programs)
Work incentive programs	315,000,000
Programs for the aging	193,000,000 (of which 150,000,000 is for nutrition)
Refugee services	132,000,000
Children's services	46,000,000
Other services for native Americans	32,000,000

SOURCE: *U.S. Department of Health, Education, and Welfare,* Fiscal Year Budget 1977 *(Washington, D.C., 1977).*

families not receiving cash payments but having an income not in excess of 115 percent of their state's median income for a family of like size, are also eligible for services at each state's option. Information and referral services and protective functions for children and adults may be offered by states without regard to income criteria.

Title XX and its appropriations do not represent the complete federal commitment to the personal social services, although its allocations make it by far the largest component. Table 12 lists additional federally supported activities which are also considered part of a personal social-services commitment.

The scale of these programs is not large if one considers the total population. The 1977 administration budget estimates, for examples, that nearly 1.5 million persons would somehow be touched by rehabilitation services and 332,000 would be "rehabilitated"; 350,000 children are expected to be served by Head Start programs alone; 170,000 individuals are expected to be placed in jobs; 290,000 daily meals will be provided to the elderly in 4,900 sites.[5] Although these figures are small when compared to the expenditures and number of persons reached through the other basic programs of income maintenance, health, and education, it is reasonably clear that an important beachhead has been established in federal policy, establishing through a 40-year evolution the principle of federal support for attention to the personalized needs of vulnerable groups, wholly apart from generally distributed welfare services. Mott has summarized the philosophical foundations for this evolution as follows.

1. Government has an obligation to assist society's most vulnerable

[5]*U.S. Department of Health, Education, and Welfare* (Washington, D.C.: *Fiscal Year Budget for 1977).*

people to attain the highest possible level of economic and functional independence of which they are capable.

2. The federal government should underwrite a variety of services,
   locally determined, to improve individual and family functioning
   through some combination of both public and privately sponsored
   services.

3. Public service funds should be expended on a priority basis for
   those with low income, although not exclusively for them.

4. Funds should not be used to substitute for other state or federal
   support of the primary human services, such as cash assistance,
   health care, public education, and the like.

5. Use of these services should be voluntary except for crisis-
   protective intervention, and the shaping of goals should include
   joint efforts of consumers and service providers.[6]

The first year of operations under the new legislation proved to be a
year of widespread confusion and disillusionment. The mandate for personal social services was substantially widened, but the sums of money
available were not increased. This passed back to the states the unpleasant
task of deciding how to distribute limited funds over a wider spectrum of
demands. The planning involved enormous short-term effort to develop
statewide plans for federal approval with little time to build up staff for
the development of new plans within the new framework. In addition, the
phasing in of the program from the federal government's perspective was
not at all coordinated with the budget appropriations and planning cycle
of state governments, so that many state plans had to be developed without
reference to changes in state legislation which would ensue. Finally, the
procedures broadened the participation of consumers through public
hearings, and this increased the number of special-interest voices legally
able to assert claims on available funds. Thus conflicts between service
providers and consumer groups endured in previous categorical programs
were introduced again, with new claimants for the same funds.

Aside from these essentially transitional dilemmas, a key policy issue
emerged which was not resolved by either the federal legislation or administration. This dilemma is rooted in the ambiguity about the nature of
the personal social services outlined at the beginning of this chapter.
Should the new program and its policies be used to lay the foundation for
a network of tax-supported personal social services throughout the country
or should these funds be used solely to underwrite a variety of services
already provided by existing public, private, and proprietary agencies?
Should an independent, personal social services program to provide homemakers or halfway houses be established in a state or should funds for this

[6]Mott, *Meeting Human Needs.* pp. 49–50.

purpose be allocated and distributed among correctional institutions and mental health agencies, in order to enable each to develop halfway houses for their categorical populations? If providers of homemaker services for the sick and disabled prefer to concentrate their efforts on relatively short-term homemaker services calling for highly skilled nursing, should these funds be used to underwrite their services for eligible populations, even though there is an unmet need and demand for less skilled, long-term homemaker services for disabled persons? If the existing providers choose to concentrate on the short-term services, should the available public funds be used to force them to develop the long-term services or should a tax-supported program be developed for the purpose?

While these policy questions may seem to be matters of turf protection or development, a more serious underlying issue is involved. A rough type of Parkinson's Law can be proposed that established services will consume newly available resources more rapidly than it is possible to expand or develop new services. Put another way, newly available funds are frequently seized upon by existing service providers to meet their operating costs and thus to displace efforts at expanding these services from other sources. If federal funds are available, philanthropic income or local appropriations may be displaced.

The beachhead to which we have alluded provides an opportunity to assure that the personal social services are, over time, available to populations requiring them. But this goal will be realized only if the policy underlying the program is able to work consistently in that direction. Lacking such a consistent direction, it is equally possible that old patterns will be maintained without any change in the nature of the social service system and, therefore, without change in the basic social policy which the legislation has promised.

If we review this evolution in the context of the interplay between societal and public policies, we have an example in which public policy appears to be ahead of the social norms which usually underpin acceptance of public programs. Although there has been no widespread evidence of civic or cultural support for the idea of the government's providing personal social services of the kind we have here considered, still the executive branch—often in collaboration with the Congress—has persistently moved in the direction of establishing just such an addition to the social services. The fact that this policy has grown almost imperceptibly does not diminish its significance.

Controversies over organizational and administrative details can readily obscure the underlying policy issues which confront this subject. Is the definition of goals for the personal social services sufficiently clear to permit steady evolution? What are the effective personal social services necessary to acheve these goals, and how will effectiveness be ascertained for a new and evolving frontier? What is to be the emphasis in evolution: to meet the needs of all persons who confront common problems regardless of social and economic status or to meet the needs of only families with the lowest incomes? A direction for public policy is shaped around such directional questions as these. A host of other dilemmas can be identified which are matters of administration and operating policy, rather than public policy as we have defined the term.

THE INTEGRATION OF THE BASIC SOCIAL SERVICES: NEW ORGANIZATIONAL APPROACHES

While the major federal effort to incorporate some aspect of the personal social services in national policy has stressed attention to the content of policy, a parallel approach has stressed organizational and structural change. As the number of basic human service programs has increased more and more concern has been expressed about the absence of any orderly or unified relationship among the programs. The feeling has grown among professionals, legislators, administrators, and the public that the proliferation of agencies and programs has somehow gotten out of control. Perhaps the earliest attempt to deal with the maze of public programs was a commission appointed by Herbert Hoover in 1929 to report on national social trends.[7] In 1948 former President Hoover headed a presidential commission to examine the organization of governmental processes;[8] and in 1959 the Advisory Commission on Intergovernmental Relations was established by act of Congress to conduct several varieties of studies dealing with intergovernmental relationships and trends.

By 1966 two concerns of the Republican administration riveted attention to the organizational forms for the social services. Despite the rhetoric of the early Nixon years, the major effort appeared to be one of controlling the rate of growth of federal investment in human services, not their reduction or elimination. The concern about total cost was soon linked to a concern about the federal government's apparent dominance in the traditional federal-state-local pattern of relationship. However, attempts to reduce the federal role in a situation as complex as the delivery of human services (which represented by 1968 close to half of the federal budget) were believed to be limited by the inability of state and local governments to take over any significant administrative responsibility. Implementation of the "new federalism" which was intended to return policy planning, and action responsibilities for human services to the states, thus seemed to require a parallel federal effort to assist the states in restructuring their

[7]Wesley Mitchell, *Recent Social Trends in the United States* (New York: McGraw-Hill, 1933).
[8]Herbert Hoover, *Report of the U.S. Committee on Organization of the Executive Branch of the Government* (Washington, D.C.: U.S. Government Printing Office, 1949).

governmental mechanisms. Federal agencies were to undergo the same type of restructuring to reduce total costs.

This attention to organizational capacity was based on a belief that some type of administrative control had to be exercised over the large numbers of independent programs which had been enacted by the legislature and that such control would result in reduced expenditures, a more efficient use of available money, and better results in the public interest.

Management theory appeared to supply the means to achieve restructuring. On the state level a variety of presumably related functions and departments were to be consolidated into "super" departments, umbrella agencies, or secretariats, something like the federal model of the Department of Health, Education, and Welfare. At the level of the federal government the staff and information capacities of the Office of Management and Budget were enlarged to represent the White House views on administrative policy for executing legislated policies and programs. Within HEW (and other executive departments) the office of the secretary was likewise enlarged with general planning and policy personnel and greatly increased data systems derived from the department's component parts. It was assumed that through the assessment of information gathered from a variety of agencies and organizations the umbrella agency and the OMB could achieve a broader perspective about policy than could be held by any one department or bureau whose staff was necessarily concerned with the implementation of a specialized, categorical program mandated in legislation.

Management devices for cost-benefit analysis, program planning, and budgeting were tested and adapted in an effort to assure that the purposes of a variety of federal programs were more clearly articulated, to assure that these articulated purposes and their implementing programs did not contradict each other, and to reduce the presumed duplication and overlapping of expenditures and personnel.

It was felt that only by such a broader perspective and attention to management practices could the whole human service enterprise be made more efficient and be moved in the direction of clear-cut goals, the achievement of which could be tested. Where progress toward achieving goals was slow and unsatisfactory, it was assumed that alternative programs or strategies could be introduced to replace the old ones.

These management concepts proved limited in their success because the operations of government are not as controllable as those of private business. Congress is the basic source of broad policy sanction and if, for whatever reasons—political, economic or ideological—Congress chooses to mandate categorical programs, the authority of the executive branch to modify how these programs are in fact administered is limited. At best the executive branch can delay program introduction or can reduce its scale by regulation. These difficulties are further complicated when the White House and the Congress are controlled by different parties with com-

peting political agendas. Programs which are seen by the Office of Management and Budget to have a common purpose and, therefore, to be susceptible to rationalization and reorganization may be viewed by Congress
to serve the needs of different populations and the interests of different
constituencies and, therefore, to be unamenable to consolidation.

The effort to limit or reduce the detail of federal control in the administration of many categorical programs was widely applauded. The
breadth and diversity of human organization in the United States is such
that detailed administration governing the delivery of services to individuals cannot readily be developed in Washington for uniform application
throughout the country. There seemed to be little way to stem the Parkin-
sonian tendency for the federal government to mandate by regulation what
child can be examined by what personnel or to mandate what individual
will be entitled to public assistance in what kind of emergency and under
what circumstances. The absurdity of this situation became manifest in
numerous ways. Federal support of training programs to develop personnel
for the human services had for a long time been carried out by grants to
state and private universities, which in turn selected the individuals to be
admitted to the training programs. But by 1970 an effort was made to
cut back these institutional grants sharply and to replace them by a program
which required individual students throughout the country to apply, one
by one, to offices in Washington for the procurement of scholarship support
to enter professional schools.

Despite such complexities in 1968 a federal agency, HUD, made a
grant to the Commonwealth of Massachusetts to study reorganization of
state government. This was followed by a variety of incentives, encouragement, and pressures from Washington to other state governments every-
where to update and improve their capacity to handle more efficiently the
flow of funds designed to deal with the social needs of residents. Most of
these pressures were in the direction of consolidating government agencies
into superagencies. In Massachusetts, for example, over 14 independent
state agencies and a large number of institutions, independent boards,
advisory councils, and commissions associated with them (which had reported directly to the governor) were consolidated into the Secretariat
of Human Services, incorporating all state programs for public assistance,
corrections, youth services, veterans' services, rehabilitation, children,
mental health, and public health. The resulting new secretariat covered
approximately half of the entire state budget and almost two-thirds of all
state employees. Even so massive an attempt at consolidation could not be
completely logical, since the human services themselves lack a tight logic.
In Massachusetts, at least, a parallel yet completely independent Secretariat
of Elder Affairs was established with very little money and very little
staff, but representing political pressures in that state. Similar anomalies
were found in other states.

By 1974, several states but less than a majority, had carried through some form of reorganization, and the peak of the consolidation effort seems to have been reached.[9] In these states varieties of independent agencies were brought together in similar umbrella structures. No clear logic underlay the kinds of agencies brought together, although most of the umbrella agencies did include public assistance, mental health, public health, and youth services.

The effort to improve organizational capability was extended down to the cities, and many metropolitan areas were also stimulated to create large agencies similar to those of state government. In all these situations a large number of independent commissions and state boards were brought under the head of one secretariat or commission. The number of senior executives in a governor's or mayor's administration was thus nominally reduced, but the span of control of each executive was broadened by the consolidation process.

These reorganizations were structural, not substantive. The line of authority from administrators of categorial or direct-service agencies now ran not directly to the governor or to a general office of budget, but through an intervening layer of administration. Data systems were introduced to improve the information which this intervening layer of administration could acquire about the broad range of services within its purview. Budgets were usually funneled through the secretariat to legislatures, even though legislatures might, in the end, choose to ignore secretariat recommendations. The staff of the secretariat was in the position to press the various constituent departments to articulate their purposes more clearly and to specify how requests for their programs were intended to achieve their results. This combination of improved data systems collected centrally and the introduction of management by objective program planning, was supposed to put the secretary and secretariat staff in a position to influence the general direction for program development in the component departments. It was also hoped that an overall look at what was being expended for what purposes would permit the secretariat to identify duplications, overlappings, and inefficiences and to reduce waste through a continuous restructuring of how manpower and funds were assigned.

This management concept gives limited attention to two serious deficiencies in the scheme. Most of the objectives of the programs being thus administered are set by legislatures. And, the broad purposes of programs in the human services are set for state governments by the federal government. Consequently, efforts to change are limited to goals of efficiency and effectiveness, and sharply conflicting views about what is an effective plan of action usually arise. Lacking real authority to decide what the

[9]Examples of this effort are reported in American Society for Public Administration, "Coping with the Demands for Change within Human Services Administration," Summary Report of Conference sponsored by ASPA and the Southeast Institute for Human Resources Development, ed. by Robert Agranoff, June 1976.

content of programs should be, the state governments have seen their effort to rationalize the system to some extent neutralized by questions as to what constitutes a more effective way of carrying out a legally sanctioned mandate.

Nonetheless, so large a reconstruction of human service structure as this effort contemplates necessarily takes a long time to evolve. Certain modifications can be noted, although they are not at all universal. At the minimum, one center in state government now at least has the capacity to know something about the system of social welfare programs in which the various departments are involved. It remains to be seen whether more knowledge on a broader front can be absorbed, analyzed, and shaped by policy and planning personnel to produce changes in the system which will be reasonably persuasive in the political controversies through which final public policy is decided.

Legislatures and all political figures necessarily are responsive to the pressures of various constituencies. If resources were unlimited, constituency wants could be mandated without limitation. But since resources are in fact limited, public policy involves hard decisions about how resources are to be distributed among a variety of equally compelling and worthwhile ends. At this stage it is not at all clear whether the purposes of programs can be modified by rational means. For example, it might seem self-evident that if a certain population of the elderly is now given the option of living independently without any help or going into an institution which is paid for by public funds, a change in policy and purpose might be clearly indicated. Such a change would involve the argument that available funds should be allotted to individuals in a set of options rather than a single option, a set which would include the possibility of diverting some of these public funds for purchase of supplementary services for delivery to elderly persons in their own homes. Unfortunately, there are many people who do require substantial institutional attention, and funds need somehow to be divided between institutional and noninstitutional supports, but the guidelines along which the division should be drawn are not at all clear. Similarly, expert and professional groups differ substantially about where the line should be drawn. And citizens themselves may disagree. They might agree that individuals should not be "forced" into institutions, but the same individuals may bitterly oppose the maintenance of very disabled persons in neighboring houses. The extent to which rational analysis of information will alter the thrust of public policy has not yet been fully tested.

On the other hand, there are more limited ways in which this movement has clearly begun a process of change. There are, for example, grave discontinuities in the way in which the existing programs are linked with each other. For example, individuals may be placed in mental hospitals for long periods of time, reach a state of readiness for return to their community, but lack families and homes to which to return. Mental health programs do not have the means or the authority to reconstruct living arrangements; departments of public welfare and other community-based programs have other priorities and are not readily able to prepare homes to receive these individuals. The result is that many persons in institutions remain in a no-man's-land without any means of returning to a community, although they are certainly ready for it. In somewhat similar fashion, a small number of families and individuals have multiple needs which have led to the situation in which numerous staff members from several agencies are in constant touch with a small number of families, each duplicating the work of others.

On such relatively minor fronts the movement toward organizational restructuring seems to have had an effect. For example, in many communities service personnel from a variety of agencies are housed in adjacent offices so that eligible persons can sort out their requirements without burdensome traveling to different offices. In a few communities the work of several related agencies has been closely integrated, with the result that staff members from separate agencies now serve under a common administrator to carry on the functions of all agencies without regard to their previous specialty. More widespread is the introduction of a case manager who is assigned core responsibility for any entitled person. The case manager is responsible for obtaining and coordinating any services required to achieve a coherent plan in the person's interests. Coordinating agreements of this kind do not have authority, and in effect, the case manager must depend upon persuasion to secure existing services. Where necessary services are completely unavailable, as in the case of long-term home care, the case manager is relatively powerless.

The best that can be said about the movement toward reorganization is that it seems to express a final acquiescence to the role of federal as well as state governments in responsibility for personal social services. Whether the delivery of these services can be made more systematic is being tested.

Confusion Between Policy Ends and Policy Means

While the central policy of commitment to the personal social services thus seems to be maintained, the outlook is somewhat less promising if one considers policies in relation to means. And policies over means have been frustrated by the lack of specificity in the more general policy goals. While the federal and state governments are committed to "doing something" about certain vulnerable populations, the end product of their efforts has not been specified. The clearest example can perhaps be seen in the case of the elderly and the severely disabled. Certainly there is no disagreement that something "should be done" for those persons who lack families and are physically not capable of taking care of all their needs by themselves. But what is it that should be done? We have clearly adopted a policy which assures access to medical treatment for all such individuals. When curative measures have been exhausted and disability remains, we can still fall back on a policy of restoration and rehabilitation. But federal policy on rehabilitation is still quite limited by a primary focus on restoration of economic independence. With minor exceptions and despite a long effort to change the policy, rehabilitation efforts supported by the federal government are intended to restore full physical independence through curative means or to restore economic independence through retraining and restoration of function sufficient to permit employment.

There is still no policy applicable to cases in which reemployment is not possible or continuing attention is required for some irreversible disability. A policy may be developing through current experiments in diverting some Medicaid and Medicare funds to provide for less costly modes of support outside of institutions, but even this more flexible use of medical funds remains based on the expectation and desirability of some ultimate increase in self-care for the individual. Federal policy is ambiguous about responsibility for persons requiring intermittent long-term care or the part-time attention of others. Is the federal policy to rely exclusively upon the families of the disabled, even though the assumption of such caring responsibilities may lead to a breakdown of the families' integrity, or is the policy to supplement the families' capacities to carry the burden? In the case of individuals without families, is the policy to increase the scope of support in their own homes or to rely upon institutions?

The federal government's commitment to the future takes the form of support of various experimental and demonstration programs intended to increase the rate of deinstitutionalization for many previously institutionalized persons—the mentally ill, the chronically ill, and the criminal offender. It remains to be seen whether the results of these experiments, demonstrations, and tests will lead to a clearer public policy about ends and means which can serve as a guide throughout the entire human service system.

Case Examples of Reorganization [10]

The movement toward organizational reform was carried out in the federal government primarily by executive effort, but stimulus through the states was carried out through congressionally funding of programs identified as capacity building, such as Serivces Integration Targets of Opportunity (SITO). Over 50 program grants were received by the states by 1972.

---

[10]Marshall Kaplan, Gans, and Kahn, "Human Resource Services in the States: An Analysis of State Human Resource Agencies and the Allied Services Act of 1972," mimeographed (San Francisco: Research Group, Marshall Kaplan, Gans, and Kahn, 1972).

Florida originally attempted to coordinate its programs through legislation in 1969, when 200 independent administrative agencies were consolidated into a loose confederacy of 25 departments under the Department of Health and Rehabilitation Services. Nine programs were included: vocational rehabilitation, youth services, aging, retardation, health, family services, mental health, children's medical services, and corrections. Little change was introduced at the delivery end, and some arrangements were provided for administrative coordination horizontally at the level of state departments only. This did not produce any substantial change in patterns of activity.

By 1970 a comprehensive delivery system was initiated in one county with federal support; most of the "integration" was administrative rather than organizational. One county (Palm Beach, Florida) sought to develop a common information system, case management for multiproblem families, across-the-board diagnostic services, a computerized client information system, common application and service forms for all departments, local planning councils, and adjacent location of facilities. However, the director of this county program had little authority and achievements depended almost exclusively upon moral persuasion. The computerized system was not developed, the staff resisted changes, common application forms proved to be burdensome and created more rather than less paper work, the planning council was a discussion group rather than a decision-making body, and the case management system worked poorly.

By 1974 a state government management and efficiency study produced further recommendations which led to the 1975 State Reorganization Act. Several alternatives were examined. A completely integrated model had wide support, but it faced objections in the Department of Health and Rehabilitation Services in that specialized services had reduced visibility, accountability to satisfy state interests was found difficult to establish, county department funding proved less amenable to total integration, and eligibility from federal sources tied to federally funded categorical programs was threatened.

The final reorganization represented one step towards integration. The office of the Secretary for Health and Rehabilitation Services retained responsibility for public information, legal services, and performance control, the latter intended to measure progress toward state-determined objectives. An Assistant Secretary for Operations administered 11 service delivery districts throughout the state. Each district contained a network of DHRS-funded services presumably capable of delivering and controlling medical services, aid to families with dependent children, aging and adult services, dependent and delinquent services, family social services, food stamps, Medicaid eligibility, services for mental health, public health and retardation, vocational rehabilitation, and SSI eligibility. Administrative outlets for these services were located in common offices where possible. Each district was expected to develop a case management unit to identify each client's needs, guide the client to the appropriate services, monitor delivery, arrange for the delivery of supporting services such as transporation, and generally assure that the client's needs, as defined at application, were met.

Parallel to these units is the Office of the Assistant Secretary for Program Planning and Development which generally supervises the administration of all the services, is responsible for program research, identifies client needs, and develops recommendations for solutions to these needs with priorities. The planning and development office develops policies and standards and provides technical assistance to the district directors. Although maintaining a presumed across-the-board capacity at state government, eight separate categorical program offices under the assistant secretary develop specific plans and standards for children's medical services, mental health, vocational rehabilitation, social and economic services, and health services. These program units are located functionally in the district but have no line authority.

By the end of 1975 this combination of some central authority, some localized integration, and some regional categorical arrangement for continual development claimed the following results: front-line delivery services were co-located and somewhat unified; unified administration reduced by 440 throughout the state the number of nonservice personnel; district operations plans covered all services, but there was no departmental program throughout the state; a single intake system for all children and youth was set up; there was a reduction in personnel and professional influence on the legislature. There was also reported difficulty in mobilizing the state facilities to respond to state or local crises.

Another quite different example is seen in Minnesota where administrative reform in the human services began officially in 1972 with the receipt of a SITO grant from the Department of Health, Education, and Welfare. The Minnesota project sought to test a continuing process of program development rather than a reform or reorganization. The Governor's Office for Program Development, under the grant, sought to build consensus for change among various forces in the human services system. The governor's office maintained a low profile, never calling itself an office for human services reform, for example.

A first step appears to have been the enactment in 1973 of legislation permitting (not mandating) county boards of commissioners to modify their county-wide planning, budgeting, and program for the human services. County commissioners were authorized to replace diverse and independent public boards by consolidated or integrated human service boards consisting of county commissioners, citizen members, and professional personnel, provided that the new boards represented corrections, health, mental health, and social services.

The county boards were to have authority to develop annual integrated budgets and plans for social services, public health, public assistance, mental health, court-related mental retardation, and day activity services for children. Several counties chose reorganization under this option.

Within two years it was ascertained by monitoring state agencies that some single point of entry was necessary at the level of state government to conform to the consolidated, single-entry units developed at the level of county government, so that the county organizations could communicate with a single state office.

In 1975 the state legislature funded a Governor's Office of Human Services which replaced the preceding Office of Program Development in order to maintain the process of continuing change. The new state office was given responsibility for monitoring the continued development of the county boards and for analyzing budget, personnel, and program activities in the various county and state agencies and the relationship between these agencies and various regulatory functions which are distributed among state agencies. A host of problems are still being studied, including: fragmentation, difficulties in accountability, the inappropriateness of levels of decision making, multiple program relationships, the interrelationship of various flows of funding into the counties, and the absence of single policy points for almost all activities.

It is evident that in Minnesota the difficulties involved in restructuring are still being considered by a process which does not test any specific model other than the county-based consolidated board. The boards are able to exercise some control over independent and diverse programs through the authority to consolidate budget requests into a single county budget for human services.

Attempts to rationalize the human services system have met many obstacles and have produced a resistance to change greater than the forces for change which have thus far been let loose. To illustrate: both federal and state legislatures are reluctant to relinquish the authority inherent in their capacity to authorize and fund categorical programs which have clear visibility; the efforts to make the human services system more re-sponsive to human need by opening decision making to more and more voices has increased rather than consolidated the demands for services, so that a race appears to be underway between the continuous enlargement of demand for more and more activities and anxiety over the increasing cost of meeting the growing demands. The belief prevalent in the early 1970s that reorganization could permit the human services to do more for more people with less has not been proven. In the course of unsettling of a basic system of categorical services, some vulnerable populations with-out strong political support are threatened with loss of help or with being overlooked as newer, more dominant, and salient interests come into play. Mothers who are the heads of single-parent families, while numerous, are less politically powerful than—let us say—spokesmen for the elderly or for the retarded; infants with severe nutritional deficiencies and severely neglected by disorganized families are at risk of being overlooked until grave damage is done; and disabled adults are frequently overlooked in the rush to provide health services of an acute and episodic nature to all, a development which in turn is threatened by rapidly escalating costs which threaten the economic stability of many communities.

Finally, the various categorical programs which have developed in the past have all evolved with strong supporting constituencies, determined to maintain their present position as regards the distribution of allocated funds. A continuing tug of war remains between these various special categories, and all of them resist any attempt to modify the traditional patterns under which they have functioned.

It cannot be said that a clear-cut policy has yet emerged, other than to argue that the commitment to some level of service delivery is being maintained. Policies of consolidating services by various mechanisms— sometimes by an attempt to merge agencies, sometimes by an attempt to use administrative mechanisms and budget procedures to coordinate programs—have all been tested and all have been found relatively wanting. What is being set up is a continuing conflict, out of which some public policy other than administrative management alone will evolve in time. The tension between a vastly elaborated network of human services, the stumbling and confusion which results from lack of careful relationship between the many components, and the concern over containment in the steady growth in expenditure for the human services may, in time, lead to a public policy concerning the means by which services will be delivered; but this does not yet seem to be on the horizon. The movement toward consolidation of human services has thus far had a relatively brief history, but the resistance to consolidation has proven to be stubborn indeed.

Despite these difficulties, one promising device appears to have emerged, that of the case manager. It is likely that the case-management idea is sufficiently useful to survive, regardless of the other forms of service policy which may evolve. To date, the case-manager mechanism is primarily limited to handling multiproblem families through one of the three alternative means: (1) the case manager primarily refers applicants according to some plan and monitors the progress of the applicant through various service units; (2) he or she acquires authority over some proportion of all available resources in an area and can authorize payment therefrom for services according to the case manager's plan; (3) a case committee made up of various service agencies operates on all troublesome cases and provides the case manager with guidance in monitoring steps to be taken by the various agency partners.

In 1977 the status of personal social services remains clouded. Federal funding remains at a fixed level, and not all states use all the funds available to them. Federal guidelines are changing almost yearly in response to the practical problems reported by the states. In the states old programs maneuver against each other to secure some share of Title XX funds. Efforts of reformers to alter the pattern of service delivery away from the old categories are incomplete. Legislation has introduced a mandate to create a new system of personal services, but the resources with which to carry through the change are not only limited but rely upon initiatives to be taken at state and local levels; and at those levels old patterns have proven stubbornly resistant to change. The absence of a clear federal policy has thus far produced much activity without significant change in program operations.

ADDITIONAL READINGS

Anderson, Wayne, Bernard Frieden, and Michael Murphy. *Managing Human Services*. Washington, D.C.: International City Management Association, 1977.

Axinn, June, and Herman Levin. *Social Welfare: A History of the American Response to Need*. New York: Harper & Row, 1976.

Kammerman, Sheila, and Alfred Kahn. *Social Services in the United States*. Philadelphia: Temple University Press, 1976.

Morris, Robert. *Toward a Caring Society*. New York: Columbia University School of Social Work, 1974.

Turem, J., et al. *The Implementation of Title XX: The First Year's Experience*. Working Paper 0990–08. Washington, D.C.: Urban Institute, 1976.

CHILDREN AND THE AGED:
DILEMMAS OF FAMILY
POLICY

Much has been said and written about public policy for the family, but the subject has always been obscured by ambiguity over what constitutes a *family policy* as distinct from a *health* or an *income* policy which serves family needs. The family policy refers to those acts that are intended to strengthen or alter patterns of family life as distinguished from acts that help individuals and so may have an indirect bearing on the family network. The possible negative effects of such policies have been examined, but positive alternatives have not been proposed. For example, some critics believe that present relief policies for mothers and children lead to the break-up of common-law families on the assumption that the male wage earner is encouraged to leave home so that his dependents can qualify for welfare payments more readily. However, the critics offer few alternative programs to provide the necessary aid.

The subject of family policy may be most vividly approached from the point of view of children and the elderly, two groups of individuals dependent upon family ties for affection and care. National effort devoted to the needs of the aged and of children has often been justified on the grounds that it is intended to strengthen family life as much as it is intended to protect dependent individuals. In the following discussion we will limit consideration of health insurance and income maintenance to the ways they do or do not support a policy for children (or the aged) when they are combined with other specific acts dealing with children's needs, especially their protective or developmental needs.

EXTENSION OF POLICY FOR THE ELDERLY TO SOCIAL AS WELL AS ECONOMIC CONCERNS

During the past 40 years and especially during the last 20, federal involvement in programs specifically directed at the wants of the elderly has produced funds or services for the following: retirement income through social security, minimum assured income in case of permanent disability, medical care through Medicare, supplementary income where the foregoing are not sufficient through supplementary security income programs, special low-cost housing, special nutritional services, special transportation arrangements, special programs for social activity, employment, or constructive activity, alteration of social role, and a larger share in the Gross National Product. Do these programs add up to a federal policy or set of policies toward the elderly in American society?

Following our earlier framework, it would appear that our national approach to the elderly does not violate policy guidelines. The elderly have been considered an especially vulnerable and disadvantaged group based on accumulated evidence that they have much less than average income, they have more severe health needs than the average, and, because they frequently live apart from their families, they have grave difficulties in coping with isolation and physical handicaps. The federal government has clearly moved in to alleviate some of these pressures and to relieve the distresses. The policy approach has been primarly the modest and supplementary role of making special income available for the elderly while relying on the marketplace functioning of our basic institutions. The median income of families with head over 65 was $7298 in 1974 and about $3000 for individuals.[1] Approximately 60 percent of the aggregate incomes earned by this population was derived from essentially private sources and about 40 percent from various governmental programs, with 30 percent of the latter derived from Social Security.[2] But does this financing add up to a line of direction for the use of governmental power? The answer is mixed.

Clearly, economic status has been improved, as has access to medical

[1] U.S. Bureau of the Census, *Demographic Aspects of Aging and the Older Population in the U.S., Current Population Reports*, Special Studies Series, No. 59. (Washington: D.C.: U.S. Government Printing Office, 1976), Table 6-6.
[2] See Matilda W. Riley and Anne Foner, *Aging and Society*, Vol. 1 (New York: Russell Sage Foundation, 1968), chap. 4. In 1974 52 percent of retired couples received income from both social security and private pensions; 38 percent received only social security payments. See Alan Fox, "Work Status and Income Change," *Social Security Bulletin* 39, No. 12 (December 1976): 15-31.

care, which will soon be discussed. But public policy for the elderly is
especially interesting in that it opened the door to a slight but potentially
significant shift in the direction of new societal norms, as well as enlarged
public policy. Primarily because of the innovative policy incorporated in
the original social security legislation, both income and medical care for
the elderly are available without means test, and federal benefits are available to at least 10 percent of the population, regardless of their financial
status. This apparent deviation from long-standing societal policy of using
government to intervene only for vulnerable and especially needy groups
has been rationalized on the grounds that the aged as a class are vulnerable
and disadvantaged and warrant this kind of extension. The effect has been
that individuals with substantial private incomes draw benefits for retirement and medical expenses in exactly, or almost exactly, the same proportion as do those with virtually no private resources.

Policy for the elderly is interesting also because it has directed attention to many essentially social problems of the elderly which are not rooted
in economic distress. Actions of both Congress, through the Senate Special
Committee on Aging, and the executive branch, through the Administration
on Aging, have touched many aspects of the life of older persons: research,
experimental programs, and locally initiated activities have been concerned
with opportunities for constructive activity, developing useful roles which
the elderly can fill once they have been displaced from the labor market,
nutritional status, opportunities for gratifying leisure activities, mechanisms to reduce isolation and loneliness, to name but a few.

This real extension and potential future extension in the range of
public social policy, so much at variance with past socially sanctioned
functions, is justified by the unusual situation which modern society con-
fronts concerning its elderly. In 1880 3.4 percent of the American population was over the age of 65, whereas in 1977 almost 10 percent was over
65, and by the end of the century the figure is expected to rise to nearly
15 percent. The average life expectancy in the population has risen dramatically. In 1900 life expectancy for males was an average of 48.2 years; in
1973 this had increased to 67.6 years. For women the comparable rates
were 50.7 years and 75.3 years. This means not that the species is living
longer genetically, but that more individuals are living longer and the
proportion of persons over 65, and especially those over 75, has increased
dramatically.

This proportionate aging of the population has been accompanied by
a phenomenal growth in economic productive capacity and in the mechanical capacity to produce the goods which a population requires. As a result, the manpower of older persons is decreasingly required for the running of the economy. In contrast with earlier times when the elderly performed a lifelong economic function, today their labor is not required by
the economy. This circumstance is most dramatically represented by
changes in labor force participation by the elderly. While the participation

of adults over 14 in the labor force has remained at approximately 55 percent since 1900, the proportion of the elderly over 65 participating in the labor force has declined from 68 percent in 1900 to 23 percent in 1975 and appears to be still declining.[3]

At the same time the American culture has changed. A primary value is now placed upon independent living residences for nuclear families, meaning that older persons maintain residences independent of their adult and married children.

The sum effect of these developments has been to create a society containing a large group of members who in the past were revered and valued, but who now lack economic and social functions. The lack of definition of their role in turn creates instability and unpredictability in their relationships to members of their families and the society in general. In a sense public policy has been expanded to include some of the responsibilities previously assumed by family relationships. Government programs, whatever their direction or scope, are now concerned with the mobility, movement, social life, recreation, economic security, health, and nutrition of the elderly. At the same time, the potential development of this policy is still constrained by the belief that these wide-ranging needs can best be met through the marketplace.

We must conclude that no guiding directions for government policy have yet emerged for the use of its influence concerning the plight of the elderly in society and the roles they should fill, how their health is to be maintained, or what the balance should be between family and private or governmental support for housing and transportation.

The role of the aged is the one area almost ignored by federal policy, except in a negative sense. There has been a continuing tendency toward earlier retirement, that is, earlier than 65, much of which can be attributed to liberalization in social security legislation.[4] Such legislation, for example, permits retirement with some reduction in benefits at the age of 62 or 60. Other liberalization has made it possible for persons under 65 who become permanently and totally disabled to begin withdrawing their income benefits as if they had already reached 65. This provision has been heavily utilized by workers in their late 50s and early 60s who become unemployed, find it extraordinarily difficult to find competitive employment, and use existing physical handicaps as a means for securing minimum income. Over all, it can be said that the elderly are effectively enabled to leave the labor force whether by virtue of their inability to find employment or as a matter of personal preference.

Minor pressures have developed to reverse this tendency toward removal from the labor force and to widen opportunities for the retired

---

[3]Riley and Foner, *Aging and Society*, pp. 39–49.
[4]Juanita M. Kreps, "Social Security in the Coming Decade: Questions for a Mature System," *Social Security Bulletin* 39, No. 3 (March 1976): 21–29.

elderly to earn small sums of money through employment without losing retirement benefits. For example, a small-scale program was set up in 1975 to provide short-term employment at limited reimbursement for 149,602 elderly through Retired Senior Voluntary Program (RSVP) programs.[5] Such actions are tokens of federal interest, but they do not yet represent a federal commitment to assure that the elderly have useful and significant roles in their communities made available to them. Whether or not such a federal commitment is required, given the natural choices which individuals have about the use of their leisure time, is untested. To say that a positive federal policy on a role for the elderly is lacking does not say that this problem has not been recognized in many circles of government. However, recognition has been expressed only in a few demonstrations of interest. In 1978 Congress acted to reinforce an old social norm to meet this issue. It passed legislation making it illegal to terminate employment for reasons of old age alone until the age of 70. It did not deal with the long-term trend to voluntary earlier retirement.

A CHANGE IN FAMILY SUPPORT POLICY

In another direction, public policy seems to have been in the vanguard of a change in societal policy. Family members had long been considered responsible for each other, and, in conformity to inherited English poor law constructs, public sources were made accessible only when families were missing or incapable of providing assistance to their members. With the coming of the Social Security Act, the elderly had access to independent sources of income. This access seems to have reinforced the already apparent tendency for families to separate into nuclear units, living independently although maintaining ties of personal association. By 1965 57 percent of all the elderly were either living alone or with their spouses. An additional 11 percent were living with other persons not related by blood ties. In 17 percent of the households, older persons and their children lived together with the older persons as heads of household and another 11 percent of the cases lived together with the adult children as heads of household.[6]

[5]*Action*, Annual Report (Washington, D.C.: U.S. Government Printing Office, 1975), p. 1.

[6]Riley and Foner, *Aging and Society*, pp. 168–169. Between 1965–1975 this trend continued although data is compiled differently. In 1975 15 percent of men and 37 percent of women over 65 lived alone or with nonrelatives, maintaining independent homes as "primary individuals"; 78 percent of women aged 55–64 years lived alone or only with spouses, as did 60 percent of women over 75 years of age. For men the corresponding figures are 88 percent and 84 percent. See also U.S. Bureau of Census, *Demographic Aspects of Aging*, pp. 47–49; Marvin Sussman, "Family Life of Old People," in *Handbook of Aging and the Social Sciences*, ed. Robert Binstock and Ethel Shanas (New York: Van Nostrand Reinhold, 1976).

Studies between 1958 and 1975, however, indicate that this tendency to live apart had not necessarily produced a weakening of family ties. Nearly 50 percent of the elderly live within 10 to 30 minutes' journey of some family member and only 5 percent live as much as a day's journey apart. More significantly, studies have indicated that affectional ties accompany this physical proximity, measured by frequency of visiting, and the like. Schorr reports that, while some older people are isolated from their families, most are a part of a family configuration.[7] Upwards of two-thirds of aged parents see their children at least weekly. Studies of middle-class families conclude that the generations have a desire to help one another.[8] Nonetheless, this maintenance of close family ties has been accompanied by a marked shift of financial responsibility for the elderly from family to tax sources. This remarkable shift, led by the initial Social Security Act for retirement, has taken place within the basic societal context we have been postulating, since the social security is premised upon individual contribution to a presumed insurance fund with benefits presumably being returned in a proportion to contributions made. However, it is important to remember here that the Social Security Act does not maintain a sequestered fund, but rather contributions by individuals constitute in effect a claim upon future tax revenues from which there is a contractual obligation to make payments.

The shift in fiscal responsibility from family to state is most clearly seen in state and federal policies governing supplementary assistance payments, first from old age assistance and, more recently, from supplementary security income. Until the enactment of the SSI legislation policies regarding filial responsibility lay within the jurisdiction of state governments. By 1970 many states made no support demands on adult children and 21 states, while requiring the contribution as a matter of law, did not make the granting of assistance contingent on that contribution. Since the remaining states which require, at least nominally, some filial contribution if their parents do not have sufficient income, also take into account the income level of potential contributing family members, the degree of family responsibility is even further reduced. Since most families in the United States have modest incomes and the vast majority of adult children of dependent elderly also have moderate incomes, there are relatively few cases in which there is a sufficient disposable margin of filial income to make feasible a demand that payments be made for the support of parents living elsewhere. On balance, it can be said that the precept that families

[7]Alvin Schoor, *Filial Responsibility in the Modern American Family* (Washington, D.C.: Social Security Administration, U.S. Department of Health, Education, and Welfare, 1960).

[8]See also Ethel Shanas, "Sociological Research Findings about Older People," in *Toward Better Understanding of the Aged* (Council on Social Welfare Education, 1958), p. 52; Gordon F. Streib, "Family Patterns in Retirement," *Journal of Social Issues* 14, No. 2 (1958); Marvin B. Sussman, "Family Continuity," *Marriage and Family Living* 16, No. 2 (May 1954): 112–120.

take care of their dependent family members has been substantially invaded and that as a practical matter families are relieved of this responsibility where aged parents are living independently, except in those relatively few cases where adult children have substantial incomes.

Recognition of this development has been obscured for a long time because public assistance, as distinguished from social security, has been identified with a deep stigma, and many older persons, even though in financial difficulty and living separately from their children, have been reluctant to apply for public assistance, even where it is available. The stigma has encouraged the maintenance of the traditional societal view of family responsibility, but it is evident that the introduction of public support for the elderly as a class has already altered one dimension of family relationships.

This type of modification of public policy has occurred slightly, but perceptibly in other fields. For example, public support for independent living of nuclear families is seen in small programs of specialized housing for the elderly. Federal policy in housing encourages the construction of special accommodations for the elderly living alone, either in public housing, in subsidized low-cost housing, or in special housing developments. In 1956 the Federal Housing Act specifically authorized federal financing for units especially designed for the elderly in low-cost public housing. In 1962 the Senior Citizens Housing Act authorized the insuring and the granting of loans for the housing of elderly in rural communities. One especially interesting program, that of rent supplements, has been mandated for the whole population, but about 25 percent of the families receiving assistance through rent supplementation in 1969 were elderly.

However, these expressions of public policy concerning the housing requirements of the elderly should not be overvalued. While it was estimated in 1970 that 1.5 million older persons lived in substandard housing [9] or in housing which they could not afford (meaning that they use a disproportionate amount of their income for rent and thus are badly nourished), by 1974 only 331,000 units for the elderly had been constructed to reduce the cost of housing and fewer than 20,000 elderly families received rent supplements.[10]

The Administration on Aging also supports a variety of other personal service programs for the elderly, but on the basis of reflexive funding. The Congress allocates a fixed sum to the states by formula. The states, either through governmental units or voluntary organizations approved by state units on aging, initiate service proposals which are contributed to by the

[9]U.S. Bureau of Census, *1970 Housing Census, Housing of Senior Citizens*, HC (7)-6 (Washington, D.C.: U.S. Government Printing Office, 1970), Table A-5.
[10]U.S. Department of Housing and Urban Development, *1973 and 1974 HUD Statistical Yearbooks* (Washington, D.C.: U.S. Government Printing Office, 1974).

federal funds when they fall within federal guidelines. As a result, specialized programs do exist, such as senior citizen centers for socialization, programs to enable the disabled elderly to remain in their own homes, friendly visiting programs, experimental transportation arrangements for the housebound, but most of them are in the nature of demonstrations with limited guidance as to purpose or objective.

It cannot be said with any confidence that this variety of programs represents a direction in policy for the federal government, except that it is prepared to intervene modestly in the distribution of resources on behalf of the elderly and in response to requests which initiated at the local or state levels. Still, they illustrate first steps which may evolve into adopted policies of public provision of leisure- time centers or of constructive activity for the elderly.

The exception to this lack of direction is in the area of nutrition. Amendments to the Older Americans Act in 1973 provided that 39 percent of funds ($99 million) appropriated under the Act in 1973 must be utilized for the provision of nutritional programs for the elderly. In many urban areas some individual and group feeding programs, such as home-delivered meals and the provision of meals in senior centers, have resulted. These programs represent a concern on the part of the federal government that the poor elderly be well nourished as a complement to health services. It also represents a readiness to have federal funds used creatively. Nutritional funds made available through senior centers not only strengthen the ability of the group centers to meet the needs of isolated and lonely elderly, but also strengthen the desire of the elderly to use those centers. The funds thereby encourage social interaction and to a degree counteract the tendency to isolation on the part of some of the elderly, especially the handicapped.

The sum effect of these actions, both the clear-cut public policies in relation to income and health and the modest demonstration innovations in other social areas, define present public policy for the elderly. The policy is seen in terms of individuals, that is, actions are taken to meet the needs of aged individuals or to relieve family members of many responsibilities; it is still not a family policy, that is, a policy addressed to the well being of that *collectivity called a family*.

ADMINISTRATIVE STRUCTURE FOR FEDERAL POLICY SHIFTS

Since this set of policies appears to deviate from the societal constraints, it is interesting to summarize briefly the sequence of events which led to the present state of affairs. The first evidence of federal policy concerns, other than those reflected in the Social Security Act of 1935, was the 1951 White House Conference on Aging, the first of its kind in the United States. The President's decision to convene the conference may

have been related to an attempt to influence the debate over health insurance for the elderly via an expansion of social security protection. However,
it is not unreasonable to conclude that the conference also represented an
extension of the executive office concern for the elderly which had its first
significant testing in the 1930s in the debate over economic security. In
addressing this conference about the responsibilities of government for the
elderly, former Governor of New Jersey Robert M. Meyner advanced views
which seemed to conform to an interpretation of public policies expressed
by the Office of the President: "The federal system is weakened when the
national government does not accept and fulfill its share of obligations. I
hope this conference will set forth fearlessly the relative responsibilities of
the several levels of government and make strong recommendations to
each for carrying them out." After arguing that governments, both
national and state, have an obligation to provide moral leadership in moving into areas where senior citizens need protection, the governor chose
to point out some concrete areas in which federal as well as state responsibilities needed to be discharged in a consistent direction. Among these
were the need to protect the elderly from the special hazards of injury on
the roads and from neglect and abuse in nursing homes. Beyond reiterating
what had already been well established, the fact that the elderly are often
poor and in need of special medical assistance, he pointed out that the
aged are, in addition, ill housed. He concluded that every state, with
federal assistance, should have an agency to take the lead in carrying out
a comprehensive program for the welfare of the aged. Although noting
that such an agency should provide leadership and coordination, he seemed
to imply that the thrust of federal government policy, as well as that of the
states, should be one of consistent responsibility for the development of a
comprehensive program concerned with the welfare of the aged, not only
their income and their health.

Successive conferences in 1961 and 1971, sponsored and supported by
the White House, expanded on these themes. They addressed themselves to
a wide range of subjects affecting the religious, morale, housing, health,
transportation, and occupational concerns of older persons and proposed
relevant federally supported programs in each area.

In addition to the conferences, the White House established an inter-
departmental committee with a special staff to prod, stimulate, and arouse
the major executive departments to give special attention to the needs of
the elderly.

These efforts were supplemented by the establishment of the Special
Senate Committee on Aging, which has over the years produced a series of
significant studies and hearings bearing on all aspects of living conditions
for the elderly.

These activities culminated in 1965 in the enactment of Public Law
98–73, the Older Americans Act, which established the Administration on

Aging, a distinctive administrative focus for the interests of the federal government.

By 1975 programs for the aging were funded at the level of $246 million, including federal support at the level of $100 million for 800 nutrition programs to provide 290,000 daily meals five days a week in 4900 local sites. In addition funds were available for the support of an indefinite variety of social services administered predominantly through 462 area agencies on aging, regional or urban governmental units responsible for contracting with private providers or actually organizing a variety of services for the elderly, including homemaker services, chore workers to maintain properties, transportation, socialization programs in senior citizens centers, legal aid services, and the like. The claim that 7 million individuals were served by these programs needs interpretation; considering the modest sums available to each area office, it is expected that a large part of this servicing consisted of giving information rather than more tangible forms of service.

In addition, the Administration on Aging supports special educational programs and training programs to equip professional and paraprofessional service providers with special knowledge about the needs of the elderly so that, presumably, their services can be more effective. Personnel trained by these funds might be employed in agencies serving only the elderly, such as the area offices on aging, homes for aged, and senior citizen centers, or in general purpose agencies serving all ages, such as public assistance, housing, hospitals.

The scope of the Administration on Aging goes still further. In this field, at least, a consistent evolution and broadening of federal policy appears to have taken place. Beginning with assurance of income security and the establishment of a comprehensive financial and administrative system for managing income security, the economic bases have been steadily broadened through Medicare to include the hazards of illness. While the nonfinancial services cannot be said to represent specific choices by the federal government, about such issues as relationship with family, the assurance of adequate housing for all, or a massive attack upon isolation or upon inactivity, at least federal policy has expressed sufficient interest to intervene slightly in the distribution of resources to attract attention to such needs. There are a set of specific public policies conforming to societal predispositions and a variety of programs, which while they do not yet constitute policy direction, do represent a clear expansion of the scope of federal government obligation. The federal government is thus engaged in the lives of the elderly far beyond the guides originally suggested by societal preferences, but the directional nature of this interest is still unclear, for federal support remains in the form of cash payments to individuals left then to rely upon the marketplace of goods-and-services providers. The family purposes which guide the structure of these services are not really clarified by federal policy.

The Impact on Federal Policy Enlargement on the Well-Being of the Elderly

The position of the elderly relative to the rest of the population as regards income and access to health services has already been discussed. With two exceptions, it is difficult to identify any effects which these programs have had on the life of the elderly. No clear causal connection can be made regarding extension of life. Some studies, such as those by Carp, indicate that housing does improve the morale of the elderly, but no extensive comparative studies have been completed.[11] The variety of specialized services funded through the Administration on Aging area offices presumably improve the well-being and perhaps the morale of the elderly, since the services at least are utilized and presumably wanted. But whether a change in health, well-being, or morale has resulted has not yet been established.

However, the two exceptions to this general conclusion lead us into the present policy choices which confront the national government. The exceptions are: (1) an increase in the ability of the aged to maintain homes apart from younger relatives and (2) an increase in proprietary nursing home beds for the sick aged. The second of these is clearly on the public agenda. There is no longer much doubt that the enactment of the social security protection and the administrative decision to make old age assistance and social security payments to vendors of institutional services, especially nursing home operators, has produced a great increase in the number of proprietary nursing home beds available in the United States. Between 1939 and 1970, this number has grown from 25,000 to 1,099,412.[12]

Part of this increase has undoubtedly been required because the growing number of older persons, especially those over 75, necessarily means an increasing number of persons with severe physical as well as social disabilities which require full-time institutional care. However, the growth of proprietary nursing homes has given rise to the charge that national policy is strongly biased in favor of institutional care for those who are completely capable of managing for themselves. This charge is justified, at least by the fact that Medicare payments for 100 days in a skilled nursing facility and Medicaid payments for indefinite periods of time have until recently been available only for older persons in hospitals or those placed in nursing homes as part of a treatment plan. Neither Medicare nor Medicaid encouraged or permitted the use of equivalent funds to supplement normal social security or public assistance benefits to help the individual secure part-time assistance to remain at home, whereas larger sums for full-time attention were made available to those

---

[11]Frances Carp, *A Future for the Aged: Victoria Plaza and Its Residents* (Austin: University of Texas Press, 1966).

[12]U.S. Senate Special Committee on Aging, *Nursing Home Care in the United States: Failure in Public Policy, Introductory Report* (Washington, D.C.: U.S. Government Printing Office, 1974), pp. 20–21.

in nursing homes. A succession of studies has indicated that, depending upon the jurisdiction and the scope of alternative services, anywhere between 10 and 40 percent of nursing-home patients are so placed primarily for social reasons. The fact that they are enfeebled does not necessarily mean that they could not have continued longer in their own homes with partial social supports which until 1976 have not been readily available. This situation appears to be the consequence of the decision to relate most medical care for the elderly to an economic program, social security, and to build both Medicare and Medicaid policies around the controls provided by the medical professions.

By the early 1970s, however, the criticisms about overinstitutionalization and about the quality of care provided in many institutions led to a continuing reexamination of basic national policy. The Medicaid administration undertook to waive its normal limitations on the use of Medicaid funds to permit payment for home-care services outside of institutions on an experimental basis. Medicare administration followed shortly thereafter, authorizing a few test experiments wherein medical funds were used to pay for nonmedical services in an effort to diminish the volume of institutional care. At this writing (1977), these remain tentative, experimental steps taken by national government and are not yet fully developed and adopted policies.

The legislative branch has introduced legislation designed to provide federal payments for noninstitutional services as part of a major effort to reverse the long-standing tendency to rely upon institutional care when individuals are not wholly capable of managing alone.[13] However, no efforts of this kind had yet been adopted by 1976.

Federal policy has had an observable effect on the ability of older persons to maintain independent households. While early fears that family ties would be loosened as a result have not been realized, a serious new policy issue has risen to the surface. When government assumes any type of financial responsibility for its citizens, responsibilities previously borne entirely by the family, the door is opened to a continuous extension or expansion of this transfer of obligation and responsibility, at least in monetary terms. Should all care in nursing homes be provided without charge to the family under any circumstances of family wealth? Should part-time, home-care services be provided for the partially disabled by tax funds, even though those services are in some 75 percent of all cases still being provided by family members without compensation?[14] A major public policy debate may be in the making over the appropriate boundary

---

[13]Examples are bills introduced in the 94th Congress by Representatives Edward I. Koch (H.R. 10324) and Barber B. Conable (H.R. 2268). In the 95th Congress similar bills have been introduced by representatives Koch (H.R. 452, 453), Conable (H.R. 2029), and Claude Pepper (H.R. 1130).

[14]See G. Eggert, R. Morris, C. Granger, and S. Pendleton "Community Care for the Chronically Ill," mimeographed (Waltham, Mass.: Brandeis University, 1975).

between responsibilities for all citizens which should be publicly assumed
and those which properly should be left to family members. The debate is
complicated by the fact that 14 percent of elderly persons lack living relatives or are completely alienated from family members. Where income
alone is not sufficient to maintain functional independence because of
illness or enfeeblement, alternative social arrangements must be provided.
But what of the much larger number with remaining family networks?
What are the proper boundaries for the division of responsibility between
families and government? It is conceivable that the precedent set in the
social security legislation will some day be extended to other services
considered desirable for the elderly without a means test, with tax support
for all persons, regardless of assets.

CHILD CARE POLICIES

The history of public policy concerning children is less clear than
that for the aging, although the history is longer. It is taken as an article
of faith that, as a society, we place the highest values on caring and
nurturing children as the bulwark of the nation's future. In reality our
policies have, for the most part, relied upon families to provide this nur-
ture, although we have also built up a surprisingly large number of supplemental services either to protect children who are at risk of neglect or
to relieve families of certain pressing obligations.

If we assume that income support runs to families and parents, that
health services are available to most anyway, and that public education is
available for all in some form, then most public actions are concerned
with special protection, usually for the poor. Neglected and abandoned
children are provided with substitute care in foster homes or in institutions, juvenile courts treat delinquency in a sheltered and protected way,
social workers keep in touch with families where neglect is reported, and
day centers are funded for children whose mothers work.

Some other programs represent first steps by government to push a
little beyond the conventions of the past. Day centers are widely employed
by middle-class families, and eligibility for use of public centers has been
slowly expanded beyond the harsh constraints of public assistance so that
a continuum of day care is becoming available for everyone. Well-baby
clinics and postnatal services attend to the medical needs of infants and
small children, at least those from poor families, so that a continuum of
medical care is available for all. Crippled children, regardless of income
status, have some access to special therapeutic programs to correct disability
where feasible. These represent a steady growth in public programs, but
as public policy they do not go far beyond our underlying norms. Most
of the programs are still limited to the poor or near poor, most are designed

to bring more equity into the lives of a vulnerable or disadvantaged group, and many services are delivered by marketplace private services, reimbursed but not guided by government.

At another level there are policies which affect all children more or less alike. Child labor laws, mainly state administered, more or less protect children from industrial exploitation. Family planning and abortion programs do facilitate some control over family size, although these are fiercely opposed. They are supported in part to satisfy parents' desires, but in part because of a belief that unwanted children or families too large for family income produce damaging environments for child development.

The evolution of federal policy has for a long time been obstructed by the peculiar division of major programs. Income programs are divided among AFDC, the Veterans Administration, and the Social Security Administration. The latter two provide income security for dependent children of social security beneficiaries or of disabled veterans. Some of these benefits, at least in the case of severely handicapped children, are attached to children directly when they reach maturity. The AFDC program is concerned only with children in low-income families. And the historic U.S. Children's Bureau (now merged into the Office of Human Development) has had the mission of monitoring the general well-being of all children, regardless of income, or class.

To these activities must be added recent federal funding of programs intended to improve the education of poor children and of all children. Head Start and Upward Bound were products of the Great Society years, in which disadvantaged minorities were found to require special educational opportunities to leapfrog over other social and economic disadvantages. Such programs were founded on the even more sweeping policy of removing all forms of school segregation, with the consequent restructuring of many local school systems by federal regulation and federal court order. In education at least, the federal policy has clearly moved far beyond social norms and has imposed a single national standard as to the social relationships in public schools. Since some of the impetus for this vast innovation came from evidence that minority children learned differently than others and since the schools' social structure was blamed for the differential, it followed that national criteria with which to measure school achievement have become more and more prominent. Although the old distrust of national control of the educational process still remains, it has been ignored in certain fields.

What must be asked is: do these activities constitute a guiding set of principles? The answer is clearly yes, for vulnerable children have been the object of much legislation. The scope of the principles has also broadened in the past decade and the old reliance on the locality and the marketplace has been breached. Education is now clearly a matter of national responsibility, at least as to achievement and social relationships in education, if not the details of school structure or curriculum.

EVOLUTION OF FAMILY POLICY

Whether or not these efforts also constitute a family policy is another matter. In a negative sense it might appear that the encouragement to mothers to enter the labor market, aided by the spread of a network of day-care centers, could be interpreted to mean that there is such a policy and its thrust is to further reduce the obligations of family members. It remains moot whether this strengthens or weakens the family. It can be argued that freeing women to work leads to freer adults of both sexes and that this, in turn, produces healthier family relationships. But the counterargument can also be made that this process, encouraged by government action, weakens family ties by encouraging successive changes as adults divorce and remarry or as family care is replaced by impersonal professional day care. If the issue is not resolved by evidence, it is at least reasonable to conclude that federal policy has slowly emerged as supporting the first of the two arguments.

A recent volume reporting the conclusions of a series of conferences comes to rather grim conclusions.[15] Kessen, in reviewing the series, says:

> In the center is the ambiguity of commitment Americans have to children. No longer an economic asset, no longer a comfort in our old age, no longer a continuation of our people in the traditional pattern of our forebears, (we must ask how long a society which exiles its old folks can preserve its continuity with the young), the American child is becoming both in his own life (as a child) and in the lives of his parents, without function.[16]

This is a harsh indictment, but not unreasonable when we consider that parents are encouraged to give up much of the daily care of their children, that children leave home early and set up independent households whether or not they establish families of their own, and that the obligation to care for aged parents is now shifted to public income supports or to the nursing home. Aside from loving each other, what functions do parents and children have for each other in times of trouble (as well as of pleasure)?

At the heart of the matter lies the dilemma of what set of values we can explicate, and whether these should be held and exercised by families, privately, or whether government should be expected to intervene actively in family life to further one or another set of values.

A common response in the past has been to build up service programs incrementally to take care of discrete difficulties as they arise: to supply medical care to children in poor families, treatment to crippled children, day care for working mothers, and so on. But now underlying social trends

---

[15]Nathan Talbot, *Raising Children in America* (Boston: Little, Brown, 1976).
[16]William Kessen, "Ambiguous Commitment," *Science* 193 (July 23, 1976): 310–311. Copyright 1976 by the American Association for the Advancement of Science.

have challenged many earlier assumptions. Our service programs have, in the past, been really concerned with the vulnerable and rejected child, at risk of being abused or neglected. But now our dilemmas concerning children and youth affect all children and we are as yet unclear whether government should act and, if so, how. A common proposal is for the further extension of discrete problem-specific public services. One such proposal, emerging from the Talbot reports, is for a universal child-family screening program under a national health service. Another is a program of regular, possibly compulsory home visiting to evaluate the care of children in all American families at periodic intervals. While not spelled out, it might be inferred that criteria need to be developed and that families not meeting these criteria will be the object of some intervention.

Looking at family policy from the point of view of children and the elderly, one can perceive a disturbing situation. Our basic social norms concerning the relative position of government vis-à-vis the family have been overtaken by unanticipated developments in our culture. Families were once the bulwark and they were treated as sovereign with respect to family needs. Government entered mainly when families, a few in proportion, proved incapable or incompetent to cope with certain stresses. In time these trends merged with a much more powerful tide, the freeing of individual members of families to realize their aspirations as individuals, not as members of close family units. If we are to acquire a new public family policy, we confront most painful choices. Can we expect the family to function as a unit without also having to perform clear functions and to bear certain responsibilities? And if we extend certain function-relieving services to everyone as a matter of right, do these really strengthen the family *as a unit* or do they free its members as individuals? And beyond this, do we want government to act on one or the other conception of family function?

Evolution of family or child care policies has been complicated by changing views about what a family consists of. Children with only one parent, adults living together without children, communal living groups or unrelated individuals, permanent liasons between individuals of the same sex are all considered families in much modern thinking. How much sustained responsibility such groupings should take for their members is not at all clear vis-à-vis the responsibility government owes to the individuals. This change in public attitude will certainly affect the future evolution of policy concerning the aged, children, or the family as a collectivity.

ADDITIONAL READINGS

Butler, Robert. *Why Survive: Being Old in America.* New York: Harper & Row, 1975.

Costin, Lela. *Child Welfare: Policies and Practices.* New York: McGraw-Hill, 1972.

Kadushin, Alfred. *Child Welfare Services*. 2d ed. New York: Macmillan, 1974.

Kammerman, Sheila, and Alfred Kahn. *Social Services in the United States*. Philadelphia: Temple University Press, 1976.

Lawton, S. Powell. *Planning and Managing Housing for the Elderly*. New York: Wiley, 1975.

Low, Seth, and Pearl Spingler. *Child Care Arrangements of Working Mothers*. Washington, D.C.: U.S. Department of Health, Education, and Welfare, Children's Bureau Publication 453, 1968.

Maas, Henry, and Richard Engler. *Children in Need of Parents*. New York: Columbia University Press, 1959.

Riley, Matilda W., and Anne Foner. *Aging and Society*, Vols. 1 and 2. New York: Russell Sage Foundation, 1969.

Shanas, Ethel, et al. *Old People in Three Industrial Societies*. New York: Atherton, 1968.

Steiner, Gilbert, and Milius. *The Children's Cause*. Washington, D.C.: Brookings Institution, 1976.

Steiner, Peter, and Robert Dorfman. *Economic Status of the Aged*. Berkley: Univesity of California Press, 1957.

Talbot, Nathan. *Raising Children in America*. Boston: Little, Brown, 1976.

SOME POLICY ALTERNATIVES

The burgeoning of national states has been accompanied by a growing optimism that governments can develop and execute policies to affect national and human problems in a positive way. Whereas in the past most governmental actions, at least in the human service arena, were reflexive (that is, government reacted to a suddenly perceived difficulty), the belief has now grown that effective and constructive steps can be taken to manage anticipated difficulties or to solve recurrent problems. Experience with policies adopted in the past has produced a belief that they can be improved upon, that better policies can be shaped and put into effect, better in the sense that they will be more effective in dealing with recurrent difficulties. Our review thus far has explored the limitations and achievements of some recent policies. It will be worth examining alternative options in the fields of health, income, aging, children, and housing.

The search for policy alternatives opens up a cornucopia of possibilities, ranging from the most utopian to the most narrowly technical. Choice among the vast range can be narrowed by deciding upon the time frame to be used. The most utopian alternatives require for their execution a basic change in social values and attitudes and therefore require perhaps even several generations to bring about the changes desired. An illustration is the view that income should be distributed according to need and not according to ability or to any contribution to society's productive capacity.

At the other extreme, narrowly technical policies can be put into effect immediately, but while they may have wide rippling effects, they do not change the nature of the problem. An illustration would be the introduction of coinsurance requirements to all health insurance policies as a means for controlling the use of health services and affecting the cost distribution between government and consumer.

This chapter will consider some alternative policies which might reasonably be adopted by governments, given the underlying social constraints discussed in Chapter 1. In other words, we will be interested in alternatives which move beyond the present structure for human service delivery, but not so far that there is no likelihood of their adoption short of a cataclysmic overthrow of present social and public institutional forms. Before considering alternative policies, it is worth examining dilemmas policy makers confront in the process of selection.

CONFLICT OF RIGHTS

Many analyses have explored the powerful influence of ignorance, limited vision, and political opposition on the selection of policy alternatives.[1] Less attention has been directed to a more basic difficulty, namely, reconciling conflicting rights. Frequently a perfectly good idea, when translated into policy for action, turns out to remedy one ill at the price of violating another right. For example in recent years housing policy has attempted to remedy the lack of adequate housing within the means of those with limited income and has been concerned with building neighborhood vitality. Several programs have produced low-cost housing, usually in concentrations in areas of the city where the poor tend to live. This, on the surface, seems not unreasonable, for the poor do tend to cluster in neighborhoods with the housing they can afford; the new low-cost housing is seen as a means of strengthening these neighborhoods and improving housing at the same time. Unfortunately the programs, where they have been effective, have produced a situation which by other criteria is seen as undesirable, namely, the concentration of the poor in delimited parts of the city. The fact that income influences population distribution and is also a positive factor in developing neighboring relationships among compatible persons and families is seen by many to be in itself undesirable. The inhabitants of close-knit neighborhoods wish to maintain the character of their neighborhoods, while improving the quality of life in them, but this

---

[1] See, for example, Peter Marris and Martin Rein, *The Dilemmas of Reform* (New York: Atherton, 1967) ; Martin Meyerson and Edward Banfield, *Politics Planning and the Public Interest,* (New York: Free Press, 1955) ; Alan Altschuler, *The City Planning Process* (Ithaca, N.Y.: Cornell University Press, 1965; Daniel Hirshfield, *The Lost Reform* (Cambridge, Mass.: Harvard University Press, 1970).

leads to separation by income class. The awkward situation thus arises that actions which follow the norms of urban social organization produce results deemed undesirable by those seeking to equalize economic and social relationships. In Boston 1976 funds for low-cost housing were recently slashed for one low-income area which had been quite successful in mobilizing, building, and occupying federal subsidized housing; the reason given for the cuts was that the neighborhood had an overconcentration of low-income families.

Such examples can be multiplied almost indefinitely. In health we find a strong desire to have the highest quality of medical care accessible to all as represented by access to complex teaching hospitals and at the same time strong desire to have health services close at hand in small neighborhoods, responsive to ethnic and cultural differences. The services made possible by the concentration of medical personnel and technology in large centers cannot be replicated in small hospital units, serving small groups of people. They would be underutilized and the cost of such duplication would be wasteful. Similarly, the services provided by small neighborhood health centers, controlled by indigenous residents cannot be replaced. A balance between the two must be found.

In programs for the elderly there is a powerful impetus to develop services attuned to their special circumstances: their slower physical pace, the content of their education (so different from present-day education), and their vocational status. Counter to this is the urgent desire to avoid age segregation, much as we seek to avoid race segregation. Senior centers usually separate users from those of other ages, but unsegregated centers usually are unable to meet the needs of the aged while also meeting the needs of teen-age youth.

The attempts to seek equity in income maintenance encounter the cross fire of conflicting rights of the very poor, the working poor, and those with higher incomes. The very poor should be assured a decent income without loss of dignity. But the working poor want to have their work efforts rewarded differentially from those who do not work. And those with higher incomes feel they should help only those who help themselves, for example, by working, which leads to the introduction of often undignified and inhumane control procedures.

Recognition of the conflicts of rights places on policy makers a new obligation: to assess the extent to which any policy aimed at redressing a violated right carries with it the likelihood of violating different, but related rights. Public policy today demands this more complex level of evaluation and is no longer satisfied by the selection of alternatives simply through power play among political forces.

The search for policy alternatives is therefore more complex than a direct attempt to correct a clear injustice. It involves attention to equally deserving but contradictory rights, awareness of the socially inherited value biases of citizen constituencies, and consideration of the time frame adopted for action. With such a framework in mind, we can turn to some policy alternatives which have been advanced in each of the areas we have undertaken to review.

OVERALL POLICY

If one moves away from specific problem policies, general policy guidelines can be derived from a comparison of the Johnson Great Society years and the later Nixon administration.[2] Despite apparent differences in the rhetoric of political debate, these two periods follow a more or less common path as to the scope of federal responsibility. Both were committed to using federal programs to help shape American life, and while there were differences in the rate of growth in federal expenditure for social welfare, a review of the budgets indicates that federal spending to that end expanded during both administrations. The major distinctions were the slower rate of growth under Nixon and the objects to which such expenditure was directed. Also, it seemed to be an implicit assumption of the Nixon administration that the federal government's role was to *govern*, not to do, that is, to set guiding rules, but not to, administer programs directly. This could explain the persistent efforts to return programs to local authority or to voluntary agencies or to the marketplace, albeit with tax support. The Johnson programs also encouraged new volunteer efforts, but public administration was not avoided. Policy alternatives which reflect such strategic differences are not difficult to identify. In health it comes to public management of insurance versus private insurance company management or support of public hospitals and clinics versus reliance on private physicians. In housing there is a choice between public construction and management of low-cost housing versus private construction with tax subsidy and private ownership and management. In income there is public assistance in some form versus unemployment insurance plus some kind of family or children's allowances.

Johnson's program emphasized the provision of goods, services, and income to the poor and the disadvantaged. The objective was an assault on poverty and improvement of the condition of minorities, especially blacks. It supported community action agencies to give poor consumers a better voice in decisions about programs; legal services, adult education, and neighborhood centers (especially for health) were developed and supported. VISTA, a job corps, a neighborhood youth corps and other vocational training programs were designed to help the poor improve their economic skills. Head Start and Upward Bound were designed to overcome educational and social disadvantages beginning at the earliest years. Many of these programs sought to change the economic, political, and social bargaining position of the poor.

---

[2]See Sar Levitan and Robert Taggart, *The Promise of Greatness* (Cambridge, Mass.: Harvard University Press, 1976) which has been drawn upon for this comparison, providing a useful elaboration.

By contrast, the Nixon administration shifted away from such changes in the socioeconomic arrangements, although it continued to increase expenditures to relieve acute distress. The Nixon program moved away from a primary concern for the poor or very poor and extended its welfare services to the working poor whose needs, did not involve actual physical subsistence. This broadening of the welfare base inevitably reduced the benefits available to the very poorest. Johnson combined social economic change with traditional welfare for the poor. Nixon abandoned the economic change elements, but his broadened relief programs, through the Family Association Plan, blurred the conventional boundary between the poor who worked and those who did not.

Johnson worked for a federally administered health insurance and secured passage of Medicare, a federally administered program for the aged. In contrast Nixon cut funds for hospital construction and for other programs, arguing that the health system needed to be reformed, not expanded. His strategy for reform was a meager program to encourage the development of privately organized health maintenance organizations and a system of physician-organized review of professional services.

In housing the two were less differentiated. The Johnson administration supported the Housing and Urban Development Act of 1965, permitted public housing authorities to lease privately owned dwellings, reduced interest rates on loans to build housing for the poor or aged, and introduced rent supplements for low-income tenants. The Nixon years continued these policies, but funding was markedly reduced.

In other social welfare activities the two sets of policies differed mainly in priorities. Funds for welfare rose under both administrations. Social expenditures, as a share of the total federal budget increased from 26 percent in 1955 to 33 percent in 1965 and to 62 percent in 1974. However, the rate of increase was slowed, as Table 13 indicates.

TABLE 13

Annual Growth of Federal Social Welfare Expenditures, 1965–1975

Fiscal Year	Rate of Increase (in percentage, Based on 1973 dollars)
1965	18
1966	14
1967	10
1968	9
1969	8
1970	15
1971	11
1972	12
1973	5
1974	8

SOURCE: *Sar Levitan and Robert Taggart,* The Promise of Greatness *(Cambridge, Mass.: Harvard University Press, 1976), p. 21.*

The changes in policy from 1964 to 1976 were, of course, a result of complex and contending political forces, but it is reasonable to infer certain policy differences that activated the two administrations:

1. Use of the federal government to correct social inequities and to guarantee a minimum standard of welfare for all versus reliance upon private economic processes and slowing the rate of government involvement

2. Commitment to maintain existing programs and to project new ones versus retrenchment or reform of existing systems

3. Belief in constant economic expansion which would produce new income, some of which could be directed to social purposes (the fiscal dividend) without unduly raising taxes versus emphasis on the limits of growth

4. Use of the federal government as an instrument with which to change the private sector (as in the civil rights movement and the creation of agencies and pathways for services which bypassed traditional state and local organization) versus reliance on established institutions

5. Categorical grant programs aimed at specific problems and populations versus general revenue sharing

6. Belief in taking risks with new experimental strategies to change the condition of disadvantaged persons, to "shape civilization," versus dependence upon shoring up existing systems, with a hoped-for "filtering down" of benefits to the poor

Put another way, one general disposition, akin to a policy direction, tends to the creation of new agencies, programs, and social institutions to deal with persisting problems. These problems would be slowly reduced as a series of purpose-specific programs are created, one after the other. Preexisting programs which may overlap the new ones can be continued, or they will slowly wither away. The counter disposition is to avoid adding still further to the complex of government agencies, and instead to rely on efforts to restructure the ways in which already existing programs and already committed funds are organized.

In many ways solution of problems by restructuring is more difficult than by creating new programs. Existing organizations and social institutions quite normally fight to maintain themselves. To change them risks arousing their combined opposition and thus increases the opponents in the political process through which every policy must make its way. But, creating new programs also runs many risks, for the costs of adding new programs may activate other interests or established agencies may feel threatened by new competition. Whatever the similarity or difference in political hazard, the policy line for guiding action is clearly quite different: different technical tasks are involved in creating new programs, as against restructuring old ones, and the constellation of political forces is quite different.

SPECIFIC PROGRAM ALTERATIVES

Health

Over the past 40 years, the adopted federal health policies have struggled to find a stable foundation for financing, the structure of service delivery, and professional control. With the exception of Medicare for the aged, our present social as well as adopted policy stance on these issues can be summarized as follows: voluntary insurance for finance, fee for service payment, private medical practice based on large hospital complexes, and self-control of professional practice by the professions.

The major policy alternative which has been advanced and fought over for at least 40 years is compulsory health insurance. The details of this struggle have been adequately described in countless articles and books so that the alternative, in its general outlines, is now well-defined.[3] With the exception of the Kennedy-Griffiths health security bill and its successor, the Kennedy-Mills national health insurance program (introduced into the senate in April 1974),[4] all proposals to extend health insurance in the United States promise only to shift the mechanism for paying for medical care. None of them purport to affect the present distribution of medical or health personnel and health facilities nor to alter the way in which health services are delivered. All proposals assume that the present system would function quite well if only the obstacle of financial means were removed, that is, that health service providers and consumers would find each other and be satisfied with what each gives the other.

Compulsory health insurance by federal legislation must be viewed as a minor modification in policy rather than a significant policy alternative. True, the infusion of a compulsory system of insurance coverage will have wide-reaching effects. It will create a large administrative apparatus to collect funds from beneficiaries and distribute them to providers; it may open up access slightly for the poorest, but will not necessarily equalize the levels of medical care given the rich and the poor; and it will

---

[3]See, for example, Daniel Hirshfield, *The Lost Reform* (Cambridge, Mass.: Harvard University Press, 1970); Theodore Marmor, *The Politics of Medicare* (Chicago: Aldine, 1970); Rosemary Stevens, *American Medicine and the Public Interest* (New Haven: Yale University Press, 1971).

[4]These Kennedy initiatives are intended to act on the medical structure only indirectly, by directing the flow of health insurance premiums, and therefore of income, through a governmental entity, not through the private insurance intermediaries.

undoubtedly increase significantly the share of the GNP going to health care and also increase the price of medical care. Insurance does not, of itself, produce a marketplace in which rising demand can bring forth more services and a reduction in price due to competition. Health services and access to them have been shown to be controlled by the way in which health providers function. The supply of medical personnel cannot be increased readily, and even when it is, the use of the supply is still controlled by providers. Between 1954 and 1974, the number of physicians produced by medical schools has doubled, and the ratio of physicians per 100,000 population has risen from 149 to 158. But this is exactly the period in which overall medical costs skyrocketed and total medical expenditures rose from 4.5 to 8.2 percent of the GNP.[5]

The Kennedy-Griffith Bill moves one step beyond this, but only a small step. It provides that the collection of insurance premiums be made by governmental agencies and that payments of benefits also flow through this agency. In all other proposals this flow is left to private insurance companies, as is the case with present private and voluntary insurance. This change is not necessarily a guarantee of significant change in policy, given the propensity of all government agencies to fall, in the end, under the control of some producer constituency. As the commerce department is inextricably tied to commercial interests, and the Federal Drug Administration to the drug industry, and the labor department to major unions and manufacturers, so it is not unlikely that a national health insurance agency would find an unavoidable symbiotic relationship with the health industry. Nonetheless, a government agency presiding over the flow of health-financing funds amounts to an element outside of the health-provider industry which could, at some future time, use its strategic position as leverage to carry out other health policies which might alter the structure or direction of medical care more fundamentally. This could come about by altering either the rates at which certain procedures are compensated or the conditions for entitlement. It remains a moot question whether such a structural change would be a real change or not, since the use of the imputed "leverage" depends upon the behavior of various political forces. The positive view has been expressed by Senator Edward Kennedy: "We must use the financing mechanism to create strong, new incentives for the reorganization and delivery of health care. . . . I say, give us the lever of national health insurance and together we shall move the medical world. . . ."[6] The opposing view has been expressed by Navarro: "In

---

[5]Alfred Skolnick and Sophie Dales, "Social Welfare Expenditures, 1950–1975," *Social Security Bulletin* (Jan. 1976) vol. 39 no. 1; and Advisory Commission on Intergovernmental Relations, *Significant Features of Fiscal Federalism 1976* (Washington: 1976), p. 17.
[6]Edward M. Kennedy, "National Health Insurance Proposals: Leverage for Change?" *New York Academy of Medicine Bulletin* 48, No. 1 (January 1972): 152.

most countries, experience has shown that the insurance system will adapt itself to the organization of medical care and not vice versa. . . . There . . . is more evidence . . . of the use of insurance programs as leverage against instead of for change in the power structure underlying the delivery system." [7]

To consider a more radical change in policy, we would have to turn to proposals for a national health service, similar to forms adopted in England, or the Soviet Union. Under such a system health services would be provided by government agencies, not by private providers paid by government by some formula. All institutions would be owned by some government unit, although, as in England, actual administration would be delegated to boards or regional authorities with substantial independent operating authority, mainly subject to the policy guidance built into allocations of funds by legislatures. Institution staffs would become civil servants and other health providers, such as physicians outside of hospitals, would be either employed or would, as in England, be paid under contracts negotiated between their organization's representatives (as the American Medical Society) and government officials.

Such a radical change has never been seriously proposed for policy debate in the United States and may be taken to lie outside the bounds of acceptability to the American electorate, at least for the near future.

At a less global level, policy could be directed at the delivery system structure directly, whatever the financing mechanism be. National policy could opt for a more total reliance upon the hospital, or medical center, as the hub of all medical care. Under such a policy, all physicians (not only most, as today) would be expected to become a part of a hospital staff organization for purposes of training, professional discipline, and access to other services. The pre- and posthospital attention which any patient requires could be provided by a medical center or controlled by it through contracts negotiated with ancillary providers. Child health and maternal health care would be supervised by the medical and nursing staff of a hospital as would admissions and transfers. Home health services and neighborhood health centers would radiate from the centers, and their staffs would be accountable to key staff at the center. Such integration could be brought about by the way in which tax funds are distributed for capital construction, as under the Hospital Construction Act, by reimbursement policies, since over 42 percent of health care is covered by some tax payment,[8] or by control over the distribution of health manpower, in which direction the National Health Manpower and Training Act of 1976 has already moved, but gingerly.

A mirror image policy could deemphasize the central role of the

---

[7]Vincente Navarro, "National Health Insurance and the Strategy for Change," *Health and Society* 51, No. 2 (Spring 1973) : 224.

[8]Skolnick and Dales, "Social Welfare Expenditures"; *Social Security Bulletin* (Jan. 1977) vol. 40, no. 1, p. 15.

hospital in favor of community- and neighborhood-based delivery systems. Small-scale experiments in this direction have already been authorized through funding of neighborhood health centers (originally a part of the War on Poverty and the Office of Economic Opportunity) and of health maintenance organizations. Taken together, these two modes of service organization are a counterbalance to the hospital, although they do not replace it. What is involved in such a policy is systematic tax funding of both capital and service reimbursement to favor HMOs and neighborhood centers, as against the hospital. The result, if ever pursued for long, would produce a less unitary system than that promised by a hospital-centered policy, with many more separate delivery centers which would be difficult to integrate, but which might be more quickly responsive to variations in consumer needs and wants.

Finally, the quality of health care can be protected by a shift away from the present reliance upon each of the professions to police its own members. All the recent measures have continued to rely upon the medical profession not only to police its members' ethical practices, but also to control the use they make of hospital and other institutional resources. The entire elaborate structure of professional services review organizations which the Congress mandated to control "abuses" in the use of hospital beds still relies upon groups of physicians and other service providers, such as nurses or social workers, to monitor the use of resources in each hospital. The only significant argument over this approach was with the AMA, which wanted to have its local societies do the monitoring, while the legislation sets up outside review groups.

Housing

In the field of housing many of the conceivable policy options have been tried over the past 20 years, so that it is difficult to propose one which lies well beyond experience to date. The one which comes to mind is also the farthest removed from an overriding American cultural bias. It is perhaps best expressed in the English evolution of their housing policies in recent decades. The British government bears the major, not necessarily the sole responsibility for a stock of good and acceptable housing, available to all with moderate or average incomes. To carry out this policy, the national treasury makes money available to local governments for building such housing, either by local government directly or by various contractual arrangements entered into locally. The housing is intended for working persons, not for the poor alone, and it is administered by a department of local government at a low level of rent, to assure that the housing is within the reach of all. Subsidies are relied on to keep rent at reasonable levels. The administration is without stigma; many middle-class families live in council-rented housing, housing designed to blend into the surrounding environment. In some industrial cities the largest share of rental housing, as distinguished from detached privately owned housing, is owned and managed by local governments. In some working-class areas as much as 75 percent of all rental housing is managed as town council housing.

An extension of this program was enacted in 1947 in the Town and Country Planning Act to cope with the problem of land speculation which often produced undesirable housing or housing for the rich, with large profits to the developer, but without producing housing for moderate-income families. Under this legislation the government recaptured, by taxation, all of the increase in land value which resulted from development and which in the past went to the developer. In effect when a piece of slum property was developed into luxury housing, the value of the land rose and this difference was taxed 100 percent. By 1964, after changes in government, a 100 percent tax was found to be too restrictive, and it was replaced by a 40 percent betterment tax.

Short of such measures, the problems of housing have given rise to many less extensive policies, all rooted in the preexisting pattern of private ownership. American policy has tried public construction and management of low-cost housing for the very poor and for the aged; it has offered tax incentives of many kinds to private developers to build housing, given rent supplements to tenants to bridge the gap between low income and high rents, and offered mortgage and other incentives to individuals to enable them to buy private housing. The cumulative effect of such actions has been to assure the construction of a great deal of housing for people with adequate incomes, but it has not succeeded well in producing housing for persons of limited means. Public housing has led to ghettos of poor families, mainly those on relief, while other housing has been priced out of the reach of working low- and moderate-income families. These policies have also been troubled by continuous uncertainty and bureaucratic complexity, as several layers of government are involved at each step of the way. Responsibility is so divided that authority is confused. And when abuses are uncovered, there is a tendency to abandon programs completely on the grounds that they are now tarnished and "unworkable." Sharp start-and-stop financing periods alternate with economic ups and downs, so that a steady flow of housing construction cannot be maintained, and the needs of the poorest are overlooked. And housing for higher-income groups is often developed helter-skelter so that transportation, roads, schools, shopping, and other environmental necessities are underdeveloped.

One alternative to this situation would be the development of a policy line which seeks as goals to rationalize housing construction, rent subsidy, and land-use control into more streamlined development. Stimulus for housing construction is needed, and a national fiscal policy (i.e., on interest rates) is required. But control of land use is a local option and the application of rent subsidies can also be considered a local responsibility. It is a moot question whether these three goals should be synchronized by federal government or by local government or by both, as is the case now. To have all three dominated by federal action violates a basic predilection in American life. Perhaps more reasonable would be to leave most responsibility for housing in the hands of the local government, with federal aid but with a minimum of federal regulation over administrative details. Wherever located, some central synchronized guidance for these three interlocking facets would represent a real change.

Income Maintenance

The United States already has so complex a variety of income-supplementing programs that the policy alternatives are limited to substituting one general system (nearly impossible) or to harmonizing those which do exist. The problem is complicated by the fact that, by now, income-maintenance policy cannot be tackled in isolation. Wages and wage-related benefits (such as health insurance), plus variations in taxation, access to income-conditioned supplementary income programs must all be taken into account. To illustrate: higher negotiated wage settlements in industry involve higher prices, which reduce either the value of income programs or require significant increases in benefit payments. But increased benefits mean higher taxes to raise the money, and some of these tax increases are inevitably imposed upon workers since the sums to be raised by taxing only the very wealthy could not be sufficient to meet the benefit increases. But this taxation could reduce worker take-home pay. A large part of the work force already pays an effective tax of at least 30 percent, counting income tax, social security withholding, and the value of the employers' social security contribution, which might otherwise be paid to the worker as wages. In Sweden, with a maximum program of income and welfare protection, the blue-collar worker who gets a 5 percent increase in real income (take-home pay) must get a 32 percent increase in pay to cover the 5 percent, plus the added taxes.

Added to this maze is the question of access to income-tested benefits, such as food stamps, medical care, and housing allowances. Between 10 and 25 percent of relief-dependent families were entitled in 1972 to five or more benefits, and a family of four may have income from these benefits averaging $6500 a year.[9] This is not a large income, but it exceeds that earned by some full-time workers. The result is that the working poor either press for inclusion in these benefits, which increases the expenditure and leads to a further tax increase, or it leads to a demand by the working group to cut benefits to those who are not working. Much of this complexity flows from the long-standing American policy that links income programs to work. Virtually all money-assistance programs are contingent on the beneficiary's being in the labor force, holding a job, seeking a job, or being temporarily out of the labor force due to illness or injury. Complex

---

[9] See Joint Economic Committee of the Congress, "How Welfare Benefits are Distributed in Low Income Areas," Studies in Public Welfare, No. 6 (Washington, D.C.: U.S. Government Printing Office, 1973), pp. 86–89.

administrative rules and mechanisms are required to assure that no one receives help who is not simultaneously trying to get work, no matter what the level of unemployment is. Large bureaucracies are necessary to monitor and enforce this linkage.

A basic policy alternative would be one which breaks this work-welfare link. Conditions under which the lack of income alone would be sufficient to generate income entitlement can be specified. The attractiveness of work can then be assumed to be sufficiently strong to draw persons from relief into work when work at reasonable pay is available. Such an approach would need to accept the reality that as much as 20 percent of the population slides back and forth between work and relief regularly, not because of sloth, but because the economy has many part-time, seasonal, or low-paying jobs which must be filled. Movement between relief and work takes place by the rules of the economy and not because relief administration is able to force people into jobs they do not want to take. Under such a policy of separation, the coordination between work and relief policies can take place at legislative levels, not in program administration. Several approaches to relief policy, under such a separation, have been advanced.

President Carter's welfare reform proposals of 1977 follow this approach. They separate income programs into two great clusters, one for those out of the labor force and one for those presumed able to work. The latter are helped to find jobs, including public service jobs, plus a slightly less generous relief rate than that provided the former.

Several policy options have been advanced or are being tried in other countries. To handle the needs of those without work, something akin to a negative income tax or the family assistance plan, proposed in the Nixon years, could be revived. Under it, all families earning less than a given sum of money would receive a payment sufficient to bring their income up to a predetermined level. Such a policy would make more general the policy embedded in the supplementary security income program whereby the aged and disabled, who are presumably out of the labor force are assured a minimum federal fixed income. Aside from the emotional reaction of some legislators to extending such a guarantee to those on Aid for Dependent Children, mostly black unmarried mothers, the plan was first introduced at too low a national level, $2400 a year. But to raise the minimum level significantly would increase costs greatly and lead to political objections that the tax level would be high. Even if such a negative income tax uses a sliding scale with benefits dropping as income rises, it is necessary to pitch the final cut-off substantially above the present relief level to avoid the disincentive which now plagues the welfare system—a 100 percent tax on earnings, every dollar earned while on relief only replacing a relief dollar, without an improvement in income.

This grand design is also flawed because it does not take into account differential needs of families due to illness, disability, age, and the like.

Such a policy could produce still another income program, but it cannot replace all existing supplementary programs. Moreover, difficulty of replacement is not limited to family variations. Some current programs, such as unemployment insurance, provide relatively higher benefits, and persons protected by these more generous programs are unlikely to accept a lesser substitute, even if more simplified.

A less complex policy involves the federal government's assuming full responsibility for all income maintenance, including the costs of AFDC, general relief, and Medicaid. To work, such a program could not merely underwrite the costs of existing state programs, which vary widely as to eligibility and payment levels. In the end, federalization would involve either a federal income floor, averaged for all states, or the case-by-case fixing of budgets by the federal government, which would be impossible to administer from Washington. A more feasible policy would be the adoption of a federal floor for all relief, especially for AFDC, which the states might supplement if they wished. A reasonable policy would be to separate slowly the responsibilities of state and federal governments and the accompanying control of money which has been associated with our present three-tier partnership, each level of government being involved financially and administratively every step of the way. In this, the federal government would be accountable for maintaining a floor under income in a means-tested program; the states would be free to supplement above the floor if their state culture, financial status, or political alignment called for supplementation and if they could raise the additional funds.

Another approach would be to extend the policy, already in force, of mandating various supplementary allowances, such as food stamps and housing allowances. Such allowances are attached to particular problems and to specific populations with those problems. They have the defect of being very much like relief in kind—the old grocery basket concept of charity—which was abandoned in the 1930s. They have the advantage of permitting a build-up of well-targeted programs to achieve specific aims, not the general income level of all persons, although that may well be the final result. Medicaid, extended to working persons with incomes too low to afford good medical care, can improve attention to health needs. Similar allowances for housing can improve housing conditions. And so on.

Still another approach involves a different kind of partnership between government and the private sector, at least as regards that majority of the population in the labor force at any time. A two-tiered benefit or pension system has been proposed, at least as regards retirement. In it government protection provides a floor, but labor/management and other industrial contracts add a tier of benefits to the floor. Federal steps to guarantee that private pension-plan benefits are vested in workers so that they do not lose protection when they change jobs, and reinsurance in case a company becomes bankrupt, are steps in this direction. Given the pervasiveness of health protection in industrial labor contracts, the two-tiered system could possibly be extended to medical care at least, as well as to retirement.

The United States is fortunate in that it already has in place a great variety of income programs. That they are confusing may be only a small price to pay for taking care of a great many distinctive needs. We are in a position to reexamine all of them to see which provides the most satisfying option for the next stage of development; and these programs permit choices in a number of different directions: federalization, partnership, a simplified income floor, decentralization of federal authority, or extension of categorical aids.

Aging

The aged already have programs in advance of the rest of the population—retirement income guaranteed, compulsory health insurance, and housing assistance. It is, however, possible to look at national policy for the aged beyond the simple level of income security. The central dilemma of the aged, other than income security, is the role they fill in modern society. At the present time national policy is based squarely on the premise that persons aged 65 years should be out of the labor force; insurance as well as employment regulations clearly are intended to enforce this view. In fact, liberalization of retirement insurance policies has increasingly encouraged workers to retire even earlier, at age 60 or 62. Labor contracts make it easy for workers to retire at 60 if they wish; and many federal and state military and civil service regulations encourage retirement as early as age 50, after from 20 to 25 years of service.

An alternative policy may be forced into our consciousness by the demographic character of our population. About 10 percent of the population are over 65. If trends continue, it is expected that the population ratio of the aged will rise to 15 percent in some parts of the country within the next decade or two and to 20 percent over a longer time span. The health of this population has improved, not so much through medicine as through public health and generally higher income levels, which produce better nutrition and better living conditions. If we add together all dependent persons, that is, children under the age of 18 and persons over the age of 65, we find that perhaps half of the population works to produce all the goods for the other half. Thus far our economy has performed reasonably well, in large part due to increased productivity, mechanization, and high technology, but it is not unreasonable to expect that the rate of productivity increase will slow down. And if we continue to have a larger percent of persons out of the labor force (the aged and children, as they stay in school longer), then the strains on the economy will begin to show. They have already begun to show in our social security system, where these very trends have required a higher and higher level of taxation on the work force, so much so that complaints and creaking in the machinery have already made themselves heard.

A major new policy shift could be taken, which would be consistent with the long-time trend in American attitudes, namely, a relaxation of the current strict retirement regulations. Small steps have already been taken, by permitting nominal earnings after retirement under social security. A more significant shift would encourage the continued employment of older persons where they wish to work and where employers wish to employ, them, without penalty to either party. Withdrawal of retirement benefits could be phased in relation to the amount of work time or benefits could be wholly drawn even if work continues in some modified form. Employer taxes could be readjusted to favor continued work or tax legislation could encourage employers to begin a phased and extended program of retirement, beginning at much earlier years, say, age 50, but continuing to, say, 70 or 75, good health permitting. Such a major shift would probably depend upon a national conviction that the available work force is not large enough for national needs and that it is in the national interest to increase the work force rather than reduce it, as we now do. Such a policy obviously depends on the availability of sufficient jobs for all to be employed, a situation which does not now prevail.

Alternatively, attention could be turned to many tasks which are now considered valuable, but not economic in the sense of fitting into our goods-production economy. Building and maintaining a pleasant environment in city and suburb, into which homes and shops can fit, information services to help all of us thread our way through the maze of organization, consumer information, and protection services, monitoring the working of chronic illness facilities like nursing homes, attention to the social needs of the home-bound disabled or aged—all come to mind as tasks which older persons, with health and interest, could perform for our general well-being. They might even be engaged to staff much of our election and campaign processes. Even if additional funds are used to provide modest supplemental salaries to retired persons, the performance of such tasks would do much to enrich community and national life.

Children

The long history of the United States Children's Bureau has produced, directly or indirectly, a wide range of services directed at children's needs: health care and education. However, the bulk of public policy is oriented to programs which serve families, not children as such, although children are the intended beneficiaries of many family-oriented programs. One long-advocated policy is that of children's allowances, intended to relieve families of economic burdens and thus to improve the condition of child rearing. Children's allowances would, in effect, be paid to *any family* with children. These would not be means-tested, but could be limited to the second child and those coming after or to only a few children in the case of very large families. Such allowances have also been used to either encourage larger families or to discourage too large families, but the long-term results of such incentives are unclear.

More relevant to today's situation is the issue of day care. With so many mothers of small children in the work force, national policy can either encourage the evolution of supplements for the mothers' care in the form of day-care centers or it can try to discourage mothers from working by disincentives to keep them out of the labor force. The latter course seems against the strong trend of this century, during which the liberation of women from legal and family constraints has led to a long-term entry into paid employment for women from all economic classes; it is, therefore, unlikely to succeed. Doubt as to its success is increased by the fact that so many mothers work to bring in a second income as a means of raising family income and economic well-being. Undoubtedly this increase in the work force and in family income has much to do with maintaining purchasing power and with the continuing consumption of goods which, in turn, provides the stimulus for increased production and for employment for men and women alike.

Day-care centers, the alternative, seem a much more reasonable policy. During World War II this was the national policy and a national network of such centers was financed with federal aid. The network was effectively dismantled at the end of the war, although many proprietary centers survived, largely for families with adequate income. During the late 1960s a means-tested measure was taken to revive such a policy, when women on relief, who could work, were trained and then assured supplementation to pay for child care where earnings were insufficient. However, this remained a relief-tainted program. The alternative national policy would be to support the development of a national network of day-care centers for children from families of all income levels. Sliding fee scales could assure some equity between those who could pay some of the costs and those who could not. A less discriminating policy would simply develop these centers as a public utility for all mothers needing them.

Some variations on this theme have been tried in a small way. Industry could be encouraged, by tax incentives or subsidy, to provide for day-care for its employees. This option is difficult to execute for the large number of persons engaged in businesses too small to undertake such programs, even with tax aid. Alternatively, the centers could become a part of the public school system, whereby schools would serve children below present school age. A start in this direction has been taken in the opening of kindergartens in Head Start and in other preschool classes in some parts of the country. The costs of local education have recently made it harder for school systems to add a new function, but a national policy could help overcome this difficulty.

A more troublesome question would have to be resolved as part of any such policy. Some proponents see the centers as places to begin early childhood education, while others see them as child-caring centers, with early education secondary. Which emphasis is finally selected determines the nature and intensity of staffing patterns and therefore the costs and manpower requirements.

DIRECTIONAL ALTERNATIVES

It may be clear by now that a number of policy options are available as alternatives to those now in effect. Few of them are so far removed from American traditions as to be impossible in the near future. They represent alternative policy options for either major political party. If any are followed, consideration would also have to be given to certain aspects of any policy choice beyond the level of problem-specific or program-specific areas. A few of these have already been touched upon and we will mention here four more such policy choices.

Personal Disposable Income Versus Government Expenditure

The United States still has some way to go before its governmental income as a percentage of the GNP equals that of other advanced industrial states (see Table 14). For example, in 1971 the United States average was lower than that of six European countries, although the American performance is better than many critics of American social policy realize. What this means, simply, is that there is a choice between how much money should be left to individuals to spend as they wish and how much they should pay to the government in order to provide for their needs without recourse to the uncertainties of the marketplace. There is clearly a contradiction in citizens' views on this matter, as seen in public opinion polls during the 1976 presidential campaign. (A significant majority of citizens polled wanted to have less government and lower taxes, while simultaneously wanting more public action to provide medical care, housing, etc.) They want to have as much income as they can get to spend as they wish, but when a crisis arises in health or unemployment, they want a government program to fall back on. Somehow, public policy must find an acceptable mean between these two extremes. One policy tilts in the direction of private income (the American tendency until the recent past) and the other in the direction of more public guarantee.

TABLE 14

Tax Revenue as a Percentage of Gross National Product, 1955–1971
Figures in percents

	Mid 1950s	Late 1960s	1971	Increase 1955–1971
United States	25.4	27.4	27.8	2.4
Great Britain	28.1	34.6	35.7	7.6
West Germany	32.4	33.7	34.5	2.1
Netherlands	28.5	38.7	42.2	13.7
France	32.9	35.8	35.6	2.7
Sweden	29.1	39.6	41.8	12.7

SOURCE: Richard Goode, "The Tax Burden in the U.S. and Other Countries," Annals of the American Academy of Political and Social Science, No. 379 (Summer 1968): 85–87; Organization for Economic Cooperation and Development, Revenue Statistics of OECD Member Countries, 1965–1971, (Paris: OECD, 1973), p. 25.

It is sometimes argued that we can have both of these wishes at the maximum, but here common sense, the attitudes of the citizens as reflected in opinion polls and how they vote, and an examination of economic data indicate that both cannot be secured to the maximum. Even an expropriating level of taxation of wealth or industrial profits would not yield enough funds to provide full government security while maintaining high take-home pay for workers, with little taxation.

Action to Equalize Income Versus Marketplace Rewards

Another related policy choice is between government action to equalize incomes and reliance on the economic marketplace to reward persons according to their contribution to the economy. Programs directed toward other specific problems do create a certain amount of equalization: minimum wage legislation and income policies determine how low the economic floor can be permitted to drop and civil rights legislation acts against racial, religious, or other discrimination. But even with these generally equalizing or equity-producing efforts, a wide gap exists between high and low income recipients in this society and, for that matter, in every other society, including the socialist and communist. The differences among societies, to the extent they exist, lie in the size of the spread between high and low.

If a policy of giving the same income to everyone in the same condition (i.e., same family composition), is quite unattainable, it is still possible to use social policy to try to smooth out glaring inequities, as we have done historically. A policy designed mainly to raise the income floor for the poorest families relieves distress, but retains relative poverty, that is, the spread does not diminish since the higher income rises as does the floor. Alternative to this would be a more assertive role by government to redistribute income in a way designed to reduce the spread. We have not really attempted direct control of the spread to date, although we have many examples of floor raising. The family assistance plan and social security, among others, involve taking funds from all, but returning relatively more to the lowest-income families at the expense of higher-income families. The progressive income tax, first enacted in 1916, goes farthest in this kind of redistribution, although its effect has been eroded by the slow addition of many preferences and loopholes which favor moderate- and upper-income families.

Nonetheless, we have seen a slight redistribution among large groups, even though the spread between individuals has not been much affected. Between 1964 and 1969 the lowest fifth of the families (in income terms) increased their incomes, while those in the highest fifth decreased theirs, a situation slightly altered between 1969 and 1974. For unrelated individuals the lowest fifth increased its share in both periods while the highest fifth decreased its share. (See Table 15). Since we are dealing in population aggregates, it is worth noting that in these periods the mean number of children per family in the lowest fifth dropped more rapidly than it did

TABLE 15
Percent Income Distribution by Quintiles, 1964–1974

Category	1964	1969	1974
Families			
Lowest fifth	5.1	5.6	5.4
Second fifth	12.0	12.4	12.0
Third fifth	17.7	17.7	17.6
Fourth fifth	24.0	23.7	24.1
Fifth fifth	41.2	40.6	41.0.
Unrelated Individuals			
Lowest fifth	2.5	3.3	4.0
Second fifth	7.1	7.8	8.9
Third fifth	12.8	13.8	14.5
Fourth fifth	24.4	24.3	24.2
Fifth fifth	53.2	50.9	48.5

SOURCE: *Sar Levitan and Robert Taggart*, The Promise of Greatness *(Cambridge, Mass.: Harvard University Press, 1976), p. 246.*

among the upper fifth. Also, the growth over the decade in the number of single-parent families was marked, meaning that, for an unknown number of units, a father's separate income could have been calculated along with that of the mother's and children's incomes to combine into a total income for the lower fifth much larger than these figures suggest. Similarly, in this period supplementary benefits in the form of Medicaid, housing allowances, and food stamps were increased. If one estimates that only a third of these in-kind supplements went to the families with the lowest fifth of income, then their real, as against cash, income would be increased by 40 percent.[10] All in all, this very slight reduction in income spread suggests that a policy for a more rapid systematic reduction is not wholly unthinkable.

Federal Versus State and Local Responsibility

Despite much rhetoric decrying the loss of local authority, the long-term trend has been for citizens and local governments to shift more and more responsibility to the federal level. The latest example is the demand by cities and states that the federal government assume full responsibility for public assistance. A reasonable alternative to this trend would be a redistribution of responsibility among the various levels of government. Our history has so intertwined these levels as to make the task most difficult. The trend to centralization required extraordinary convolutions of legalisms to secure federal financial participation without violating the Constitution. As a result, except for social security, most welfare programs are nominally state and locally planned, but all levels are involved in funding,

[10]See Sar Levitan and Robert Taggart, *The Promise of Greatness*, pp. 246–247.

and state regulations and procedures must conform to federal rules. To disentangle the web would require the specification of at least some social services as wholly state or local responsibilities and others as wholly federal. This would involve a clean division of fiscal responsibility commensurate with taxing power, so that functions considered to be state or local would be wholly funded by state or local taxes. Some steps have been taken in this direction. Supplementary security income leaves funding and regulation of base income for the aged and handicapped to the federal government. Supplementary payments above the minimum are a state responsibility, although the administrative responsibilities are still rather tangled. Medicare for the aged is wholly a federal obligation, whereas unemployment insurance is administered by the state with federal help. A division of duties vis-à-vis housing has already been discussed. Federalization of AFDC could be traded off against the states' assumption of full responsibility for other personal social services, not financial in nature, such as home care or day care for children and the elderly or the disabled.

Decentralization, a concept so appealing to American ears, cannot be made real without some such devolution of authority, accountability, and financial burden, but the present situation in state and local taxing power makes their assumption of financial responsibility difficult. All that an alternative policy could work for is a slow untangling of the thread of association and partnership. Not to do so bespeaks a policy of continuation of present policy, which means at least three layers of administrative decision making for each program and confusion about the boundaries of local responsibility.

Pay-As-You-Go Versus Deferred Payment Social Welfare System

Retirement insurance, the bedrock of our current welfare policy, is a good example of the choice that must be made between a pay-as-you-go or a deferred payment system. At present persons currently employed pay in taxes enough to pay for the benefits earned by people who are now retired. But inflation and rising expectations introduce serious tension into the system. The illusion is maintained that each person has contributed and therefore has earned his benefits, this is true, except for the fact that the money each individual pays in does not pay for his or her own benefits; what each person pays in pays for benefits of those already retired. This is further complicated by a tendency for each generation to anticipate its own retirement by increasing the benefit structure while its is working, not realizing, perhaps, that the payments for the increased benefits are made by the next generation of workers. To proceed in any other fashion would require that social insurance be recast in full insurance terms or "funding" payments, meaning that payments made by workers would be invested in a fund solely for the use of future payments. Today amounts in excess of one year's payments go into general funds and are spent for current government operations, as are other kinds of taxes.

The alternative to this unpleasant procedure is to subject the level of future retirement payments to whatever future generations of workers will approve via appropriations from general revenues. This strategy has been urged by many critics, on the assumption that the political pressure to make higher rather than lower levels of appropriations will safeguard the rights of retired workers.

Thus we see that, at both the general level of policy and the problem-specific and program-specific levels, there are real conceptual alternatives. But each alternative presents policy makers with troublesome choices between valid claims made by different segments of the citizenry. These tensions tend to prevent adoption of significant shifts in policy from one administration to another, but rather encourage slow incremental changes, each building on the preceding policy consensus. Still, the more powerful alternatives are there, to be adopted if there is political will and strength.

THE RADICAL ALTERNATIVES

In the 1960s a new line of more radical analysis of social welfare policy began to emerge in the United States. The alternatives derived from this analysis have not been advanced as concrete proposals for quick adoption or even as subjects for contemporary policy debates of national government. Rather, they represent a radically different way of perceiving the social problems of the times. Some of them are derived from Marxist analyses of society; others represent a desire to simplify the modern condition and to create human-scale, face-to-face, self-help forms of social organization to replace national shaped bureaucracies.[11] In some respects, they purport to avoid the awkward choices which are embedded in the conventional alternatives just discussed.

The best-articulated radical alternatives do not usually deal with specific social or welfare policies, in the sense of guiding principles linked to the execution of specific programs. Instead, these alternatives outline a view about the causes of social and personal difficulties, that they are mainly due to distortions of a capitalist society in which exploitation of many by a few is inevitable, no matter how much effort is made to obscure that exploitation by palliative measures of liberal social welfare. This viewpoint argues that social work (or welfare) as now organized is not benign, that what is good for the agency supercedes what is good for the client, that social workers do not "run" social agencies, and that client problems

---

[11]This section touches only slightly on the subject. See such texts as: Frances Piven and Richard Cloward, *Regulating the Poor* (New York: Pantheon Books, 1971); Roy Bailey and Mike Brake, eds., *Radical Social Work* (New York: Pantheon Books, 1975); Bill Jordan, *Paupers*, Boston: Routledge & Kegan Paul, 1973); Jeffrey Galper, *Radical Social Work, The Politics of Social Services* (Englewood Cliffs, N.J.: Prentice-Hall, 1976). For an earlier period, see especially all issues of the periodical *Social Work Today*.

are not psychological or inherent in their personal defects. Social welfare in America is characterized as a set of institutions which attempt, ineffectually, to resolve contradictions between consumption and production. It is assumed that such contradictions would not arise in a socialist society or that they would be resolved differently.

Case data is presented about the defects in present welfare operations, including the ways in which agency policies injure or neglect clients, the ways in which agency rules coopt workers into anticlient attitudes, and the failure to eliminate income differentials among all classes. From this evidence, the approach concludes that the existing sociopolitical-economic order must be replaced by a socialist society. Therefore, all actions should be directed toward this replacement, or this revolution. Elaboration of this policy stance is often couched in political-strategic terms, not in programmatic terms. The transfer of power and the upending of social control is seen as the outcome.

Another radical alternative stops short of an explicit political alternative, but urges the view that clients are claimants on social institutions, not helpless beneficiaries. As such, the policy stance seems to be one of stressing client strengths, not weakness. All things must be done which will help clients learn how to express and claim their rights from resistive social agencies. This approach differs from the more articulate Marxist analyses in that it stops at getting agencies to respond to needs (at least as far as the literature goes), whereas the Marxist view sees such demands only as pressures which should ultimately lead to the dissolution of these agencies and their surrounding social structure and the replacement of both agency and society by new socialist forms.

The articulation of such radical alternatives does not fit readily into the framework of analysis used thus far, for at least two reasons. First, and most seriously, the radical analyses enunciate a very general policy stance, the replacement of a capitalist by a socialist society. The explicit character of socialist policies has not yet been presented in terms of specific problems, such as programs for an income system, for the mentally or chronically physically ill, or for the delinquent. If such approaches no longer claim that a socialist society eliminates such human difficulties, neither do they present the skeletal outline of how a program and a policy for such areas would differ from current capitalist approaches.

The concrete discussions to date have focused on two levels only: political strategy to transform society and individual social-worker practice within that strategy. Although programmatic and national policy details are not available for review, it is worth noting the kind of practices being urged on social workers. From this point of view, the social worker's function is to instruct clients in the radical or Marxist analysis of their situation so that they may (1) understand their alienation as caused by capitalist exploitation) and learn the sociopolitical reality which shapes their lives; (2) build up their self-esteem and resist hegemony (i.e., resist being submerged into the norm); (3) acquire personal and collective capacities to transform that reality into socialism by practical struggles, which would eliminate the need for "helping" social welfare institutions.

This is a sketchy summary of a few key arguments, omitting the details which make such analyses provocative. Whatever evaluation of their solutions we may make, they are valuable in a consideration of alternatives in that they force us to confront failures in present policies and programs and to examine the cause of the failures. The case descriptions are poignant and moving as they expose agency behaviors in which desperate human needs are distorted or ignored by staffs caught up in the crazy quilt of programs, regulations, and attitudes.[12] Unfortunately, for the purposes of social policy analysis, a great void still exists between the preamble goal (or policy stance) of building socialism and the case-by-case social worker practice injunctions published by the radical social welfare writers. The preamble goal shares much of the passion and symbolic generality of the American Constitution and Declaration of Independence, while the case critique echoes similar criticisms launched by social workers over the past hundred years. The difference between the more radical and the "liberal" alternatives lies in underlying causal analysis: is socialism the essential prerequisite to improvement? If it is, the explicit social welfare content of that alternative, as seen in proposed sectoral policies and programs (not only in attitudes) remains to be launched.

ADDITIONAL READINGS

The more familiar policy options are discussed in references listed at the end of the preceding chapters. However, there has recently emerged a small body of literature which defines itself as "radical social welfare." The following are a few representative references.

Bailey, Roy, and Mike Brake. *Radical Social Work.* New York: Pantheon Books, 1975.

Cloward, Richard, and Frances Piven. *Regulating the Poor.* New York: Pantheon Books, 1971.

Galper, Jeffrey. *The Politics of Social Services.* Englewood Cliffs, N.J.: Prentice-Hall, 1976.

---

[12]See, among others, case descriptions by Frances Piven and Richard Cloward in Bailey and Brake, eds., *Radical Social Work;* and in Jordan, *Paupers.*

TOOLS OF POLICY ANALYSIS: PREPARING FOR A POLICY PROFESSION

Until recent times science and technology have only indirectly affected the process by which public policy has been shaped; they have not, when directly used by policymakers, affected the setting of goals or the selection of guiding principles. Of course, science and technology have transformed many aspects of contemporary living, and these changes have created problems with which policymakers have had to grapple, using primarily the processes of political exchange and maneuver. The first major federal effort at technical policy planning was the creation in the 1930s of the National Resources Board which sought to derive from data it assembled new ways to deal with pressing economic, social, and political issues. But it was not until the end of World War II that there emerged a significant scientific interest in the exact tools which might be developed to help governments deal with national concerns. Stimulated by physical and social scientists' concern over nuclear policy, new attention was paid to the social needs of the postwar world which in time led to the proliferation of federal and state programs for human welfare. This in turn led eventually to the application by business and administrative students of their tools for "scientific" management of large enterprises.[1] Science and business both contributed to the development of social policy planning technique.

---

[1]For an interesting review of the steady, if slow, march of the U.S. government toward formal planning, see Otis Graham, *Towards a Planned Society* (New York: Oxford University Press, 1976).

THE FUNCTION OF PLANNING TECHNOLOGY

We have concentrated thus far on tracing patterns of societal norms, public policy, and social policy. If, as argued to this point, various elements of the national government sometimes mount a sustained effort to shift the boundaries of societal norms in order to move in some new direction, then the tools which are available for use in the effort need to be understood. The nature of the means by which change can be effected is the basis of a conflict between what could be called the rational and the political views of the processes of government. The rational view holds that certain techniques can be brought to bear on decision making which will displace political power plays. The political view argues that a democratic society depends upon the continuous expression of citizens' wants in a contest between varying opinions on how to meet these wants. The political view sees the rational approach as too autocratic and technocratic and expresses a lack of confidence in scientific means, while the rational approach sees political mechanisms as too emotional, erratic, and unstable. The truth probably lies somewhere between these extremes. Planning technology does contribute objective input to decision making and leads to more comprehensive approaches to problem solving, whereas political mechanisms invariably leads to more subjective, compromise solutions, since bargaining among competing interest groups lies at the heart of that process. A blend of the two is undoubtedly in the making and therefore a better understanding of the technical tools now available is necessary.

Discussions of policy tools often mix administrative and management devices with techniques useful in framing policies of a general nature. The following discussion will be limited, to the extent possible, to a few techniques or tools which are especially useful to policymakers who do not wish to rely exclusively on managing political forces to secure action on intuitively derived policies. Such tools are intended to complement political power with empirical evidence and rational analysis.

Policy tools, at their present stage of development, can do little to influence the underlying aims or broadest purposes of government. One party or administration may be committed to government intervention for the well-being of its citizens or for redistribution of income, while another party may be committed to containment of the national state and the undisturbed operation of the marketplace. Such fundamental guides to public action are derived from the backgrounds and histories of persons and institutions which hold these views and are seldom altered by technical devices.

At best, technology may be useful in helping policymakers or political leaders choose the more effective means with which to carry out the underlying purposes. The federal government can be more or less active in welfare by administering programs itself, by fostering administration by other governmental jurisdictions, or encouraging voluntary efforts. It can act directly by mandating services, or it can act indirectly by altering the flow of its funds in one direction or another, without administrative control. It can act to redistribute income by manipulation of tax rates, by control of incomes and prices, or by providing compensatory, in-kind services to some part of the population. These alternative means, by which first principles of policy are carried out, are another level of guiding principles of policy, not administrative devices, and they can be influenced by technolgy.

Some technical means now available also serve to influence, albeit slowly, the underlying aims of policy by uncovering needs or potential trouble spots in advance of public awareness. If reliable, such advance knowledge could conceivably affect the underlying aims of political parties. Certainly in the 1930s the economic decline, which was not anticipated, led to a major shift in readiness to accept active federal intervention in hitherto private or local governmental domains. Participation in World War II had a similar effect. Untested is the conclusion that, if these events had been anticipated earlier, the shift in direction could have been introduced sooner. We can assume only that earlier identification of impending disaster might alter the tempo and shape of policy evolution.

The tools to be considered are those which are believed, at least by their proponents, to be useful in helping policymakers decide the best use of their resources to further the basic purpose of their policies. In this sense resources usually means allocation of funds, but the definition need not be so circumscribed; regulations, reassignment of personnel, and taxation are other resources with which government can effect its ends. The uses and limits of the following mechanisms will be discussed.

1. Assessment of the state of a system: needs identification, systems analysis, opinion polls, advocacy, surveys, social indicators

2. Decision making: program planning and budgeting systems, cost benefit analyses

3. Prediction: demographic projection, simulation, econometric projection

4. Outcome evaluation and research

5. Logical analysis

ASSESSMENT OF THE STATE OF A SYSTEM

The oldest and most widely used device for social welfare purposes is that of needs assessment. It is, however, a mechanism which lacks sharp definition and has a quite primitive technology to draw upon. It is full of subjective biases which each assessor brings to data and which alter what the assessor considers a valid "need." At its most primitive level, need assessment takes the form of simply adding up the number of persons in a situation perceived as a problem: number of persons with incomes below a given level, number of infant deaths, number of dilapidated houses, and the like. Such evidence may be useful in attracting a policy-maker's attention or in mobilizing political support, but it tells little if anything about what should be done, or the priority to be assigned to each distress, or the relationships among them.

A somewhat more sophisticated version was developed in Philadelphia in 1956, using the title "needs/resource assessment." [2] Numbers are counted as in the simpler version, but types of difficulty are first classified as to whether they involve the adjustment capacity of individuals or the social, educational, or cultural development of groups in the population. Then each problem is weighted to indicate the proportion of persons affected and the severity of the distress. For example, a rare fatal disease will be weighted more heavily as to severity than one which has transient effects on many thousands, but will be less heavily weighted as to the pro-portion of persons affected. To this is added a weighted estimate as to the proven efficacy of programs of intervention to deal with each distress: a serious condition for which there is no known effective remedy will be less heavily weighted than one for which there is a proven remedy. The sum of these calculations is intended to produce a numerical ranking of prob-lems and remedies which can help in the allocation and direction of resources. The process is encumbered by the subjectivity of the weighting, but it at least places in the open the subjective kinds of judgment which are made every day.

A much more sophisticated methodology is that of systems analysis.[3] In its simplified form, this requires that policy makers first enunciate their basic objectives. Data are then assembled about persons, organizations, and programs known to be involved in this objective in any way. It is assumed that these components constitute a "system" of parts so inter-related that changes in the behavior of one will affect the behavior of the others. These data are organized to show where people move through the provider system, how the units handle them, and what happens to them. At its present stage, this device requires a large investment in data gathering so that a population of consumers can be identified and tracked as they move through various provider units. It produces little evidence as to whether the problems of users are "solved," but does give useful insight into whether existing providers are at least receiving and helping persons

[2] See Health and Welfare Council, Inc., "Needs/Resources Study," mimeo-graphed, 1956; also Joseph Lagy, *Priority Determination Plans*, Vancouver: Community Chests and Councils of Greater Vancouver Area, mimeographed, 1960.

[3] For discussion of this approach, see: Phillip Boffey, "Systems Analysis," *Science* (November 24, 1967), pp. 1020–1030; Alfred Blumstein, "Systems Analysis and the Criminal Justice System," *Annals of the American Academy of Political and Social Science* 374 (November 1967) : 92–100.

presenting problems and whether there are bottlenecks or gaps in access. It relies on a conviction that if service providers receive and retain consumers, then the consumers' needs are being met adequately.

Opinion polls or the accumulation of data about consumer wants through specialized advocacy groups represent another, half-technical, half-political means of assessing the state of a community or its welfare system. Opinion polls do provide some insight into what citizens and consumers consider important at the time they are polled, but their views about what should be done are strongly biased by the kinds of questions put to them and by the way questions are phrased. Respondents are also limited by what they have experienced, so that the process is unlikely to turn up clues to alternative courses of action. Respondents with unmet medical needs are unlikely to suggest new ways of delivering medical care, although they may express preferences between existing arrangements. More serious than any of these defects is the doubt whether responses of this kind are equated with actions which consumers may take. Except in the electoral process itself, where opinion and votes may be congruent, the match between opinion and action is poor. Respondents may say they "need" a neighborhood health center, but may not utilize it if one is established.

Advocacy groups may mobilize evidence about any number of "needs" or consumer wants, but they are inevitably focused on specific problems— the very poor who need income, the disabled with specific handicaps. Although unmet distress can be made more visible, relationships among needs cannot be determined by such means.

A final tool for purposes of assessing the state of a system is social indicators.[4] Indicators consist of quantitative data that serve as indexes to important conditions in society. Ideally they provide a picture of both the nature and the state of a system or of a society, a picture sufficiently standardized to permit measurement of changes over time. Constructing indicators is difficult because many phenomena about which trend data are desired are not readily quantified. Further, there are biases about statistical data chosen for measurement, and technological and social changes continuously introduce new factors which must be added to fill out the picture but which erode the possibility of measurement over time. Indicators have also been taken by some to imply a statement of policy or a commitment to a particular policy rather than being an objective measure of trends. A rise in divorce can be taken to mean that family life is weakened and that we should reverse the trend, but, equally, it can mean more freedom for women, which should be helped along. Indicators, to be effective, must measure the same phenomenon over a long period of time,

---

[4]See Raymond Bauer, *Social Indicators* (Cambridge, Mass.: MIT Press, 1966), chaps. 1, 2; Eleanor Sheldon and Wilbert Moore, *Indicators of Social Change* (New York: Russell Sage Foundation, 1968); and Judith Wins de Neufuille, *Social Indicators and Public Policy* (New York: Elsevier, 1975).

so that changes can be identified. But in our present elementary stage of evolution our understanding changes frequently, so that pressures build to change the bases of what is being measured, in effect eroding the very utility that indicators promised.

Despite these difficulties, indicators are constantly being elaborated, and are used by public officials to sense the direction that the past has taken in order to work out the future. A case in point is the indicator of poverty or of employment. Base lines have been developed to measure the long-term movement of employment, but they have had to be re-examined regularly as uncontrolled social forces change the nature of the labor force. For example, if we take into account the entrance of house-wives and teenagers into the work force, we seem to be sliding back in our capacity to employ all who want to work. If we were to adhere to earlier criteria about work, we would find that the number of jobs has increased over the years so that proportionately many more are now employed than was true twenty, thirty, or fifty years ago. Both indicators are correct, but leave to policymakers the dilemma of deciding if we should be satisfied with trends and keep to past lines or be vastly discouraged and adopt some radically different orientation. Such difficulties need not be discouraging, for they force all of us to consider how we can continuously work for greater perfection in our social order; but they do not give guidance as to what course of action will lead to that end. All of these devices, in effect, tell policymakers whence we have come and at what point we have arrived.

DECISION MAKING

Decision-making techniques were first developed in industry and in public administration where the directors of formal or of single-purpose organizations had to make choices affecting the survival of the organiza-tion. In time the principles underlying these administrative processes be-come elaborated so that they could be applied, at least experimentally, to larger systems, such as the national government or the work of a single government department.

Program planning and budgeting systems (PPBS) represents one of the best publicized attempts to apply a specific systematic process to policy development.[5] The system is simple conceptually, but extraordinarily com-plex and difficult to use in real situations. Simply put, persons sitting in central policy-making positions, such as the Office of Management and

---

[5]See David Novick, ed., *Program Budgeting* (Cambridge, Mass.: Harvard University Press, 1965), for a discussion of the original application of the con-cept; and Robert Mayer, Robert Moroney, and Robert Morris, *Centrally Planned Change* (Urbana: University of Illinois Press, 1974), pp. 163–169, for an assessment of its limitations. Also, Elizabeth Drew, "HEW Grapples With PPBS," *The Public Interest*, No. 3 (Summer 1967).

Budget or the Department of Health, Education, and Welfare, set in motion a long-term process whereby the units accountable to them can organize their allocations and activities in the most efficient manner to achieve broad objectives. For those in the central position the system also provides continuous feedback of data so that they can know how subordinate units are behaving and if they are moving toward the general objectives laid down by policy. The process forces all, from the top to the bottom of a system, to be more and more explicit about what they are trying to achieve and to synchronize their efforts. To decision makers at the top, it gives data about duplication, contradiction, and omission in the use of resources. It may not of itself create policy, but it provides a better basis for deciding, what gets attention.

There are five major steps in PPBS:

1. Appraisal and comparison of various government activities in terms of their contribution to national objectives. For example, Aid for Dependent Children, social security for dependents of disabled beneficiaries, and the Veterans Administration all operate vast programs providing funds for children. The system purports to encourage looking at all of these in relation to each other and in the context of some objective, be it health or economic security of children.

2. Determination of how given objectives can be obtained with a minimum expenditure of resources. In the example just given, duplications in benefits, gaps in the organization of services and other inefficiencies can be revealed in examining the relationship of the work of the major agencies. Such examination thus could produce a different pattern of service and expenditure in each agency so that it reinforces the work of the others without duplication.

3. Projection of government activities over an adequate time period. The system assumes that altering programs takes time, since vast bureaucracies cannot function while undergoing rapid change. The lead time in federal appropriations requires at least three years between the initial work on an agency budget and the time the budget will be acted on by the Congress; and, for practical purposes, a four- or five-year lead time is more reasonable.

4. Comparison of the relative contributions of private and public activities to national objectives. The private sector, including business, philanthropic agencies, the family, and informal associations, plays a crucial role in achieving any objective of government. The relationship between the two sectors needs to be thought through.

5. Revision of programs, budgets, and objectives in the light of experience and of changing circumstances.

These steps are clearly conceptual in nature and to become operational require specific and extensive data. Much of the early effort to introduce PPBS was devoted to inserting a new information system into a wide variety of agencies so that information from each could be made compatible with that provided by the rest. This introduced marked strain in the work of government agencies, since each had to continue old data patterns while trying to add new ones, thus contributing to the exploding volume of paper passing in government operations. Once data systems are installed, complex computerized devices become necessary to absorb, store, and permit rapid retrieval of the data for policy purposes. It is not surprising that the early efforts to introduce this device in the federal government led to enormous strain and some displacement of effort away from program purposes and toward data-assembling almost for its own sake. Less time or energy was left, in the short term, for analyzing or acting on any conclusions which the data suggested.

The PPBS contains another defect characteristic of many technical management processes; a risk of deflecting attention from objectives to process, even after data processes are in place. In HEW, for example, PPBS led to the current emphasis in federal policy on coordination of the work of several agencies. While coordination is clearly necessary, it does not necessarily achieve the objectives for which programs were first installed. The balance between achieving objectives and coordinating activity is little understood, and PPBS has not yet resolved the tension between the two.

Cost benefit analysis is one aspect of PPBS which antedated it in evolution.[6] It is an economic instrument designed to measure the balance between the costs of a particular course of action and the benefits which may be derived from it. Its great usefulness lies in its capacity to produce a comparison of the relative costs and benefits of several courses of action. For example, choices can be made between two or more programs, each of which tries to accomplish the same objective. A general program of health education regarding high blood pressure or alcoholism can be weighed against the clinical program which focuses on a smaller population identified as high risk. Where it is applicable, it is a priceless tool for decision makers.

Unfortunately, its application to large-scale policy choices is limited by

[6]For a discussion of the application of cost benefit analyses to social programs, see: "Cost Benefit Analysis for Government Decisions," *American Economic Review,* May, 1967; John Hill, "Cost Analysis in Social Work," in *Social Work Research,* ed. Norman Polansky (Chicago: University of Chicago Press, 1930) ; and Michael Borus, "The Economic Effectiveness of Retraining the Unemployed," in *Retraining the Unemployed,* ed. Herman Somers (Madison: University of Wisconsin Press, 1968).

some of the same factors which limit the use of PPBS. The costs of any course of action are difficult to ascertain if one wishes to go beyond simple bookkeeping. Out-of-pocket costs (for staff, rent, capital construction, and the like) and the value of service benefits can be calculated. But every social program also has a built-in cost known as opportunity cost, that is, given limited resources, following one course of action means that another course cannot be followed and the opportunity to get results from that other course is foregone or lost.

The choice to increase cash income to all the poor may make it impossible for an administrator to reserve funds to pay for specific programs, such as reducing infant mortality by funding pre- and postnatal childbirth clinics. An even clearer example is the choice between improving housing conditions for all low-income persons and trying to prevent tuberculosis by providing health services to a smaller number of vulnerable persons.

Costs may also be external to the program, that is, a program may have side effects that can all too easily be overlooked, but whose costs a policymaker must take into account. A policy to safeguard the privacy of delinquent children may have the side effect of concealing particular cases whose records show they need attention of some kind. Or a program to produce a great deal of housing quickly may destroy neighborhoods and introduce extra costs of social disorganization.

Closely related to these external costs is the difficulty of measuring the benefits in social programs. We are far from certain that we can prove that social programs deemed by many to be good do in fact influence the lives of their recipients for the better. Even when observation tells us that a course of action must be good, it may be difficult to translate this good into the quantitative terms a cost benefit analysis requires. Most of this flaw, however, lies not in the tool but in the primitive state of social intervention. We have difficulty in proving that a network of community centers for young people makes much difference in the rate of juvenile delinquency or that social centers for the aged improve the morale of old people. Most evaluative studies reveal that persons not using such services come out about as well as those who do, by any measure of well-being now in use. The same can be said for the widely popular counseling programs. They are believed by all to help those who use them, but this is a highly selective population. When the behavior of large numbers of persons is compared, it has proven difficult to establish that those using counseling get along, in the aggregate, much differently from those who do not. None of this proves that the services are not worthwhile for individuals, but policy choices are concerned with effects on large populations, so that there is still difficulty in applying this tool to programs dealing with human beings and their behavior.

Despite these obvious limitations, the way of thinking which cost benefit analysis stimulates becomes invaluable. Policymakers and planning staff attuned to such mechanisms can transfer the way of thinking to choices which do not lend themselves readily to absolute quantification. Certainly, all persons intuitively try to balance the costs and gains attached to any important decision. What this technique does is to translate this intuitive process into an open one, so that planners can be more conscious of what is involved in each of several courses of action. Over time, and with more practice, these tools can be improved and made even more technically useful.

PREDICTION AND FORECASTING

In troubled times everyone wants to know where we are going, but recent experience forces us also to be skeptical as to whether we can ever know. Hope overtakes doubt, and most Americans, while maintaining a strong skepticism, are also willing to suspend disbelief partially. The field of economics, which is considered to have made the greatest progress in forecasting among the social sciences, has been reported as relying on these mechanisms: (1) the loaded deck method (foretelling the future by what has happened in the past); (2) symptomatic techniques (reading clues or straws in the wind); (3) the form book (looking up what someone else has said); (4) the awe of computers (feeding data into a computer and accepting the output of the machine, which in fact reflects the subjective decisions as to input); (5) soothsaying (seers who rely on psychological or experienced insights.[7] If this is what prediction is like in the most developed science, what can we say about the field of social welfare policy?

By contrast with the foregoing tools, which are closely identified with organization management concepts, forecasting can be said to symbolize the long-term future for policy analysis. If government is ever to go beyond the stage of reacting to recurrent crises and the political pressures of self-interest, if it is ever to escape the heavy burden of acting on yesterday's experience alone, then the capacity to anticipate future events is crucial. There are two elements in this form of prediction: assessing what future states or conditions are likely to be and then anticipating the behavior of institutions and individuals, given those future conditions.

Policy planning approaches this set of tools with utmost caution, and properly so. Attempts to anticipate the future have failed many times. Demographers in the 1930s predicted a decline in birth rates, but birth rates exploded in the 1940s and no one predicted the subsequent falling off thirty years later. The attempts to predict the behavior of the economy or of the stock market have not been successful, although economics is a much better established "science" than is social welfare. The rush of women into the labor force and the prolongation of life for adults who survive childhood diseases or adult respiratory infection was not anticipated.

---

[7]Adapted from Leonard Sills, "The Art of Forecasting Is Ancient, Arcane," *New York Times*, January 3, 1977.

Despite these disappointments, and with due caution, one may probably say that human beings and their governments are now in a better position than ever before to anticipate future events under conditions which permit our institutions to get ready for change, rather than being overwhelmed by them. This is not to say that social intelligence or political will necessarily act upon advance knowledge, but the potential is in sight.

Three tools are worth noting for this purpose: demographic projection, modeling or simulation, and econometric projection of the relationship between unemployment and inflation (the Phillips Curve). All of these techniques require that certain assumptions be made and held stable, but within these assumptions certain future events can be predicted with modest assurance.

Demography offers the richest and most fertile field upon which to draw for policy-planning purposes. The behavior of masses of people does change, but not so rapidly, in ordinary circumstances, that the behavior of the recent past can be ignored. Even changes in child-bearing habits are likely to change only from generation to generation. Within certain upper and lower limits, therefore, it is reasonable to project into the next two or three decades the shape of the population in the United States, barring worldwide catastrophe. If we can expect that the proportion of children in the population will grow or remain stable, we can at least anticipate the level of educational facilities which must be maintained and the rate at which youth enter the labor force and demand jobs. At the same time, prolongation of life permits an estimate of the relative aging of a population, the number of years adults are likely to be available for work, and the number of years they must be maintained in the economy after they withdraw from work. Such evidence permits calculation of demand for and use of schools, housing, transportation, and the like. The information does not tell us whether children will want to continue in school for longer or shorter periods of time, or whether adults will want to quit work earlier or stay on longer, or whether adults will continue to live in familiar communities or will want to move on constantly to newer parts of the country. But the data do tell planners enough to warn them when difficulties are likely to confront society. What is needed is a sense of historical continuity on the part of government officials and of citizens so that anticipatory action will be highly valued and permitted in our political process.

This can be illustrated at two ends of the age spectrum. If the number of fertile women of child-bearing age is known and if we assume that patterns of child-bearing are reasonably stable for one generation, we can anticipate whether in the next generation the demand for primary school buildings and teachers will go up or down. If it is expected to go down, planning and policy can temper the enthusiasm to build new facilities. Buildings can be designed simply and built to last a short time, or they can be built solidly and designed to permit adaptation to other uses when they are not needed for schooling small children. The training of teachers can be organized so that an oversupply does not continue to be trained long after the demand drops off. Even better, training and contracts can be organized so that changes in demand, say from primary to secondary school, can be planned for. By reallocation of manpower great peaks and troughs of under- and overemployment of teachers can be avoided.

If we can anticipate that the number of aged and retired persons is going to surpass the number of workers (who support those who retire), we can begin rethinking retirement policies and employment and insurance arrangements. In this way we can avoid being locked into a rigid situation where people are forced out of work when we need manpower or are kept at work when their labor is not needed; and we can, with difficulty, also adjust the comparative benefits of the working and nonworking populations to fit the relative burden to be carried by those of working age. Many options, ranging from modifications of insurance benefits to employment and industrial incentives, can at least be considered.

It is, however, not sufficient to know what future conditions will be; it is also necessary to assess how social institutions will behave. Here we can draw upon the findings of the social sciences and studies of organizational behavior. These studies and findings have not yet been codified, even in primitive form, but some steps have been taken in this direction by Berelson and by Rothman [8] and some evidence is available. None of it is startlingly new, but the information can be used. Thus we know that bureaucratic organizations are very difficult to move into changed work patterns and that several years must be allowed even if the smallest changes in behavior are to be attempted. Rapid changes usually produce chaos and strong resistance. Labor contracts and civil service introduce rigidities since benefits once acquired cannot be easily changed without countervailing incentives being introduced. Classic examples are found in the tendency of all organizations to elaborate and refine their work when demand slacks off, so that the same number of people do more and more things for fewer and fewer people. The well-known Parkinson's Law is apt: work expands to fill the time available for its completion. In effect, if there is a fixed work period, the less there is to do, the more time people will take to perform a task.

There is also a tendency for each work function to be subject to more and more "professionalization" by its workers. All of us prefer to be supervisors or consultants, rather than working at the bottom of the ladder, doing the hardest work. Some tasks are considered "black" or undesirable and only the most strenuous counter incentives attract workers to such tasks as garbage removal, dishwashing in restaurants, or caring for the physical needs of very old, enfeebled persons. Finally, there is the well-known

---

[8]See Bernard Berelson and Gary Steiner, *Human Behavior* (New York: Harcourt Brace Jovanovich, 1964); and Jack Rothman, *Planning and Organizing for Social Change* (New York: Columbia University Press, 1974).

Murphy's Law (if anything *can* go wrong, it will) which imposes a high barrier to the transfer of any successful experiment to mass application. Success in a social experiment usually depends on the dedication and commitment (and genius) of its first proponents. But when this idea is to be spread widely, it depends for its operation upon quite ordinary people, who usually lack commitment or innovativeness. There are flaws as well as strengths in organization, and both can be anticipated.

These aspects of organizational life were most recently observed in federal efforts to reorganize, to simplify, and to streamline government operations. Large and small agencies of government and in the private sector each have developed their comfortable patterns of function, satisfying their staffs and their managers and the people who use them. Unsatisfied are the people who do not use these programs and those who wish to change patterns to save money or to get different results. PPBS foundered at the level of the federal government, as much as for any reason, because the bureaus and agencies resisted the changes which were being urged upon them from higher authority. The extreme was seen in one state where the state executive office gave up the attempt altogether to modify the pattern of its agencies and converted PPBS into Management by Objective, only asking that each executive identify the objective he had for his department and then try to achieve that self-identified objective as best he could.

This recital of what we have learned about the behavior of organizations is overly pessimistic, because we have also learned what it is that organizations do well and how. It is the challenge of prediction to use this knowledge, not to ignore it, in shaping long-term policies to meet the kinds of problems which demographic analysis indicates can be anticipated. The combination of demography and knowledge of organizations does not deserve to be called a "tool" for policymakers, but the combination of knowledge about future conditions and behavior of organizations at least provides the raw material with which policy staffs can shape their policies more soundly.

In 1976 the Joint Center for Urban Studies, Harvard-MIT, completed a useful exercise in forecasting which suggests direction for the future in this technique, mainly because it illustrated how many hitherto unmanageable social factors can be made specific for forecast use.[9] The objective was to project American housing needs from 1972 to 1980 in a form usable in determining national housing policy. This effort sought to go beyond a previous major forecast effort by the federal government, that of a blue-ribbon committee chaired by Edgar Kaiser, in several ways. (1) It separated social deprivation and market demand. It did not assume that

---

[9]Bernard Frieden and Reilly Atkinson, "Forecasting the Nation's Housing Needs," *Working Paper No. 30* (Cambridge: Joint Center for Urban Studies MIT-Harvard, February 1975).

inadequacies necessarily had an effect on housing demand. (2) It sharpened
the definition of housing deprivation, adding households where the cost
of housing was so high as to affect families adversely. (3) It examined a
number of specific metropolitan housing markets to estimate the future of
each and used these estimates to arrive at a national figure. This stratagem
was in contrast to earlier efforts which treated housing as a national market
and did not account for local variation.

The forecast used the following units of data, among others: aging of
a population over time, mortality rates; new household formation rates,
including an allowance for reduction in overcrowded households and the
social trend to single-person households, migration rates to and from metropolitan areas, replacement rates for normal losses due to fire and the like;
changes in the desire to upgrade housing, rates of occupancy in below-
grade housing, including housing too costly for income; and rates of
normal construction in the private marketplace. It was also recognized that
the impact of some factors was more difficult to estimate, such as a change
in the desire to locate in more attractive surroundings and the occurrence
and effect of periods of economic recession.

Errors in the resulting estimates could be checked to a limited extent
before 1980 by two means. Some data could be simulated for an earlier
period and then checked against actual experience, and over the three
years of the exercise, newest data about housing starts and household
formation could be checked with late census bureau reports. The authors
found that some errors cancelled each other out, with the result that the
final estimate seems more likely to fit the reality than would otherwise be
expected. They found that they had estimated the volume of new housing
starts too high, but had been low in their estimates of new households
formed, mainly of unattached persons.

The study, though costly and time consuming, seems to justify the
confidence that such projections can be improved as to social policy
issues and can be useful in policy planning. Without claiming absolute
reliability, the method is probably much more accurate than unsystematic
peering into the future intuitively or waiting for massive distortions in
housing supply to be discovered after the fact.

A quite sophisticated technique which can help predict future situations is simulation, which involves building quantitative models of social
systems. Information is gathered about the variables in a situation and is
run through a computer to see what results are produced by any change in
any variable. In many ways, this is an effort to reconstruct real-life situations descriptively and then manipulate the pieces to see what results from
different combinations. Of course, the reliability of the result depends on
gathering sufficient data on the right variables. A simple illustration would
be to test by simulation what would happen if the first entry into mental
health services were to be shifted from, say, the psychiatric clinic or hospital to the schools or to the police. Would more or different cases be

identified? Would more or fewer patients be routed to and accepted by treatment centers? Would different kinds of personnel be able to perform the same tasks and with what different results? To attempt such simulation would require data about many disparate phenomena. How do police or school teachers handle mental problems as compared with psychiatric personnel? Where do troubled persons naturally go on their own initiative to get help? To what kinds of initial advice do they listen? How do psychiatric personnel react to referrals from nonmedical sources? The great advantage of the simulation technique is that it avoids even more costly and risky experimentation on human beings. It is analogous to laboratory experimentation in the development of drug therapies before the results are tried on people.

As is true of many other techniques, the costs of simulation are not insignificant. In a well-known case, a model was constructed of the pathways by which all troubled persons found their way to a network of mental health agencies in southern Illinois. This involved laboriously collecting data on all applications and referrals in a large geographic area. Once these data were assembled and the pathways traced, it was discovered that the real point of first contact for most patients was the sheriff's office. With this information in hand, it was possible to simulate changes in agency behavior and client reactions if the sheriff's office were added to the network of mental health agencies. Thus it was possible to peer into the future, to see what would happen in real life if this step in the mental health network were mandated and made explicitly a part of mental health programming.

Closely akin to simulation are games, usually designed to test out how organizations and individuals would behave in given situations. The same plan specifies a particular situation and the persons or groups usually involved, for example, agency staff, average citizens, city councilmen, legislators, social workers, doctors, and advocates of minorities attempting to get a larger share of resources in the reallocation of funds to meet children's needs. The actors who play the parts of the participants in the situation are briefed on the known and expected patterns of behavior of the persons or groups. The actors are then set to work to solve the game problem. Incentives and rewards and punishments can be built into the game rules and the way the actors resolve the problem can be taken as a reasonable simulation of what real-life actors would do in a like situation.

Finally, an example of prediction technique can be taken from economics, well in advance of anything yet available for social welfare, but suggestive of a path for future evolution. The econometric projection known as the Phillips Curve is held by many to predict the behavior of the economy as regards employment and inflation. Based on certain analyses of the behavior of several economies, the technique postulates that in a given set of economic circumstances, an increase in inflation by government action will reduce unemployment, whereas a governmental effort to increase employment beyond certain limits will increase the rate of inflation. In other words, the curve makes explicit the trade-off which policy makers can contemplate between jobs and inflation. Mayer, Moroney, and Morris have proposed an adaptation of this device to social work, wherein it is suggested that the trade-off for policy makers lies in the amount of control which citizens or political figures will accept as related to the seriousness of the social problem confronting them and the evidence that the control will lead to a solution of the problem.[10] The more severe the problem and the more assurance there is that a given course of action will reduce it, the more likely it is that citizens and officials will accept controls necessary to launch a new problem-solving intervention.

From these examples—demographic projection, simulation, prediction of organization behavior—it is reasonable to conclude that social policy personnel do have some tools to help anticipate the future, however limited their accuracy may be. The Phillips Curve precedent also suggests ways in which the available tools could be improved upon.

OUTCOME EVALUATION AND RESEARCH

The term *evaluation* is used here to mean relatively rigorous scientific efforts to assess the outcomes of social programs in terms of their effect on the persons to whose needs the programs are addressed. This is quite different from customary evaluations of social welfare, which measure success and public acceptance by the number of cases handled or the number of personnel added. Evaluation as used here calls upon the best methods of social science research, and such research requires the time, patience, and deferred rewards which policymakers can seldom afford. Instead of proposing that research is a policy tool, it is here suggested that the results of research enterprises in social welfare constitute a vast pool of information upon which policy personnel can draw.

Such research does present certain problems to the policy maker which should be recognized at the start. Social science research is still in its relative infancy, and the evaluation of many programs has often been conducted with less than suitable criteria. Even more risky is the tendency of researchers to consider single programs as examples and to criticize the underlying theory of a program on the basis of a few cases. In recent years program evaluations have been publicly funded, especially of large-scale publicly funded experiments. One illustration is the evaluation of massive experiments undertaken in educating underprivileged children to overcome the social disadvantage under which many of them labor. The research findings have been almost uniformly disturbing. Head Start was found

---

[10]See Mayer et al., op. cit. for a simplified discussion of the potential application of this curve to social welfare.

to have only short-term and transient effects. No changes in school situations or methods had much effect compared to the effect of changes in non-school factors such as home and friends. Other studies have found little or no change, as measured by children's reading or their work, when resources are increased, when school organization is changed, or when teaching methods are altered. Manpower training programs have been found to have at best marginal effects on future work experience of the trainees when compared with the experience of those not trained by such programs. Large-scale public housing programs have often proven to be collecting points for poverty, crime, and illness. And most careful studies of psychological and emotional counseling fail to find much benefit traceable to the counseling itself.

This discouraging recital might seem to argue that all social programs are without merit. The difficulty lies in the nature of most social science research, which usually is fueled by a desire to probe awkward questions and to study subjects for the sake of the intellectual excitement the search affords. Such research usually tries to prove that a given statement is false, not that it is true; proving the null hypothesis is most valued. Given the limited development in research technique applicable to policy questions, the disappointing results may also be attributed to faulty measurements as much as to faulty programs. What these research findings are useful for, despite their limitations, is their warnings about what not to do, about what may be fruitless effort. Such research thus helps clear away the underbrush of an infinite number of bright ideas, leaving to policymakers the opportunity to search out more promising alternatives.

Apart from such uses, evaluation of this character, when conducted skillfully and used delicately, can be used to help correct or to improve adopted programs as they evolve. Questionable findings do not have to lead to complete abandonment of programs or of policies; they can help to assure that by constant improvement the programs can achieve the desired results in the long run. The political situation makes the adoption of such a view of evaluation difficult for most policymakers, for any criticism of a program is likely to be used by political opponents as a sign of the policymaker's ineptitude.

That this risk is worth taking is seen by some positive results in recent policy research. The Congress has long debated the use of a negative income tax to reform income maintenance programs. One serious objection, other than its possible cost, has been that it would adversely affect the labor market, that is, that workers once assured of a decent income without work would withdraw from the work force. Careful studies were undertaken under rigorous experimental conditions to measure the effect of introducing a negative income tax to specific populations. The experiments and the evaluations were funded over a long enough period of time to permit reasonable assessment. The finds were interesting, but not astounding. Compared to a control population not receiving the income assurance, the test population gave no sign that many were tempted to quit the labor market to enjoy the presumed comforts of marginal income. Only a small percentage of persons did withdraw, mainly women or second wage earners who had entered the labor market to make ends meet for their families, perhaps to the neglect of their children.[11]

Another study used a broader sweep of evaluation than that usually relied upon by social researchers. Levitan and Taggart reexamined the range of programs spawned by the Great Society efforts of the Johnson Administration.[12] Whereas most research into individual programs, such as Head Start, Model Cities, and so forth, suggested that they had done very little, these authors used different measures: instead of looking to see whether poverty had been abolished, they noted that, overall, the especially poor and disadvantaged and the black minority benefited in quite measurable ways. They secured much more open access to health service, and they succeeded in getting a more equitable share of health services than before. Their access to better education was measurable, or at least their education was less different from that of middle-class families than was true before the Great Society spurt. On this kind of measure, income, housing, and the opportunity to share in the decision making of programs affecting their lives (through Community Action Agencies) were all improved. While these gains may not have abolished poverty or even reduced the gap between the poorest and the richest, it could not be said that the programs had no positive effects. Thus, with a shift in the measurements, one could honestly conclude that there were some retrievable gains in certain programs upon which improvements could be grafted in future.

LOGICAL ANALYSIS

Finally, a few words should be said about a method for policymakers of a quite different order, that of analysis of a situation using intelligence and reflection. Management systems, computer technology, and techniques of data collection and research are only aids to intelligent analysis, not substitutes for it. One of the greatest hindrances to the effective use of intelligent analysis is the haste with which many actions are taken. Policymakers are harassed by overwhelming duties, many of them concerned with insignificant details of travel, meeting many people, and producing or reading quantities of routine documents. Little time is left to reflect on the meaning of experiences and of observations, or, for that matter, to think over the meaning of research findings, social indicators, and the quantities

---

[11]Joseph Pechman and M. Timpane, *Work Incentives and Income Guarantees, The New Jersey Income Tax Experiment* (Washington, D.C.: Brookings Institution, 1975).

[12]See Sar Levitan and Robert Taggart, *The Promise of Greatness* (Cambridge, Mass.: Harvard University Press, 1976).

of data which computers and the mass media make possible. Large quantities of information are useless unless they are reduced to some order and unless there is time to consider intelligently their meaning or significance. Analysis supplies this vital ingredient to policymakers and for their staffs. Short of an exposition about the art of reasoning and of logic, it is difficult to know what to say generally about the art of analysis, as contrasted to the art of quantifying data. Two examples may help clarify the distinction.

In recent years policymakers have struggled to chart an acceptable course of action concerning the health of the nation. During this time the costs of medical care have been inflated beyond all belief, and health or medical services constitute the fastest growing part of the GNP. This has led to numerous complex proposals to contain or to control the costs of medical care, ranging from increasing the share the consumer pays for insurance to reduce use, to increasing the tax share, to limiting the use of hospitals, and to mandating what physicians should be paid. In all of this work few people took the time to look at the health system and the population in relation to each other. Long reflection and examination of old data led many to recognize simultaneously a flaw in the reasoning which governed most efforts at cost control. The flaw was simply a gap between the makeup of the present-day population and the aims of the medical care system.

The medical system is based primarily upon diagnosis and treatment of curable conditions and to a much lesser extent upon prevention of illness. But while our medical technology has become a wonder of complexity, our population has changed. The largest number of health conditions which demand attention are now chronic illness of all kinds, for which current medicine has little or no cure. Some two-thirds of all medical effort, meaning the effort of hospitals, physicians and nurses, and the like, are devoted to conditions such as arteriosclerosis, stroke, spinal cord injury, genetic and birth defects, enfeeblement of old age, heart failure, renal failure.[13] Most of these conditions remain with patients for as long as they live, often for decades. The conditions are not susceptible to cure or reversal, although sometimes their progress can be retarded. These patients continue to return to hospitals and doctors who can do little for them, but who must see them in simple humanity, and they are paid for it. When self-care gets difficult, the patients are routed into nursing or custodial institutions at a disproportionate rate.

It has taken long reflection to recognize that the traditional health system is out of kilter with the current situation in two respects. The nursing institutions are largely proprietary and are on the borderline between

---

[13]Monroe Berkowitz et al., *Public Policy Toward Disability* (New York: Praeger, 1976) and *Evaluation of the Structure and Functions of Disability Programs* (New Brunswick, N.J.: Bureau of Economic Research, Rutgers University. June 1975).

medical care and nonmedical custodial care, but their operations are largely funded by public health tax dollars. And more significant is the almost complete absence of supportive services which could help disabled persons remain with their families or in their own homes with supplemental help, in preference to full-time institutional care. These two gaps seriously disrupt the functioning of the health system and a disproportionate number of persons who might get along with part-time supplemental care in their own homes are shifted to more costly full-time care in institutions. Only after analysis and reflection were these flaws clearly identified, and then the panoply of data systems could be put to work to secure evidence with which to shape remedies.

Another example can be seen in the unwieldly complexity of government programs which surround citizens at all levels. There are so many programs that even expert professional staffs require still more specialized information experts to help them find what they need in the maze. And the maze depends upon an almost impenetrable accumulation of regulations which bind city, state, and federal government into some kind of partnership, but one in which the responsibilities of each are unclear. Lacking clarity, there has emerged a buck-passing phenomenon in which officials at each level of government are in danger of losing sight of the objective of their welfare programs; instead, they focus on the best ways to reduce their share of the cost while shifting a greater share to another level of government. The result has been not only to displace the goals of public action, but to give rise to a proliferating staffing pattern in which as many or more persons are needed to supervise and monitor the system as are involved in the delivery of the services to the ultimate consumer.

Finally, time to think about the possible short-term consequences of any policy or program can be used to bring together units of knowledge which, when viewed simultaneously, can identify risks and hazards not at first manifest. A useful example is seen in the 1977 proposals of the Carter administration for welfare reform. One proposal was to consider total family income when deciding eligibility for any income supplement to which an individual family member may be eligible. On the surface this appears to be a logical policy in order to strengthen the sense of family responsibility for its members before public income support is resorted to. On reflection, it becomes clear that such a policy is most likely to encourage individual members of a family to leave home in order to qualify for benefits to which they consider themselves entitled. The experience of the Aid to Dependent Children program comes at once to mind. In that case the exclusion of families with two parents from entitlement has encouraged desertion by husbands when their earnings prove insufficient to meet family needs.

The dilemmas which ensue are by now widely recognized, but the inappropriate confidence in computer technology and management systems has led to an almost total reliance of government on efforts to increase the amount of data being collected, and at the same time to reorganize the machinery of government, before the purposes to which the machinery is to be put are clearly thought through. While great effort has gone into installing data systems and trying out mechanical devices to clear the confusion, it has only recently become obvious, as a result of reflection and analysis by many, that these are not the first essentials of future policy-making. Analysis has not yet produced useful leads in this area, but the problem is becoming more clearly defined.

Analysis of this kind can be useful at two levels at least. For one thing, it can help policymakers to fine tune policies they have already launched. A program of health insurance can be modified in its particulars to balance more equitably the care needs of the chronically sick and the therapeutic needs of those with curable conditions. And for more complex issues, such as the proper division of accountable responsibility between levels of government, a start can be made to think through governmental relationships which can promise better attention to human needs, rather than to shifting cost burdens.

Analysis of this kind involves an improved welding together of science, values, and human judgment. To quote Hammond and Adelman:

> Judgments find their expression in the forming of public policy because it is during that process (of endless debate) that the products of science and technology are integrated or aligned with human values. . . . The key element is human judgment. . . . The fact that an essential element in policy formation remains a mystery has serious consequences. . . . Means must be found to avoid both poor judgments and self-serving judgments. . . . Two general methods have been recognized for these purposes: (1) the adversary method by which scientists with differing judgments are pitted one against the other in front of a judge or a jury, and (2) the search for scientists who have somehow gained a reputation for wisdom in the exercise of their judgments.[14]

These authors go on to propose a third method, whereby the criteria for judgment are rendered somewhat more objective. They are quoted not so much because their suggestions are necessarily the best possible, but because their concern with the subject brings into public view once again the importance of judgment in the policy process, a quality not replaceable by other tools or techniques.

TOOLS AND PROFESSIONAL POLICY CAREERS

This brief review of the technical potential in policymaking serves to show that there is a professional or quasiprofessional role in policy-

---

[14]Kenneth R. Hammond and Leonard Adelman, "Science Values and Human Judgment," *Science* (October 22, 1976), Vol. 94, No. 4263, pp. 389–395. Copyright 1976 by the American Association for the Advancement of Science.

making which, by its existence, confirms that careers for policy personnel do exist in social welfare. It has been long known that policymakers are persons with political skill who acquire positions of influence and power and employ a variety of aides drawn from quite diverse and even nondescript backgrounds. What can be presented convincingly now is that policy careers exist and that it is possible to begin the task of equipping persons for performance of this role rather than relying on the accidents of fortune and influence alone.

By now, policy roles number in the few thousands, less than the several thousands of planning positions and millions of managerial positions which can be identified in America life. Staff to conduct policy analyses are found in, to name the most obvious, state and federal offices of budget; the staffs of mayors, governors, and presidents; the staffs of legislators; planning units in departments of human resources, welfare, or health; and regional planning commissions.

As staff filling these positions acquire a better sense of their functions and of the political milieu in which they operate, they will be ready to learn how to use the rudimentary tools and techniques now available. When the limitations of the latter are recognized, the functionaries will press for and will contribute to the fashioning of better tools for policy analysis. These improvements can come about because they are developed by practitioners of what is still largely an art; and they can then be taught to others. Policy staff can enter into dialogue with scientists of all kinds, to encourage them to develop and bring forward improved tools for testing. In the last analysis, some symbiosis between the scholar, the thinker, and the doer must result. For some time to come, the policy practitioners may be expected to move back and forth between the world of makers of policy and the world of students of policy.

ADDITIONAL READINGS

Caro, Francis G. *Readings in Evaluation Research.* 2nd ed. New York: Russell Sage Foundation, 1977.

deNeufville, Judity Innes. *Social Indicators and Public Policy.* Amsterdam and New York: Elsevier, 1975.

Dror, Y. *Ventures in Policy Sciences: Concepts and Applications.* Amsterdam and New York: Elsevier, 1971.

Epstein, Irving, and Tripodi, Tony. *Research Techniques for Program Planning, Monitoring and Evaluation.* New York: Columbia University Press, 1977.

Glennerster, H. *Social Service Budgets and Social Policy.* New York: Harper & Row, 1975.

Kahn, Herman. *The Next 200 Years.* New York: Morrow, 1976.

Mishan, E. J. *Cost Benefits Analysis.* London: Allen and Unwin, 1972.

Novick, David. *Program Budgeting.* Cambridge, Mass.: Harvard University Press, 1965.

Rivlin, Alice M. *Systematic Thinking for Social Action*. Washington, D.C.:
      Brookings Institution, 1971.
Stein, Bruno, and Miller, S. M. *Incentives and Planning in Social Policy*. Chi-
      cago: Aldine, 1973.
Wildavsky, Aaron, "Rescuing Policy Analysis from PPBS," *Public Administra-
      tion Review*, March-April, 1969, pp. 189–202.
Williams, Walter. *Social Policy Research and Analysis*. Amsterdam and New
      York: Elsevier, 1971.

INDEX

79 80 81 82 9 8 7 6 5 4 3 2